# INSTRUCTOR'S MANUAL

*to accompany*

# LITERATURE AND THE WRITING PROCESS

## *Tenth Edition*

### Elizabeth McMahan
*Illinois State University*

### Susan X Day
*University of Houston*

### Robert W. Funk
*Eastern Illinois University*

### Linda S. Coleman
*Eastern Illinois University*

## PEARSON

Boston   Columbus   Indianapolis   New York   San Francisco   Upper Saddle River

Amsterdam   Cape Town   Dubai   London   Madrid   Milan   Munich   Paris   Montreal   Toronto

Delhi   Mexico City   São Paulo   Sydney   Hong Kong   Seoul   Singapore   Taipei   Tokyo

*Instructor's Manual* to accompany McMahan/Day/Funk/Coleman, *Literature and the Writing Process,* Tenth Edition

10 9 8 7 6 5 4 3 2 1–OPM–16 15 14 13

www.pearsonhighered.com

ISBN 10: 0-321-91612-3
ISBN 13: 978-0-205- 91612-9

# CONTENTS

# Anthology of Short Fiction

## PART III   WRITING ABOUT POETRY

### The Art of Poetry: Art Insert

### The Art of Poetry: Questions for Discussion

### Anthology of Poetry

### A Portfolio of War Poetry

### A Portfolio of Humorous and Satirical Poetry

## PART IV    WRITING ABOUT DRAMA

### *Anthology of Drama*

### *A Portfolio of Humorous and Satirical Plays*

## CRITICAL APPROACHES FOR INTERPRETING LITERATURE

# Instructor Resource Center

## GETTING REGISTERED

To register for the Instructor Resource Center (IRC), go to **www.pearsonhighered.com** and click **"Educators."**

1. Click **"Catalog & Instructor Resources."**

2. Request access to download digital supplements by clicking the **"New users, request Access"** link.

Follow the provided instructions. Once you have been verified as a valid Pearson instructor, an instructor code will be emailed to you. Please use this code to set up your Pearson login name and password. After you have set up your username and password, proceed to the directions below.

## DOWNLOADING RESOURCES

1. Go to http://www.pearsonhighered.com/educator, sign in using your Pearson login name and password. On the top menus, search for your book or product by either entering the author name, title, or ISBN. You can also search by discipline.

2. **Select your text** from the provided results.

   Literature and the Writing Process, 10/e
   McMahan, Day, Funk & Coleman
   ©2014 | Pearson | Paper; 1240 pp | Instock
   ISBN-10: 0205902278 | ISBN-13: 9780205902279

3. After being directed to the catalog page for your text, click the **"Instructor Resources"** link located under the **"Resources"** tab.

4. Click on the **"Show Downloadable Files"** link next to the resource you want to download.

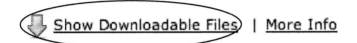

A pop-up box will appear showing which files you have selected to download. Once you select the files, a window will appear asking you to accept the provisions of the copyright. Read the terms and conditions and then click the **"I accept, proceed with download"** button to begin the download process.

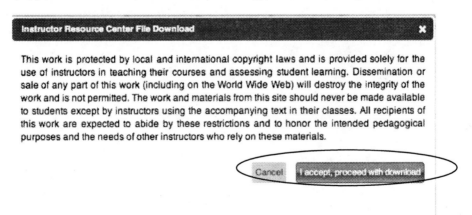

5. Once you have clicked on the button "I accept, proceed with download," the download will automatically begin.

6. **"Save"** the supplement file to a folder you can easily find again.

Once you are signed into the IRC, you may continue to download additional resources from our online catalog.

Please **"Sign Out"** when you are finished.

# INTRODUCTION

This Instructor's Manual reflects our belief that a student-centered classroom provides the best environment for learning. We have found peer involvement useful in helping students to discover a thesis, to invent ideas, to improve first drafts, and to catch editing errors. We also consider class discussion the best method of encouraging literary understanding. Students can begin by making connections between their own lives and the literature they read. Once they become engaged and interested, they can proceed to analysis and evaluation.

They will finally learn to interpret literature by continually asking themselves pertinent questions about the works as they read. Our text provides a list of such questions for each genre (designed to elicit meaning from any piece in that genre). You will want to encourage your students to use these lists whenever they read selections in the three anthologies (on short stories, poetry, and drama).

In this Instructor's Manual we supply responses to the discussion questions and to the exercises in the writing chapters, and possible answers to the postreading questions in the literature anthologies and portfolios. Your students may come up with different but equally good answers. We frequently offer suggestions for classroom activities that involve using a workshop situation (with students divided into groups helping each other solve problems in writing about or interpreting literature). We also include commentaries on all the selections in the anthologies and portfolios, along with additional questions for discussion and writing, as well as suggestions for "Making Connections" among selections by both theme and form. At the beginning of each part, we offer "Activities for Creative and Critical Thinking" for each literary genre.

## Getting Started

On the first day of class, you need to initiate the class activities you will want to use during the semester: if you want students to speak, write, and work in groups, you need to do those things today. We like to begin with a round-robin introduction in which each person (including the instructor) gives his or her name, one interesting statement, and one boring statement about his or her life. Before we start, we emphasize that the purpose is for everyone to learn everyone's name, which is easier when we have a little information to connect with the name. If you use this method, announce that you will ask a few people to name everyone when the exercise is over (though missing a few doesn't mean flunking). This activity helps to break down inhibitions and sets a friendly tone.

Because it's important to get students writing from the start of the course, you might use an activity that involves writing to help students get acquainted. Pair students up and have them converse with each other for ten minutes or so. If you want, write these questions on the board for the pairs to use in their conversations:

1. What does everybody know about you?
2. Is there anything that very few people know about you? What is it?
3. What would you like your classmates to know about you?

Tell them to take notes, and give them five more minutes or so to write up a brief paragraph about their partner. Then ask them to read their paragraphs to the class—or collect the paragraphs and read them aloud to the class (disregarding errors, of course).

These two activities will ease the way into using group work and peer review. They may take time from routines like going over the syllabus, but they are more valuable in the long run. Remember, students are going over syllabi in four or five other classes concurrently, and not much of that will stick anyway. If you close with a specific assignment, your students will be assured that you do have a plan. Discussing the syllabus may be more sensibly done in the second or third session when the class membership is more stabilized.

### Reading and Writing Right Away

At the end of the first class, you should give a specific assignment. For example,

> Read the first story in the book, "Eveline," pp. 3–7, and be prepared to discuss your reactions to the story.

If you want students to do some writing for the next class, ask them to write at least two paragraphs on Eveline, the title character: What do they think of her? You can also ask them to react to the ending: Were they prepared for the way the story ended? What questions do they have about it? Or give them a choice. Explain that short writings like this will be done frequently throughout the course to aid discussion and focus students' thoughts. When the students come to class, divide them into small groups (from three to six, depending on your class size) and have them read their papers to each other and try to come to a consensus about Eveline and/or the story's ending. This consensus will be reported to the class as a whole. Reconvene the class and listen to the reports. These discussions will lead naturally into assigning the rest of the chapter for the next class meeting.

### Using Reading Journals

Many instructors have their students keep a reading journal: a record of their impressions of, thoughts about, and responses to the literary works they read. A journal is an excellent place for students to experience the process of writing. Journals don't involve the usual pressures associated with most college writing assignments, and they provide a low-risk opportunity for student writers to pursue their ideas and explore their thoughts.

If you decide to assign reading journals, you have several ways to go about it. You can ask students to keep a journal in which they record reactions to and thoughts about assignments and reading selections. These entries can then be used as a springboard for class discussions or as prewriting for writing assignments. Journal entries might also be written in class during the last ten or fifteen minutes as a follow-up to a discussion or to get ready to discuss a different idea the next time. You can also provide prompts for writing that encourage students to make connections between the readings and their own experiences.

Many instructors collect and read their students' journals every week or so, although you can set several deadlines throughout the semester when you will pick up journals. You can stagger the deadlines, collecting journals from only certain students at any one time. You don't have to read and respond to every entry, but you need to make the journals seem worthwhile or the work will be slack. You can give bonus points for substantial entries or base a grade on a minimum length. We have found that assigning at least 10 percent of the semester grade to a journal and setting a minimum number of entries (e.g., three one-page entries per week) for a C works rather well. You can reward those students who write more and deduct from the grade of those who don't write enough.

# RESOURCES FOR TEACHING LITERATURE

## *Useful Works for Teachers of Literature*

Adler, Mortimer J., and Charles Van Doren. *How to Read a Book*. New York: Simon, 1972. Print.

Bevington, David. *How to Read a Shakespeare Play*. New York: Blackwell, 2006. Print.

Brunel, Pierre, ed. *Companion to Literary Myths, Heroes, and Archetypes*. Trans. Wendy Allatson and Judith Hayward. London: Routledge, 1996. Print.

Bunge, Nancy L. *Finding the Words: Conversations with Writers Who Teach*. Athens: Ohio UP, 1985. Print.

Byer, Jackson R., and Mary C. Hartig, eds. *The Facts on File Companion to American Drama*. New York: Facts on File, 2003. Print.

Eagleton, Terry. *How to Read a Poem*. New York: Blackwell, 2006. Print.

---. *Literary Theory: An Introduction*. 2nd ed. Minneapolis: U of Minnesota P, 1996. Print.

Forster, Thomas C. *How to Read Literature Like a Professor: A Lively and Entertaining Guide to Reading Between the Lines*. New York: HarperCollins, 2003. Print.

Guerin, Wilfred L. et al. *Handbook of Critical Approaches to Literature*. 4th ed. New York: Oxford UP, 1999. Print.

Harmon, William. *A Handbook to Literature*. 10th ed. Upper Saddle River: Prentice, 2005. Print.

Kimmelman, Burt, ed. *The Facts on File Companion to American Poetry*. New York: Facts on File, 2005. Print.

Lipschultz, Geri. "Fishing in the Holy Waters." *College English* 48 (1986): 34–49. Print.

McMahan, Elizabeth, Robert Funk, and Susan Day. *The Elements of Writing About Literature and Film*. New York: Macmillan, 1988. Print.

Shaw, Valerie. *The Short Story: A Critical Introduction*. London: Longman, 1983. Print.

Werlock, Abby H. P., ed. *The Facts on File Companion to the American Short Story*. New York: Facts on File, 2000. Print.

Young, Gloria L. "Teaching Poetry: Another Method." *Teaching English in the Two-Year College* 14 (1987): 52–56. Print.

## *Online Resources for Teachers of Literature*

*Electronic Resources for Literature Teachers*. http://people.ku.edu/~kconrad/ eleclit.html
> A diverse collection of select resources, including sample literature sites, online journals of interest to teachers of English, and online teaching resources.

*Literary Resources on the Net*. http://.andromeda.rutgers.edu/~jlynch/Lit/
> Maintains a generous collection of literature syllabi and other course materials.

*World Lecture Hall*. http://web.austin.utexas.edu/wlh/
> Publishes links to pages created by faculty worldwide who are using the Internet to deliver course materials. For anyone interested in online courseware.

# PART I
## COMPOSING: AN OVERVIEW

## Chapter 1   The Prewriting Process [pp. 2–16]

In this opening chapter, we focus on analytical reading—on giving careful attention to the literary text and asking pertinent questions about it in order to derive a thorough understanding of the meaning. At the same time, we assume that students will be writing about this work, so we introduce them to several useful invention techniques that will help them discover what they want to say about the piece when they get ready to write.

### *Who Are My Readers?* [p. 6]

The issue of audience can be a tricky and elusive one for many students. Writing a class paper presents a special problem in audience awareness. They know they are writing for the instructor, who is their most artificial and most attentive reader. They know the teacher is responsible for evaluating the students' work and will read their essays no matter how bad or good they are. But the writing that students do in class should prepare them for writing they will do in other situations and for other audiences. They need to get beyond the captive and limited audience of an instructor and learn how to write for an audience of general readers.

The general reader—also called "the universal reader" or "the common reader"—is essentially a fiction, but a very useful one. It is helpful for students to imagine a reader who is reasonably informed and generally attentive, one who will keep reading the paper so long as it is interesting and worthwhile. If students can focus on such a reader, they can gauge how much detail and background information to provide. The general reader knows a little about many things but lacks specific information on the topic the writer wants to present. In the case of writing about literature, it's very helpful to ask, "How well do my readers know the literary work?"

The best way we know to help students develop and refine their audience awareness is to use student writing groups. (See pp. 47–49 in the main text and pp. 16–17 in this manual for suggestions on the use and operation of peer groups.) Sometimes we assign a short paper in which students are to explain or interpret a piece of literature for younger readers or for readers who have not read the selection. Or you might ask students to choose a favorite selection and write a recommendation for readers who aren't familiar with it, as in a movie or book review. The goal is to interest the audience in the reading but not spoil it for them.

Here is a checklist of questions that may help students to analyze their audience and define their purpose, especially if they are working in groups.

1.  How well do my readers know the work? What details and information will I need to supply? What questions will they be likely to have?
2.  Will my readers be interested in my ideas? How can I get them interested?

3. Will my readers be in agreement with my interpretation? Do I have to be careful not to offend them?
4. How do I want my readers to respond? What do I want them to get from my essay?

**Prewriting Exercise** (letters to and from Eveline) [p. 7]
The purpose of this activity is to teach students the concept of audience. But from reading, or hearing the students read, their letters, you will also be able to see how well they understand the characterizations in the story.

**Prewriting Exercise** (about purpose) [p. 8]
These four assignments may prove too taxing for students to complete individually. Instead, you may want to assign this section to groups of three or four students to complete as a project—checking, revising, and approving one another's work.

**Reading and Thinking Critically** [pp. 9–10]
Not all reading is critical reading. Asking questions while reading is the best way to develop the abilities to analyze, make inferences, synthesize, and evaluate. You can also suggest some of these other techniques to promote critical thinking and reading:

- Make predictions as you read.
- Note any changes of opinion you have as you read and reread.
- Pay attention to patterns—and to elements that disrupt the patterns.
- Look for any significant shifts in meaning, tone, plot, or point of view.
- Mark passages that are especially memorable, ones that you might use in a paper.
- Identify the selection's most important images, symbols, and scenes.
- Think about the writer's options; imagine ways the writer could have done something differently.
- Compare the selection with other works that are similar in some way; make comparisons to movies, songs, TV shows, or advertisements.
- Look away from the text occasionally and jot down your reactions.
- Freewrite for five to ten minutes immediately after reading a selection.
- Think about how you would describe this work to a friend or relative.

**Self-Questioning** (inventing ideas) [pp. 10–11]
Here are some possible responses to the invention questions.
1. Eveline's home life is dreary, routine, and oppressive.
2. In her new life with Frank, Eveline expects to gain freedom, respect, adventure—and maybe love.
3. Since Eveline apparently knows very little about Frank or Buenos Ayres, her expectations seem to be based mainly on hopes and wishes.
4. The dust is a symbol of the dry stagnation of Eveline's life.

5. Dusty cretonne, a yellowing photograph of a priest, a broken harmonium, a "coloured print of the promises made to the Blessed Margaret Mary Alacoque" (which would be promises of lifelong virginity): these suggest decay and the denial of a vital life.

6. Eveline is "over nineteen." Probably she is around twenty years old, a time when one usually reaches adulthood and is making life decisions.

7. Eveline's father is an alcoholic, selfish, demanding tyrant, who—like most of his kind—has moments of tenderness. His being in "a bad way" means that he is drunk.

8. Eveline sometimes thinks of him as an overgrown child in need of care, like the rest of her siblings. But she also fears his violence and resents his making her beg for money to feed the family.

9. Eveline's mother led a "life of commonplace sacrifices closing in final craziness." Eveline identifies so closely with her mother that she has adopted her dead mother's self-sacrificing role in the family.

10. Eveline feels sorry about the pitiful quality of her mother's life and respects her memory. But at the same time, she wants to avoid being trapped into simply reliving her mother's dreary existence.

11. Eveline's mother, influenced by her religion, believes that pleasure in life must be paid for later with pain. When she says, "The end of pleasure is pain," she may be thinking of sexual pleasures, which, for a woman, can end in the pain of childbirth and the toil of caring for the child. She seems to be simply worn out by having too little money to care for too many children.

12. Eveline's father knows about good-for-nothing men who make promises they may not keep, and sailors have a reputation for having "a girl in every port." Her father also has a good reason for wanting his daughter to stay at home instead of marrying, since she takes care of him and his young children.

13. Frank is purposely not well defined in the story. He seems cheerful and devoted, but Eveline has not known him long: "It seemed a few weeks ago."

14. Eveline surely has a romanticized view of what married life with Frank will be like. Yet her father might justifiably be concerned that she is too inexperienced to marry and move to a foreign land.

15. Eveline has been a virtual slave to her father, seemingly because she promised her dying mother "to keep the home together as long as she could." But the modern reader sees her as having quite fulfilled her duty to her father by now.

16. Eveline holds conflicting views that she has a "right to happiness" and that she has a duty to keep her promise to her mother to serve the family. Her sense of duty to others wins out over any sense of her right to a life of her own.

17. Although she feels affection for her brothers, one is dead and the other is gone all the time decorating churches.

18. Eveline is "like a helpless animal," paralyzed by the lights of an oncoming car. She seems incapable of exercising free will. She is afraid of freedom, the unknown, and the spiritual consequences of breaking her vow to her mother.

19. Eveline's terror paralyzes her and overwhelms any other emotion she might feel at the dock. Also, Frank has seemed to be more a symbol of freedom than a real person. To respond with "love or farewell or recognition" would require that she see him as a human being.
20. Answers will surely vary here. One might say that running away to a new life is Eveline's one chance for happiness, and she refuses it—rightly or wrongly—out of fear. Others might say that eloping to Buenos Ayres with a lighthearted drifter whom she barely knows is not the wisest decision a woman could make.

### Directed Freewriting / Problem Solving / Clustering [pp. 11–13]

The material generated through these invention methods will be similar to the information resulting from the questions earlier. You may find that one technique works best for you and that your students prefer another. Encourage them to try the various methods so that they will have more options for discovering ideas to write about.

### Finding the Theme / Stating the Thesis [pp. 15–16]

You will surely want to discuss this essential material with your students and be sure they understand the difference between a *topic* and a *thesis statement*. Tell them also not to worry if at first they cannot discover the theme of a piece. It takes practice in analytical reading to develop the ability to see how the parts of a literary work dovetail to reveal the meaning of the whole. We offer further help with determining theme in later chapters.

### Making Connections

Compare Eveline to Connie in "Where Are You Going, Where Have You Been?" Consider their reactions to the men who want to take them away from home. Which one made the smarter decision?

## Chapter 2   The Writing Process [pp. 17–29]

Organization, which requires hard, clear thinking, is one of the most difficult elements of the writing process for students to handle. Most writing specialists agree that compiling a formal outline is unnecessary, but most also agree that devising some plan is essential. Students should understand, though, that the plan can always be modified as the writing proceeds.

The plan can be as simple as recording the main points of the essay in the order to be followed. But we feel strongly that these points should be stated as sentences, not merely as topics, in order to make clear the direction of the writer's thoughts (as well as to make sure that those thoughts *have* some direction). Students who merely jot down topics sometimes experience difficulty in keeping their essays unified because, as they write, their ideas veer off in directions not relevant to the thesis.

In this chapter, we suggest ways to organize an essay about a literary work and offer advice about how to develop the ideas in this plan.

### Writing Rituals May Help in Getting Started

Most experienced writers perform—perhaps unconsciously—little rituals that help them get started. Some people, for instance, always write in the same place—in a comfortable chair, at a desk, at the kitchen table, perhaps lying on the living room rug. It does not matter where a person writes, but having an established place may help to get the process going when writing needs to be done. Some people sharpen pencils before they start or find a favorite pen. Some always compose at the keyboard. Some get themselves a cup of coffee or a soft drink to keep their strength up during this arduous undertaking. You may want to discuss writing rituals with your students. If they have none, suggest that they try to establish some just in case these preparations may help to spark the writing process.

### Arguing Your Interpretation [pp. 17–18]

Here is a chance to relate writing about literature to good principles of writing in general. With your class, discuss the meaning of these terms: *claims*, *evidence*, *reasoning*, and *refutation*. Look for an editorial or letter to the editor in the school or community newspaper as an example, and invite students to assess the elements of the piece's argument.

### Building an Effective Argument [pp. 19–20]

For many people *argument* is a negative term. Perhaps it makes them think of unpleasant shouting matches and bitter disagreements. We hear and see these nasty, noisy clashes on the radio and TV all the time. But these are not examples of good arguments. They substitute volume and name calling for reasoning and evidence. So it's important for students to see that arguing is a constructive process, one in which they identify an issue for possible debate, take a position on that issue, analyze their position, and try to persuade others that their position is worth sharing or at least reasonable. The general procedure we outline on page 19 will guide them through this process. This plan is one they can use throughout college.

Be sure to make the connection that persuading readers of a point of view on a literary work is similar to persuasion of any sort. Literary critics may have some advantage because the readers usually do not already have firm opinions of their own: a good argument can stand on its own rather than working upstream against preexisting judgments. Chapter 3 goes into more detail about the connection between argument and interpretation.

### Questions for Consideration (using adequate detail) [p. 21]

We think the sample paragraph is adequately developed. Here are the details used to support the main point (the topic sentence):

- Eveline's brothers and sisters are grown.
- Her mother is dead.
- Her father will be alone.
- He has a drinking problem.
- He is getting old.

- She thinks he will miss her.
- She feels she is abandoning her father.
- She has written to him to ease the blow.
- The letter soothes her conscience.

Students may mention the following additional details as possible support for the main idea of the paragraph:

- Tizzy Dunn and the Walters (possibly former friends of her father) are gone; also gone is the priest who was his school friend.
- "Latterly he had begun to threaten her"; she apparently forgets this fear—or discounts it, even though "now she has nobody to protect her."
- "Sometimes he could be very nice"; she remembers when he took care of her one day when she was sick and when he played with the children on a picnic long ago.

The writer introduces personal opinion in the final sentence: "Eveline *seems to* feel . . ."

Most students will probably agree that the interpretation is valid, but some may disagree about whether Eveline's younger brothers and sisters (entrusted to her care by her dying mother) are indeed "grown up" by the time she considers leaving with Frank. Some might argue also that Eveline writes the letter to her father, not out of consideration for his feelings, but as a means of avoiding a bitter confrontation with him.

### Class Activity on Introductions and Conclusions [pp. 23–25]

You will want to be sure your students understand all of the material in this chapter—especially the section on distinguishing critical details from plot details so that they can successfully maintain a critical focus in their papers. But since an effective opening and closing are crucial to the success of an essay, you may want to give your students extra practice in writing these special kinds of paragraphs.

Ask your students to devise a thesis statement for a paper about a work of literature they have read recently. Then have them write only the introduction and conclusion for such a paper. After they have completed their paragraphs, you could have them exchange papers and do peer evaluation. Write the following questions on the board and ask your students to respond (concerning a fellow student's paper) in writing.

ABOUT THE INTRODUCTORY PARAGRAPH
1. Is the main point of the (intended) paper made clear?
2. Is the topic introduced gracefully? Or is it too bluntly stated?
3. Is the thesis itself interesting? Or is it too obvious?
4. Would you want to continue reading a paper that began with this introduction?
ABOUT THE CONCLUSION
1. Does it simply repeat the introduction?
2. Does it convincingly establish the main point of the paper?
3. Does it have an emphatic final sentence?

### *Ideas and Suggestions for a First Writing Assignment*

You may want your students to apply some of the procedures for prewriting and drafting that they have been studying in these first two chapters. We suggest having them write a draft of an essay about Kate Chopin's "Story of an Hour" [pp. 236–37]. Here are some directions you might give them.

1. Read the story.
2. Then turn to Chart 6-1 at the end of Chapter 6 and see how many of the questions you can answer after a single reading. But do not be discouraged if you can respond to only a few.
3. Reread the story, paying attention to the details. Then look once more at the questions in Chart 6-1 to see how many more of them you can answer.
4. Use one or more of the prewriting techniques discussed in Chapter 1 to come up with ideas for writing. You can use self-questioning, directed freewriting, clustering, or whatever works for you.
5. Then devise a thesis (or claim) and draw up a list of details to develop and support it.
6. Write a draft of your interpretation.

If students have problems coming up with an approach to this story, here are some ideas for writing that might help them.

1. In interpreting the story, focus on Mrs. Mallard's life and character to show why she reacts as she does to news of her husband's death. Why was she previously unaware of the "subtle and elusive" thoughts that come to her as she sits in her room? Why do other characters misread her reaction?
2. Focus on the imagery—the appeals to the senses—that Chopin uses to surround Mrs. Mallard. Write about how the sights, sounds, smells, and sensations contribute to the reader's understanding of Mrs. Mallard's experience.

You can, of course, also use the questions for discussion and writing that follow the story [p. 237].

Other stories in the *Anthology of Short Fiction* that might provide students with interesting characters to analyze or respond to are Langston Hughes's "Salvation," Sherwood Anderson's "Hands," Tillie Olsen's "I Stand Here Ironing," John Updike's "A & P," and John Steinbeck's "The Chrysanthemums."

## Chapter 3   Writing a Convincing Argument [pp. 30–45]

This chapter expands the concept, introduced in Chapter 2, that interpreting a literary work involves making an argument. As a way of thinking about how the elements of argument apply to interpreting literature, a discussion of a controversial work or an element in a work might be useful. We don't mean a classroom debate on an issue, but an exploration of where we get our opinions and why we accept some interpretations and not others. Here's a reading and writing activity you might use (or adapt); you might want to assign it before assigning the rest of the chapter.

Have students read the story at the end of the chapter, "Love in L.A.," and write a paragraph (or a page) in which they express their reactions to Jake, the main character. Tell students to be prepared to share their writings with the class. You could also use a class website to carry out the first part of this activity. Some questions you might pose: What do you think of Jake? What kind of person is he? Is he a positive or negative character? What are his good and bad qualities? Do you know people like him? Would you consider having him as a friend? If you were Mariana, would you have given your number to him? Then ask several students to read their assessments of Jake out loud. Or put them in groups of four or five to read and discuss their interpretations. Chances are they will not agree about Jake: some will like him more than others do. Then ask them to explain how they arrived at their opinions. At this point you might ask them to go back and look at the story again—to find particulars that support and explain their reactions. Also ask if the reactions of other students have caused them to rethink their feelings about Jake.

The point of this activity is not to reach agreement about Jake but to illustrate that interpretations vary and to encourage students to analyze why and how they form opinions about what they read. After reviewing and discussing the rest of the chapter, use the sample student essay to show how one student explained and supported his interpretation of Jake.

### Interpreting and Arguing [p. 30]
An interpretation will be more effective if it is controversial, but it doesn't have to be controversial in the usual sense, like the arguments for and against capital punishment. Both the student papers in Part I (on "Eveline" and "Love in L.A.") argue for interpretations that few people would come to harsh words over. But there are other ways to interpret these stories, and an awareness of this fact gives the process of writing about literature some dynamic tension. Once students have roughed out their interpretations, have them ask this question: What other way(s) can this selection be interpreted? Even if they never directly refute other views, the question will help firm up their own opinions.

### Identifying Issues [pp. 31–32]
Many students won't be familiar with writing a literary essay that addresses an issue. But identifying an issue—and formulating a claim (or thesis) about that issue—will help students to write papers that do more than summarize content and make obvious points.

In Chapter 3 we define an issue as a question with no obvious or clear answer. You'll want to give students plenty of practice in asking questions about literary works, a prewriting process that's explained and illustrated in Chapter 2 of the main text. This questioning is a vital part of argumentative writing. You can illustrate the value of identifying issues by referring to the debates on some current hot topics. For instance, a key issue in the debate about capital punishment is whether or not the death penalty acts as a deterrent to violent crime. How you answer that question will determine the way you

11

argue your position on this topic. An issue, then, is a pivotal point around which an argument develops. Here are some other debates and possible key issues:

> Immigration: What effects do illegal immigrants have on the economy?
> Same-sex marriage: How will gay marriage affect the nuclear family?
> Abortion: When does life begin?
> Capital punishment: Does the death penalty deter crime?

You don't need or want to debate these topics. You just want to demonstrate what an issue is and how it determines the direction of the discussion.

Issues in literature aren't necessarily as clear-cut as they are for social problems and political debates, but the interpretation of a literary work will often depend on answering one or two key questions. On pages 31–32 we illustrate how two students identify several important questions in developing their interpretations. The questions and writing prompts that we provide throughout the book will guide students to issues they can use for arguing their interpretations. Here are some examples:

| | |
|---|---|
| "The Year of Silence" | What does the story suggest about noticing, remembering, and forgetting the sensory environment we live in? [p. 427] |
| "The Lesson" | Why doesn't Sylvia get the point of the lesson? Why is she angry enough to want "to punch somebody in the mouth"? [p. 345] |
| "The Red Convertible" | Why does Lyman send the car into the river? Why are the car's lights left on? [p. 365] |
| "My Papa's Waltz" | What is the speaker's attitude toward his father? [p. 499] |
| "Mending Wall" | How does the speaker feel about walls? [p. 611] |
| "Latin Women Pray" | What are the women praying about "year after year"? Why do they never get it? Why do they persist? [p. 657] |
| *Othello* | How do race and racism contribute to Othello's downfall? [p. 967] |
| *Trifles* | Describe your reaction to the decision made by Mrs. Peters and Mrs. Hale to hide the dead bird from the men. Did they do the right thing? [p. 978] |

Chapter 17, "Writing About Dramatic Structure," offers additional instruction about defining and using issues in a literary interpretation [pp. 754–55].

## Making Claims [p. 32]

As we point out in the main text, a paper's main claim is the same as its thesis, a term that students may be more familiar with. We think the term *claim* is stronger because it implies that the writer must prove something: a claim is debatable, but a thesis statement might not be. In addition to the main claim, writers make smaller supporting claims, which are analogous to "topic sentences" in the terminology of a conventional academic composition.

If you work with students to identify key issues in a selection and to phrase those issues as questions, then it's usually easy to see that claims are the debatable answers to those questions. Sometimes a student may come up with a claim first. It's helpful, then, to ask, "What key question about the work does your claim answer? What issue does your argument resolve?" We think that the more students understand the relationship between issues and claims, the better able they'll be to argue their interpretations. You should probably not expect students to produce full-blown arguments early in the semester. It's more realistic to start by giving them plenty of practice in formulating issues and experimenting with making various claims about the literature they read.

### Using Evidence [p. 33]

We're tempted to say that writers can never have enough evidence to support their claims. That's an overstatement, of course, but we have found that it's important (and often necessary) to challenge students with questions like "Why do you think that?" and "Where did you get that idea?" It's also important to let students know that you are not denigrating or dismissing their interpretations; you just want them to recognize the value of using solid evidence to support their ideas.

There are two pitfalls that you may want to help students avoid in their use of evidence. The first is quoting or summarizing long passages from the literary selection, which often amounts to padding and usually detracts from the main argument. Audience awareness is the key to avoiding this problem: remind students that their readers have already read the selection and don't need extensive quotations and detailed plot summaries to see where the interpretation comes from.

The second potential pitfall is relying too much on the ideas and opinions of others. Many instructors limit the use of background materials and secondary sources, especially early in the semester. The first two student papers that we present in Part I (at the end of Chapters 3 and 4) were written by students who used only the primary text to develop their interpretations. In Chapter 5 we demonstrate how one of those students expanded and substantiated her initial observations by using quotations and paraphrases from the published criticism about the work she had interpreted.

### Using Reasoning [pp. 33–34]

Reasoning is essential to interpretation; it involves making connections and drawing conclusions. We don't think it's necessary to spend time studying enthymemes, syllogisms, or logical fallacies in a course on writing about literature. As we point out in the main text, reasoning simply means *explaining* how the evidence relates to the claims. Inexperienced writers will sometimes point to pieces of evidence and assume that their readers will understand what the evidence shows. The examples we present on pp. 36–37 in the main text illustrate the basic pattern of making a claim, citing the evidence, and explaining how the evidence supports the claim. Without that last step, the interpretation doesn't get made.

### Answering Opposing Views [p. 34]
Some people think that any mention of a different opinion or an alternative position weakens their interpretation. But in many cases a weak argument can be made stronger by recognizing and using alternative interpretations to advance one's own position. In Chapter 13, "Writing About Persona and Tone," we demonstrate how looking at different reactions to the speaker in "My Papa's Waltz" can lead to the formulation of a productive thesis or claim about the poem and its tone.

The two examples on page 35 in Chapter 3 illustrate how the student writers use opposing views to set up their own interpretations. The rhetorical formula is a rather simple one: "Other readers may think . . . but I think. . . ." But it is not enough, of course, just to acknowledge or describe the opposing view; one has to *argue* against it—i.e., to present a convincing interpretation, with evidence and reasoning.

### Organizing Your Argument [pp. 35–41]
In this section we present an all-purpose outline for arguing an interpretation [p. 38] and several variations (or alternate approaches). We think that outlining is an important step in presenting a clear interpretation. That's why we present the sample plans for two student papers [pp. 36–37]. We also show how to flesh out an outline by subdividing the major claim into minor supporting claims and indicating the specifics that support these claims [p. 37]. We also believe strongly in the value of making an outline of the first draft—as a way of checking the arrangement of ideas and the sufficiency of the evidence. See pages 49–52 in Chapter 4, "The Rewriting Process."

### Using the Inductive Approach [pp. 36–37]
The inductive method is the easiest way to develop an interpretation of a literary work, primarily because it mirrors the way that most people read and respond to a selection. The major requirement for a strong inductive argument is that the evidence be sufficient and relevant. Just a few points and quotations won't sustain an interpretation. A prewriting activity, like freewriting or clustering, will help to expose an inadequacy of evidence. Rereading with the major and minor claims in mind—and taking notes—are essential steps in using the inductive process.

### Making a Counterargument [p. 38]
A favorite strategy of literary critics is to review the major interpretations of other critics, refute and reject them in some way, and then offer the writer's own new and improved interpretation. Obviously, this approach will work only if the critic is familiar with a wide range of other interpretations. For most student writers this would mean doing research and reading a number of secondary sources. The example that we give in the main text [p. 40], however, is built on hypothetical (but reasonable) answers to the key issues in "Eveline." Students can get some interpretations to argue against from class discussions and small-group work. But when they consult secondary sources, they may have to look

14

again at their claims and revise their interpretations extensively, as Wendy Dennison did in her essay on "Eveline" [see Chapter 5, pp. 86–90].

As a short essay assignment, a journal activity, or an essay exam, challenge students to write a counterargument in response to an interpretation that you give to them. For example, ask them to argue against the claim that Jig, the young woman in the story "Hills Like White Elephants" [pp. 276–79], will give in to her lover and have an abortion. Or argue against the claim that the Duke in Browning's "My Last Duchess" [p. 670] unwittingly reveals too much of his cruel nature and has blown the chance to get a new duchess with a big dowry. At the end of Chapter 13 [pp. 508–10], you will find a student response to the poem "To an Athlete Dying Young," which you can also use in a counterargument assignment.

### *Arguing Through Comparison* [pp. 38–39]

Comparisons of literary selections, or of elements within selections, can be effective in clarifying and advancing an interpretation. But merely comparing one theme or one character to another isn't necessarily meaningful. A successful comparison, like any successful argument, begins with a clearly articulated, focused, and significant claim. You'll want to stress that comparisons should make a point, that they should support a claim. The examples on pages 40–41 focus on comparing the main characters from two different stories, but the goal in both cases is to identify important insights about the characters and to explain the themes these characters exemplify.

Clear organization is also crucial to the success of a comparison argument. On pages 38–39, we explain and illustrate the two major options for organizing a comparison: the block pattern and the alternating pattern. A third option is to mix the two patterns, presenting most of the comparison in a block pattern and then summarizing the minor claims in an alternating pattern, which will highlight and emphasize the key similarities or differences. Whatever approach a writer takes, outlining—both before and after composing a draft—will save everyone a lot of grief.

### *Sample Student Essay* [pp. 39–42]

This essay of about 550 words is a model for your students to examine and perhaps follow. The annotations in the margins identify claims, evidence, refutation, and conclusion, elements discussed in the text directly before the sample paper. The story "Love in L.A." follows the student paper, and if you wish you can have students read this very brief piece before the paper. However, we believe that reading the paper will spark students' interest in the story. After reading both, they can decide whether they agree with Carter's interpretation.

One way to discuss the paper is to look at the general statements, such as "Jake's self-concept is built on lies," and then have students identify the specific details that Carter uses to support each one. This impresses upon the class that each generalization needs specific support. For instance, how do we know that "Mariana isn't buying any of his lines"? What other support could Carter use as evidence of Mariana's thoughts?

You can also note the way the conclusion ties back into the introduction. It restates the main idea about self-delusion and reuses an image from the introduction, the traffic jam in which nothing is moving forward. In this way, both the major claim and the minor claim are brought together as part of the concluding comments. After students write the first draft of their own papers, they can tinker with the opening and closing to match them up in a similar way.

## LOVE IN L.A. by Dagoberto Gilb [pp. 43–45]

One fruitful way to approach "Love in L.A." is through the characterization of Jake, on whom the story focuses. While we are given no physical description of him, we know he's wearing "less than new but not unhip clothes," and we can assume he must be fairly good looking because Mariana, whose brand-new car he has just crunched, continually smiles at him. He "sounded genuine," as he cons her into believing his effortlessly smooth string of lies. Jake has no job but fantasizes about the luxurious car he would drive and the exotic lifestyle he would lead if he had the "advantages" of "a steady occupation." In reality, we know he has been at loose ends for quite some time: "one of his few clear-cut accomplishments over the years" is that his aging Buick is "clean except for a few minor dings." The Buick is sturdy, not easily damaged, doesn't sustain even a scratch—just as Jake is untouched by scrapes, like this accident, which he caused through his daydreaming. The setting of the story is apt since Los Angeles is a city famous for its crowded freeways and ubiquitous cars. And although cars are essential for many L.A. residents, for Jake a luxurious new car has become the object of intense longing. Ironically, the freedom he enjoys by being jobless is what keeps him from any realistic hope of achieving his dream. We see throughout the story that appearances and showiness matter to him, but truth and ethics count for nothing. His life is stalled, just like his car on the freeway.

The title perhaps has a double meaning. It may suggest Jake's love for sexy cars as well as his lust for Mariana, neither of which involves real love in any meaningful way. The final paragraph neatly captures the essence of Jake's character. Having dodged his responsibility for the accident, he drives away, reveling in his freedom, dreaming about an "FM stereo radio and crushed velvet interior and the new car smell" that would make his life perfection. But we suspect that he may eventually have an awakening and discover that, in the words of Kris Kristofferson, "Freedom's just another word for nothing left to lose."

### Questions for Discussion and Writing

1. Does Jake have anything in common with his Buick? How about Mariana and her new Toyota? Does she share any attributes with her car?
2. What do you think the title means?
3. Do you think Jake might feel guilty about how he scammed Mariana? What might he regret?
4. How much of what Jake says and does is a "performance"—of pretending to be somebody he isn't and trying to fool an audience? How about Mariana? In what ways does she pretend to be someone different and to put on an act for Jake? Write an essay arguing for this interpretation of the story.
5. How does the last paragraph capture the essence of Jake's character?

### Making Connections

Compare Jake with the father in Ron Hansen's "My Kid's Dog." Which do you find more unprincipled?

Compare the encounter between Jake and Mariana to the one between Betty and Bill in the play *Sure Thing* by David Ives.

# Chapter 4   The Rewriting Process [pp. 46–67]

Nancy Sommers's award-winning article, "Revision Strategies of Student Writers and Experienced Adult Writers" [*College Composition and Communication* 31 (Dec. 1980): 378–88], reveals that student writers typically do little revising—even when they *think* they have. Their alterations fall into the category of editing—cosmetic changes—rather than a true "re-visioning" of the writing. So, you will probably need to monitor your students' revising process by looking at drafts and suggesting improvements if you want to be sure that they learn to revise in a meaningful way.

The sample student paper that appears in its first draft in Chapter 2 and in its revised version at the end of this chapter provides a good model of an essay that is much improved by revision. Our student Wendy outlined her first draft and discovered that she had a paragraph that lacked support and a couple of points out of place. Making these changes produced a far better paper, and the effort proved well worth her time, raising her grade considerably.

We are sold on outlining after the writing [see pp. 50–52 in the main text]. Since many writers need to discover and refine their reactions and ideas as they write, they can't make detailed plans before they begin a draft; the after-the-writing outline lets them see whether their first draft is orderly and coherent or whether it wanders around, has underdeveloped paragraphs, and repeats ideas.

The exercises in this chapter concern revision at the sentence level—not as crucial as global revision but still essential for effective writing.

## Revising in Peer Groups [pp. 47–49]

Not all teachers are comfortable with using student writing groups, but the practice has several significant advantages: students develop a greater sense of audience; they become more involved in the class; they see writing that is better and worse than their own; and the instructor doesn't have to do all the work of leading discussions and responding to papers. Here are some general recommendations and points to consider concerning pairs and groups.

1. Think carefully about whether you want students to stay with the same partner or group for most of the semester or change around. Stable groups promote more rapport and commitment, but they can grow stale or develop interpersonal problems.
2. Have students stay with the same partner for peer review of essays, but occasionally put pairs together or tell students to solicit a second (or even a third) opinion from another partner. If peer advice is contradictory, as it sometimes is, allow the

students to decide which suggestions to follow. Doing multiple peer responses will virtually assure that everyone gets some good advice. And sorting out the bad feedback from the good is a valuable learning experience.
3.    Provide structure for the groups or pairs, especially in the early stages. Suggest a goal for the peer response work, such as, "Check to see whether your partner's essay has a good, clear thesis," or "Look for places where a concrete example or detail would help." Let groups know whether their goal is to report back to the class or to brainstorm ideas for writing outside of class.
4.    Be active during pair and group work—don't sit behind the desk. Wander around and eavesdrop or sit in on a group once in a while. Be open to individual questions as you walk around the classroom.

### *Peer Evaluation Checklist* [p. 48]
These questions are designed to help students learn to evaluate their own or other students' papers. We have found that learning to be good editors helps students to become good writers. You might find it useful to duplicate this checklist, leaving spaces so that your students can write directly on the sheets during peer evaluation sessions.

### *Combining for Conciseness: Sentence-Combining Exercise* [pp. 55–57]
Responses will vary, of course.
1.    The second common stereotype, usually symbolizing sexual temptation, is the dark lady.
2.    As the title suggests, Kate Chopin's short story "The Storm" shows how the characters react during a cyclone.
3.    Because Emily Dickinson's poetry can be extremely elliptical, readers often have difficulty discovering the literal meaning.
4.    There are three major things to consider in understanding Goodman Brown's character: what the author tells us about Brown, what Brown himself says and does, and what other people say to and about him.
5.    Most of the humorous incidents that inspire Walter Mitty's fantasies fall into two groups, the first illustrating his desire to be in charge of the situation.

### *Varying the Pattern* [pp. 57–58]
Emphasis is usually achieved when the most important information is placed near the end of the sentence. Advise your students to shift less important modifiers (whether words, clauses, or phrases) to the front of the sentence. For example, in the first sentence of the exercise, "when she was a child" should be moved out of the emphatic or "stress" position at the end and placed somewhere earlier in the sentence. The most important information (and the most surprising) is that Wharton was "not allowed to have paper on which to write," and that should be placed at the end of the sentence.

### Exercise on Style [p. 58]

Students will be able to combine sentences in several ways; here are some likely constructions.

1. Edith Wharton, who was born into a rich, upper-class family, was, as a child, not allowed to have paper on which to write.
   Or: Born into a rich, upper-class family, Edith Wharton, as a child, was not allowed to have paper to write on.
2. Because her governesses never taught her how to organize ideas in writing, she had to ask her friend Walter Berry to help write her book on the decoration of houses.
3. When she was 23 years old, Edith married Teddy Wharton, who always carried a one-thousand dollar bill in his wallet—just in case she wanted anything.
4. Although her good friend Henry James helped her to improve her novels, Wharton's books invariably sold far more copies than his.
5. Following World War I, she was presented the highest award given by the French government—the Legion of Honor—for her refugee relief activities.

### Exercise on Passive Voice [p. 60]

Answers may vary somewhat.

1. Creon brutalizes Antigone because of her struggle to achieve justice.
2. Antigone's tirade against his unbending authority did not convince Creon.
3. The play pitted male against female.
4. Society may experience considerable benefit if someone wins even a small point against a tyrant.
5. Creon's exercise of iron-bound authority causes the tragedy.

### Exercise on Word Choice [p. 61]

Responses will vary, of course; here are some possibilities.

1. The first sentence of "A Good Man Is Hard to Find" foreshadows the grandmother's violent end at the story's conclusion.
2. The family's conversations reveal their self-absorption and ignorance.
3. Lying, untruths, and self-deception abound in this story.
4. Three sinister-looking strangers approach the family after their car accident.
5. Each character speaks in a comically disturbing idiom.

# Chapter 5   Researched Writing [pp. 68–103]

We placed this chapter in the first part of the book so that it will be available whenever you and your students are ready to undertake researched writing. We strongly recommend that you assign and discuss Chapters 1 through 4, but we think you may want to skip over Chapter 5 and come back to it later, after students have written about literature on their own.

One of the challenges of researched writing is deciding how much weight to give to secondary sources. Even experienced writers are intimidated by the views and opinions of critics and scholars; they feel they don't have anything to say about a literary work that hasn't already been said. This feeling often results in a researched essay that amounts to little more than a compilation of quotations and paraphrases with very little input from the student writer. For this reason, we suggest that you follow the procedure illustrated by the sample student paper in Chapter 5: have students write a draft of their argument or interpretation before they consult secondary sources. That's what our student Wendy Dennison did with her analysis of "Eveline," and we think it's a good way to ensure that a student's own ideas and opinions will not get lost in the time-consuming business of finding sources and documenting them. In this paradigm, students use secondary sources to expand and support their understanding of a literary work, not as a replacement for their own thoughts.

## *Focusing the Coverage*

Another common problem with research assignments is the tendency to take on a topic that is too broad for the time frame and the available sources. Beginning with a response statement or preliminary draft will help to keep the coverage manageable. Another approach (which also works for writing that does not rely on research) is to identify a problem to be solved and focus it with a *thesis question* to be answered. Students will write with greater engagement if they can discover some problem concerning a literary work, one that genuinely interests them and that they can set out to solve in their writing and research. For example, someone writing about *M. Butterfly* [Chapter 19] might wonder, as most readers do, if Gallimard was really ignorant of his lover's biological sex for twenty years. A question that focuses this problem might be phrased like this:

Is Gallimard genuinely deceived about Song's biological sex, and if so, how and why?

And the thesis statement would then involve the writer's solution of the problem:

Gallimard's complete commitment to the illusion of heterosexual romance with Song allows him to feel that he is finally a real man in several ways.

If the writer is more interested in the literary techniques used by the playwright, he or she might conceive of the problem in this way:

How is the opera *Madame Butterfly* used in the play *M. Butterfly*?

The student who wrote the essay on *M. Butterfly* [pp. 874–80] became interested in a cultural analysis and phrased her thesis question this way:

How are sexual and racial stereotypes active in Gallimard's life story?

The three casebooks—on Langston Hughes [p. 552], Joyce Carol Oates's story "Where Are You Going, Where Have You Been?" [p. 199], and the character of Amanda in *The Glass Menagerie* [p. 813]—can also help you to limit the scope of a research project. The background and critical perspectives in the casebooks introduce students to working with secondary sources without having to identify and locate these materials themselves. This saves time and puts more focus on the actual writing. You might begin by having students draft a preliminary analysis of the Oates story or a response to a poem or story by Hughes, without referring to the additional materials. Once the students have a draft of their own ideas, they can then incorporate ideas and opinions of the critics whose essays are excerpted in the casebook. They will get experience using paraphrases and quotations, and you can monitor their skill at integrating and citing their sources accurately and effectively. If you wish, you may then ask them to locate additional sources to support and enrich their discussion. You can use this kind of controlled research assignment early in the semester, as preparation for writing a more extensive source-based essay later on.

### *Helping Students Complete a Documented Paper*
Most students find procrastination a major problem when they attempt to write using secondary materials. Setting a clear schedule with well-defined checkpoints along the way will help these students enormously. Here is a list of checkpoints you might want to have them meet. Assign your own dates.

1. Discuss chosen topic in conference with you—at least, those who are having trouble deciding on an approach.
2. Turn in thesis question or problem for approval.
3. Prepare a preliminary draft of the argument or interpretation to get feedback from peer groups and instructor. Another option is to have students turn in an outline or plan for approval at this point.
4. Turn in a preliminary bibliography so you can check for relevance and form.
5. Bring to class a substantial number of note cards or electronic notes—to be sure they are making progress and handling paraphrases and quotations appropriately.
6. Pass open-book quiz on MLA style; a sample quiz is included at the end of this chapter in this manual.
7. Bring a section of the rough draft along with note cards or electronic notes to class—or have them bring notes and actually write a section in class—so that you can check how well they are integrating sources and how accurate their documentation is.
8. Bring a draft of the paper to get feedback from peer groups.

Also call your students' attention to the suggestions about conducting research [pp. 69–74], taking notes [pp. 74–77], devising a working outline [pp. 77–78], writing a first draft [p. 78], organizing notes [pp. 78–79], and rewriting and editing [pp. 83–85]. These brief discussions reinforce the importance of following a process and emphasize the idea that good writing develops in stages.

### *Using the Online Catalog* [p. 70], *Indexes and Databases* [pp. 71–72]
The library's computers provide an overwhelming number of sources and service options. With so many possibilities, it's important that students take an orientation course if they

haven't already done so. You may want to arrange a tour or an orientation session with your school's librarian. Many libraries can tailor their presentations to fit the needs of a specific assignment, so even students who already know how to use the online services can benefit from such a session. Libraries are also constantly updating their resources, so each year new research tools are available. Students will also have to spend some time with these data systems to find out how they work and how useful they are. But it's time well spent. Once students get the hang of it, they will be able to research a topic with astonishing ease and thoroughness.

### Using the Internet [pp. 72–74]
The Internet and the web give students access to a great deal of information that is often more current than anything available in printed sources, and the web's hypertext feature allows a user to explore a topic quickly and thoroughly. Nonetheless, there are a couple of serious pitfalls in using the web that you might want to point out.

First, it's difficult to know how to judge the vast array of information that's available. Students will find research reports, online journals, and government publications. But they will also find unsupported opinion, propaganda, inaccurate information, and tasteless junk. Anyone can publish on the web; there is no editorial board to screen the material. So, researchers must apply sound judgment in evaluating each of their electronic sources, just as they would the print sources that they find in the library. Encourage students to check the information against other sources and carefully consider the credentials—and the biases—of the person or organization supplying the data. The suggestions [on pp. 73–74] will help them. In addition, your librarians may have created and posted additional vetted, discipline-specific website recommendations. You many want to institute a policy of not allowing the use of Internet-only sources without approval.

Second, searching on the Internet, especially on the World Wide Web, can eat up a lot of valuable time. Because it's easy to move from site to site through numerous interlinked sources, it's possible to spend hours browsing the web. Students' time might be better spent reading their source materials, taking notes, and writing the paper. To avoid wasting time, students should always go to the web for specific purposes, skim the sites first, and note the size and downloading time of a document before printing it out. (The slow downloading time on some equipment can consume a lot of time.)

### Using Reference Works in Print [p. 74]
Scheduling a library tour may provide a student's first trip to the library and can introduce the class to the print and other materials the university makes available to students. A quick scavenger hunt activity can be a useful start to good library habits.

### Working with Sources [pp. 74–75]
We still think that note cards are a productive way to record secondary source material. They're highly portable and can be easily arranged and rearranged when it comes time to construct a working outline. But the electronic age has made the note card method seem

22

outdated and inefficient. Today's students may prefer to highlight useful passages from photocopied or downloaded sources and type them into a computer file. They can then use the cut-and-paste function to group ideas and to help them visualize the arrangement they might follow in their paper. If they have also typed out the sources of these quotations and/or paraphrases in MLA style, they can then cut and paste them alphabetically on the Works Cited page.

### *Using a Research Notebook* [p. 75]

A research notebook, though a more significant investment of time at the research stage, becomes a history of students' actions and thinking for the final paper. Students find themselves shaping their ideas and claims as they progress and are set to write a draft at the end of the process. You can instruct students to begin their notebooks with these entries:

1. Write down your topic and record your thoughts about it. Explain why you are interested in the topic and what you want to learn about it.
2. Discuss the topic with your instructor and with others who might be familiar with it. Record their reactions and use their feedback to explain how you can limit the scope of the topic to make it more manageable.
3. Formulate several questions that you will try to answer with your research.
4. Outline your search plan: Where are you likely to find relevant information? What kinds of sources will you be using? Which ones will you look at first? Which indexes and databases should you use?

Then, as students read and take notes, they use the divided-page format to record the results of their research.

Instructors who use this method of conducting research think it is more efficient than starting with index cards because a student can keep all the information in a single convenient place, which the instructor can check from time to time to monitor progress and give advice. More important, the response side of the notebook shows the evolution of students' thinking and lets them articulate questions that arise as they read and process the information from secondary sources. This procedure steers students away from a cut-and-paste style of research writing because it encourages synthesis and analysis throughout the project. At the same time, it also helps writers to identify which ideas are their own and which ones they picked up along the way—an important distinction that guards against inadvertent plagiarism and allows them to claim their own views and contributions with confidence.

### *Summarizing, Paraphrasing, and Quoting* [p. 77]

Most students will benefit from practice on how to write an acceptable paraphrase. You can use the critical excerpts in the three casebooks or David Huddle's essay on the formal characteristics of Robert Hayden's "Those Winter Sundays." If you want, photocopy a page or two from a critical article, perhaps about a work that you've already covered in class. Ask students to write paraphrases of two passages from these works of criticism;

you can even specify the passages to work on. To get students in the habit of best practices, you might include instructions on appropriate attribution and citation methods at this stage. Have them prepare their individual paraphrases and then meet in groups to compare results.

### Devising a Working Outline [pp. 77–78]
Even professional writers disagree about the value of outlining. But whatever your thoughts and feelings about outlines, you need to consider their advantages as an efficient way for your students to create and evaluate the organization of their writing. Sometimes an outline is a good way for students to move from the prewriting and early research stage to making a draft. Such an outline can focus thinking, keep writers on track, and get them to think about how well the parts of an interpretation fit together. Or for writers who want to get their ideas down on paper right away, they can outline after they complete their first drafts to check for inadequate and inconsistent coverage—and decide where to place support materials from secondary sources. See pages 49–52 in the main text for more detail on the use of after-writing outlines.

Realize, too, that outlines come in many forms, some more flexible than others. Sometimes a simple listing of main points and their relevant supports will give all the direction a writer needs. For the more complicated task of researched writing, you may want your students to construct a formal outline that lays out the main ideas in full sentences and breaks them down into detailed subdivisions. Such outlines take time and effort, but they provide a solid basis for writing a complete and nearly finished draft. Whatever form you require of your students, let them know that any outline they make is a tentative plan that can be revised as they draft and redraft their writing.

### Integrating Sources [pp. 79–83]
Stress that all three parts of in-text citations are crucial because readers need to know where the writer's own ideas stop and the views and opinions from the sources begin— and end. Advise students not to be afraid to let their sources show—that's the whole point of a researched essay—and encourage them to use lots of attributions to introduce and highlight their research (see p. 80). It will help if you give students a number of models to study and replicate. Some teachers use anonymous examples from student papers they've collected from previous classes. One of our colleagues uses an in-class exercise in which students select three note cards (or entries printed out from their computer file) on a particular subtopic or subject heading, each from a different source; they then write a paragraph on that subtopic, summarizing the main points and integrating quotations and paraphrases. The instructor then has students meet in small groups to review the effectiveness of these paragraphs; she also collects the paragraphs and uses them, usually in conference, to help students improve their skills at synthesizing researched materials.

### Avoiding Plagiarism [pp. 82–83]
Students often commit plagiarism, both intentional and unintentional, because they are pressed for time and feel unsure of their own ideas and interpretations. The best way to

counter these problems is to take students through all the steps of the writing process—prewriting, drafting, revising, and editing—and to monitor each step. That's why we like to have students draft an essay in which they work out their own thoughts and opinions first (even if it's just in directed freewritings) and then consult secondary sources to support their views (as the sample documented essay in the main text illustrates). Use the list of checkpoints given earlier in this manual (p. 20) and collect or review the materials produced at each point (notes, research notebooks, outlines, source cards, drafts, and so forth). A simple checkmark system or a grading rubric sheet can help you keep track of the progress a student makes on the way to completing the final version. Including a peer-review step also helps to ensure that students are working on the essays themselves, especially if you require them to make peer evaluations in writing and to submit these written evaluations with their revised drafts. Make sure that students understand that successfully completing all the stages of the process, including writing a peer response for someone else, will be part of the final grade.

### Explanation of the MLA Documentation Style [pp. 95–103]
This section gives details on what to include in parenthetical citations and how to prepare the list of works cited, with sample entries for the most commonly used sources.

### Citing Online Publications [pp. 100–102]
For complete, authoritative explanations of the MLA style for citing online sources, see the *MLA Handbook for Writers of Research Papers* (7th ed.). An excellent online guide for citing electronic sources can be found on the Library of Congress website at **www.loc.gov/teachers/usingprimarysources/mla.html**.


# PART II
# WRITING ABOUT SHORT FICTION

## Chapter 6   How Do I Read Short Fiction? [pp. 106–11]

Although you may not have time to assign all of the papers suggested in the following chapters on fiction, poetry, and drama, we think it advisable to assign your students to read every chapter in order to receive an adequate understanding of all the fundamentals of literary analysis. Each chapter also presents a practical approach to writing about literature and includes explanations of various revising and editing techniques.

At the end of this brief introduction to the study of short fiction, your students will find the useful list of "Critical Questions for Reading the Short Story" [p. 111]. These questions can serve as an invention heuristic to develop material for writing about any of the stories included in the anthology.

### Writing Activities for Creative and Critical Thinking

The following projects will help students to integrate their reading of and writing about short stories. These are suggestions for exploratory writing, for playing with texts and language—designed to deepen an awareness of the cognitive and imaginative processes involved in reading literary texts. You can use these activities at any point in your students' study of short fiction.

- Write a continuation of a short story. Tell what happens next.
- Rewrite the ending of a short story. Choose a point in the action and change the direction of the plot.
- Rewrite the story from the point of view of a minor character.
- Change the sex or age or race or sexual orientation of a character from a story and rewrite the story—or a selected scene—accordingly.
- Work out the shots for filming a short story. Or prepare a script for dramatizing a key scene from a short story: describe the set and the characters; write the dialogue and the stage directions.
- Select a character from a short story and write a letter to him or her. You might offer some advice or express your support. Or write a letter *from* a character, in which he or she explains something to the reader (or the author).
- Select a character from a story and write an advertisement in which this character would endorse a product or service. Describe the ad and write some dialogue for the character to speak. Explain why you picked this particular product or service for the character to endorse.
- Write a letter to the author. Tell the author what you think of the story, or ask him or her to explain something about the story to you and your classmates.

# Chapter 7   Writing About Structure [pp. 112–29]

Although we focus in this chapter on discovering and writing about structure in a literary work, we believe that acquiring an understanding of how fictional pieces are designed should help students learn to structure their own essays. We suggest that whenever you discuss the pattern that underlies a literary work, you need to remind your students that the principle of structuring an essay is essentially the same, so that they can consciously relate this new understanding to their own writing.

In this chapter we discuss the most common forms of narrative structure, with cross-references to poetic structure in Chapter 15 and dramatic structure in Chapter 17. Since the structure of short stories is usually concealed (or underlying), students who plan to write about the structure of a work need to focus on plot and look for underlying clues: flashbacks, space breaks, patterns of repetition, contrasting details, beginnings and endings—and, of course, the title. These elements, then, can provide the framework for the student's own essay on the structure of a literary work.

### Prereading Activity

Ask students to come up with different senses and definitions of the verb *carry*. You might consult a dictionary and prepare a list of meanings for them to consider. *The American Heritage Dictionary* gives twenty-six transitive definitions and five intransitive ones. Ask students to look for as many uses of the word as they can discover when reading the story. What does "carrying" mean to the soldiers? Why do they carry so many different items?

## THE THINGS THEY CARRIED by Tim O'Brien [pp. 114–26]

This powerful story about the Vietnam War uses the things—both tangible and emotional—the soldiers carry to convey the unbearable burden of that senseless war. The listing begins with personal items and then moves to weapons and equipment— "whatever seemed appropriate as a means of killing or staying alive." Most telling are the intangibles that he takes up last: fear, exhaustion, disease, "emotional baggage," memory, even "the weight of the sky." About their battle equipment, they felt "a silent awe for the terrible power of the things they carried." As Bobbie Ann Mason observes, it all adds up to "the weight of America's involvement in the war." The central incident involves the company's first casualty. From start to finish, the story is punctuated with details of that sudden and senseless death. The main character, Lt. Jimmy Cross, carries a heavy burden of self-imposed guilt, since he holds himself responsible for Lavender's death. He thinks he failed to maintain strict discipline in his squad because he had been distancing himself from the grim realities of the war by fantasizing about a girl back home. At the end we see him focused on duty to his men, determined never to be caught off-guard again, as he relinquishes love for leadership, and the squad resumes "the endless march, village to village, without purpose, nothing won or lost." But the actual loss is unbearable.

### *Finding Patterns* [p. 126]

Once students have written their responses to our questions, you may wish to discuss their answers in class. Here are some suggested responses.

1. Each part of the story describes burdens the soldiers carry, which are material, emotional, psychological, and existential "things."
2. Blank linear spaces separate parts of the story visually. There are eleven parts. To save time, you could assign pairs or triads of students one part each, ask them to title their sections, and then write the titles on the board. While giving the parts titles, students will realize that the different "things they carried" serve as themes for the parts.
3. Jimmy Cross's date with Martha is the earliest episode described, and that is done in retrospect. Mainly, all of the episodes take place on April 16 and the morning of April 17, the tunnel mission and its aftermath:

> Date with Martha to *Bonnie and Clyde*
> First week of April—Jimmy gets good-luck pebble from Martha
> Mid-April—Mission to clear tunnels in Than Khe area
> April 16—Lee Strunk goes into the tunnel, Ted Lavender goes to pee, Jimmy
> daydreams about Martha, Lee comes back up and during celebration,

Lavender is shot in the head

April 16—Men smoke Lavender's dope while waiting for helicopter to take his body away

April 16—Chopper takes Lavender's body away

April 16—The soldiers burn Than Khe

April 16—Soldiers march for hours

April 16, evening—Jimmy digs foxhole and weeps, Kiowa retells Lavender's death

April 17—Jimmy burns Martha's letters and photos and makes new resolutions

4. Jimmy's thoughts of Martha structure the beginning and ending of the story. The changes in his feelings about Martha are part of the overall change he undergoes, mostly through his guilt about daydreaming of her when Lavender got shot in the head. Students can point out many clues that show how Jimmy makes more of the relationship with Martha than there really is through most of the story. However, he shows doubt about his own fantasies, so he is not fully deluded about the thinness of their real relationship.

5. The soldiers we meet in the story are

Jimmy Cross
Dave Jensen
Henry Dobbins
Ted Lavender
Norman Bowker
Rat Kiley
Kiowa

Mitchell Sanders
Lee Strunk

You might choose to assign pairs or triads of students to find information in the story about one of these characters and then pool their findings in a class discussion. O'Brien leaves out the majority of detail about their home lives, perhaps to emphasize their disconnection and alienation from civilian life in the United States. They seem suspended like snapshots in an unreal setting, though we are allowed glimpses of their individuality, particularly from descriptions of the things they carry and from their individual responses to Ted Lavender's death.

6. The story of Lavender's death is retold six times, each time with richer detail (both factual and emotional). The men's reactions to the death reveal their characters and illuminate the situation in Vietnam. Lavender's death is important in tipping the balance of Jimmy Cross's ambivalent feelings about Martha and his attitude toward leadership of the group.

***Grouping Details*** [p. 127]

The assignment of identifying a repeated element of the story (a scene, theme, or event) and then finding supporting details lends itself well to in-class activity. Students will be aware of recurring elements from the "Finding Patterns" questions.

First go over the Martha theme and the details listed on page 127. Read the thesis that grows from these. Ask students, "What is the difference between the list of related details and the thesis?" The answer is, of course, that the thesis makes an assertion or claim about the meaning and details; it puts forth an interpretation of Jimmy Cross and the change he undergoes.

Now take another recurring element of the story and list details as a class through brainstorming. Write the list on the board. Suggested elements include Ted Lavender's death, psychological burdens, idiosyncratic things the soldiers carried, and ways of dealing with stress and danger. Then, develop a thesis sentence that evolves from the details identified.

***Integrating Quotations Gracefully*** [pp. 128–29]

You may want to advise students at this point to consult Chapter 5 on researched writing. Our instruction there is directed toward integrating quotations from secondary sources into an essay, but the technique (except for acknowledging the sources) is the same. They will find in that chapter many further examples of graceful ways to combine quoted material with their own writing.

***Making Connections***

➔ Read Alice Walker's "Everyday Use" beginning on page 152. What is similar about the structure of "Everyday Use" and "The Things They Carried"?

➔ Compare and contrast structure, settings, and themes in "The Things They Carried" and "The Red Convertible."

➔ Compare this story with the poems in the "Portfolio of War Poetry," especially "Dulce et Decorum Est" and "Six National Guardsmen Blown Up Together."

***Websites***

➔ *Tim O'Brien's Home Page.* Provides a wide assortment of resources, including research links for students. **www.illyria.com/tobhp.htlm**

➔ A reading guide to *The Things They Carried*, including study questions. **www.readinggroupguides.com/guides_t/things_they_carried1.asp**

# Chapter 8 Writing About Imagery and Symbolism
## [pp. 130–64]

Discovering and interpreting images and symbols is a skill that takes time to learn. If students in high school have been involved in discussions of these important elements, they will take to it enthusiastically and perhaps even go a bit wild. You may need to encourage those who are unfamiliar with looking beneath the surface of a literary work. Remind them to look for recurring images and find associations that give symbolic meaning. Everyone will probably profit from consulting Cirlot's *A Dictionary of Symbols* or any of the other useful books mentioned on page 132 of the text.

## Prereading Activity

Discuss *rituals*. A ritual can be a prescribed form or order for conducting a religious or solemn ceremony, but it can also be any detailed method of procedure that's followed faithfully and regularly. Ask students if they have any of their own rituals—like getting ready for a date, preparing for an athletic event, cleaning their room. Why do they follow a set procedure? Is there an element of superstition in these (or most) rituals?

## Interpreting Symbols [pp. 139–40]

1. Personal responses will vary. This would be a good topic to consider in a prereading discussion, although the subject matter might be sensitive. Students might prefer to write on this question in their reading journals.
2. The townspeople know that the unlucky person who draws the black dot will be killed, but whether they understand the social purpose of the ritual is left vague. The implication is that the people don't want to face the cruelty of their actions. The ritual seems to be reenacted out of fear and a blind adherence to tradition.
3. The uncertain history of the lottery suggests that the violent ritual has been around for a long time and that the townspeople don't care to examine their behavior, and its origins, too closely. The precise meaning of the lottery is not important to the townspeople; what is important is the tradition that binds them together and focuses their repressed aggression on a single object. That Mr. Summers asks a question that everybody knows the answer to underscores the mindless nature of the ritual: they go through the motions without reflecting on what they're doing and why they're doing it. A stylized question-and-response formula is part of many religious rituals.
4. The black box is a symbol of the tradition the townspeople follow. The color black conventionally signifies evil. The box is clearly an icon (i.e., a sacred or revered image), as the details of its history suggest.
5. The stones mentioned at the story's opening foreshadow the ending and add an unspecified but threatening note to the early description. Historically, stoning was the fate of outcasts from a community (as in the Christian story of Mary Magdalene, who was saved by Jesus from being stoned as a harlot). Though the outcasts had supposedly violated the community's rules or laws, many times they served as scapegoats. Mrs. Hutchinson is an extreme example of a scapegoat, since she has not transgressed.
6. Although the characters are not fully developed, they do present a variety of viewpoints. (The fact that few of them have first names suggests that they are types.) Old Man Warner (who is always called "Old Man") serves as a rigid conservative who doesn't approve of any change in the traditional ritual (perhaps partly because he has escaped the black dot for seventy-seven years). Mr. Summers, whose sunny name is surely ironic, is a civic booster who enjoys his priestlike role in the ritual; he represents the dutiful liberal who bends the rules a little but never questions the value

of tradition. Mr. and Mrs. Adams can be seen as ineffectual radicals who point out that some communities are giving up the lottery but who do nothing to change their own community. Mrs. Hutchinson, ironically, is a well-liked, cheerful woman who seems to enjoy the ritual (until the end), though she forgets about the date and arrives late (which also seems ironic). The name *Hutchinson* may be significant for its association with Anne Hutchinson (1591–1643), a religious liberal who became one of the founders of Rhode Island after her banishment from Massachusetts Bay Colony. Hutchinson stressed individual intuition in finding salvation; she also criticized the Massachusetts Puritans for their narrow concepts of morality. Although Tessie Hutchinson does not stand up to her community, it is interesting that her name recalls a New Englander who was once tried and banished for speaking out against established authority. This historical association may also suggest parallels between "The Lottery" and the Salem Witch Trials.

## Exercise on Thesis Statements [p. 140]

This exercise works well in small groups of three or four because the discussion of each revision will bring up criticisms and suggestions beyond what each individual could generate alone. Answers will vary, but here are some possible revisions.

1. Shirley Jackson's "The Lottery" presents a compelling indictment of the practice of blaming innocent people for society's ills.
2. The ritual of the lottery itself serves as a symbol of a society dominated by unexamined tradition.
3. The impact of Shirley Jackson's "The Lottery" depends largely on the contrast between the placid, ordinary setting and the horrifying conclusion.
4. The characters in "The Lottery" symbolize the conflict between tradition and progress.
5. Shirley Jackson's "The Lottery" explores the dangers of conformity and mob action.

## Ideas for Writing [pp. 140–41]

The responsive writing suggestions ask students to examine their understanding of and experience with two key concepts in the story—traditional rituals and scapegoats. These assignments can be used to stimulate discussion and generate material for further writing.

Each of the critical writing assignments calls for a general statement (thesis) supported by analyzed examples. You may want to talk through a sample essay or outline of this type before your students begin to write [see Chapter 4].

## Sample Student Paper [pp. 143–51]

Here are some possible responses to the questions in the margins of the finished version:

Todd dropped "incongruities" from the thesis because he discusses only one incongruity, and it's a supporting detail rather than the main point.

The opening sentence was revised for conciseness and exactness.

"Jackson does this" was vague and general; "Jackson creates tension" uses more precise language and makes a definite point.

Todd improved the opening sentence of the second paragraph by identifying the black box as the "controlling image" and specifying the connection of the box to death. Both of these revisions sharpen the point of the topic sentence.

Changing "grew" to "growing" makes the series ("faded," "splintered," "growing shabbier") grammatically parallel (they're all participles).

Adding the information about the townspeople's failure to see the need for change makes this sentence more relevant to the general thesis.

The elimination of sarcasm is an improvement because the opening had not prepared the reader for a sarcastic tone; thus, the passage was confusing in the uncorrected draft.

The word "selfishness" narrows the focus of the paragraph to a specific aspect of human nature.

Todd moved the last paragraph of the draft because it was one more example of Jackson's use of symbols, not a conclusion.

Todd replaced the informal phrase "in a nutshell" to keep the tone consistently serious.

The last two sentences in the final version refine and reflect the thesis from the opening paragraph, bringing the analysis full circle and giving it a sense of unity and closure.

## Making Connections
➜ Compare the use of symbolism in "The Lottery" with the use of symbolism in "Everyday Use" by Alice Walker.

## Videos
➜ *The Lottery*. 18 minutes, color, 1969. Available from Filmic Archives.
➜ *A Discussion of the Lottery*. With Dr. James Burbin. 10 minutes, color, 1969. Available from Filmic Archives.
➜ *The Lottery* and *A Discussion of the Lottery* together on laser disc. Available from Filmic Archives.

## Audio
➜ *The Lottery*. Read by Shirley Jackson and Maureen Stapleton. 1 cassette. Available from Caedmon Records.

# Chapter 9   Writing About Point of View [pp. 152–64]

When reading fiction, we often overlook the fact that we're seeing the world through someone else's eyes—eyes that control our view of the plot, characters, and setting. And behind these eyes is the author, manipulating events and providing or withholding information. It's important to make students aware of point of view and to understand that writers choose a point of view to achieve particular effects.

## *What Is Point of View?* and *Describing Point of View* [pp. 152–54]

No brief summation of point of view can account for all the variations and subtleties of this narrative technique. Our system should be sophisticated enough to introduce students to the main uses of point of view, but they may need further explanation as they encounter the numerous refinements in prose fiction.

One way to get students to see how point of view affects writing is to have them develop a brief narrative from more than one point of view. For example, ask them to describe a break-up scene between an engaged couple from the personal point of view of one of the people involved (first-person); then ask them to render the same scene in a more objective way or in a way that does not give access to the consciousness of either person. You can also have students rewrite the opening paragraphs of a first-person story (e.g., "A & P" or "I Stand Here Ironing" or "Why I Live at the P.O.") from a different point of view, or have them rewrite a third-person opening (from "Seventeen Syllables" or "Hands" or "The Grave," for example) in the first person. This experiment in composition can become a valuable group activity in which comparisons of different versions may raise productive observations about point of view and its effects.

## *Looking at Point of View* [p. 154]

The basic question to ask about the first-person narrator is this: Why does Walker choose to tell the story through Mama's point of view? One reason is that Mama knows the background that Walker wants us to know. She knows what happened to Maggie and Dee in the past; she also knows the history of the quilts, which are symbolically important in the story. In other words, she supplies the facts about the history and heritage that Dee wants to reinterpret. For instance, she knows that Dee was named after her Aunt Dicie, not after her oppressors—which sets up the wonderfully comic exchange they have about Dee's name. Her practical, down-to-earth presence punctures Dee's pretensions; she's the necessary other side of the cultural conflict that the piece is based on. Since we have no access to Dee/Wangero's inner life, we have to understand her indirectly through details that Mama observes but doesn't interpret, such as the hair, the names, the handshakes, and the iconography of the everyday objects.

The irony of the story is that Mama does understand her heritage, which is one of putting useful items to everyday use and enjoying their beauty in that context. Perhaps she also understands to some extent what Dee/Wangero is up to—and simply resists. It's a kind of passive-aggressive thing, where she pretends to misunderstand, as, for instance, when she garbles Asalamalakim's name, referring to him as Hakim-a-barber: "I wanted to ask him was he a barber, but I didn't think he was, so I didn't ask." When it comes to interacting with her visitors, she becomes a great comic character.

Mama—uneducated, large boned, snuff dipping, and "man-working"—seems to fulfill the stereotypical image of African Americans that the Black Nationalists (represented by Dee/Wangero, Hakim-a-barber, and the farmers down the road) were trying to change. So, it is tempting to conclude that Mama represents Walker's point of view in the cultural conflict. Clearly we are meant to sympathize with Mama and cheer her on when she gives the quilts to Maggie. But in a 1973 interview, Walker explains that her feelings are more complex:

> I really see that story as almost about one person, the old woman and two daughters being one person. The one who stays and sustains—this is the older woman—who on the one hand has a daughter who is the same way, who stays and abides and loves, plus the part of them—*this autonomous person,* the part of them that also wants to go out into the world to see change and be changed. . . . I do in fact have an African name that was given to me, and I love it and use it when I want to, and I love my Kenyan gowns and my Ugandan gowns, the whole bit, it's part of me. But on the other hand, my parents and grandparents were part of it, and they take precedence.

## Prereading Activity

Discuss the meaning and importance of *heritage*. What do students consider their heritage to be? Do they have any possessions or heirlooms that have been passed down in their family? Are these items strictly personal, or do they have any larger cultural significance? You might follow up this prereading activity with a postreading discussion of Responsive Writing Idea 3 [p. 162].

## Analyzing Point of View [p. 161]

These answers are not definitive; good answers will vary.

1. Mama is a strong, hardworking, down-to-earth woman who can "kill and clean a hog as mercilessly as a man." Some might see as weaknesses her second-grade education, her being 100 pounds overweight, and her lack of "a quick and witty tongue," and perhaps Mama does. But we see that she has a lively sense of humor, and that, given the way she lives, her lack of education and her surplus of pounds have not in any way held her back. We admire her. Being called only Mama, as well as the absence of any mention of a husband/father, emphasizes her authority as the matriarch of the family.

2. Maggie is probably too shy and too nice to make an effective narrator. She would probably cut Dee too much slack. And Dee/Wangero is blind to her family heritage, so she would present a very biased perspective. She would, in fact, be an unreliable narrator, if she were telling the story.

3. Certainly we feel sorry for Maggie—disfigured, lame, "not bright," and with low self-esteem—but we are taken by her sweet disposition and gentle nature. She is a foil (almost the exact opposite) for Dee/Wangero, who is intelligent, physically attractive, and well-educated—but we are revolted by Dee's cruelty and selfishness. We deplore Dee's behavior when the house burned and are put off by her condescending attitude toward her mother and sister. We cheer for Mama when she gives the quilts to Maggie.

4. The past tragedy of the fire is crucial in understanding the character's actions: the heartlessness of Dee/Wangero and the shy goodness of Maggie. We are not told how the house caught fire, but Dee/Wangero's satisfaction in seeing it burn casts suspicion on her, especially considering her thoroughly despicable character. There is, of course, no evidence that she set the fire. Walker pared down what she presents in the story and gives us just enough to understand the situation and the conflict.

5. The African names, dress, and hairstyles stem from the Black Nationalist movement of the 1960s in which black people in this country were encouraged to go back to their African roots, to adopt the African culture and heritage. Hakim-a-barber is in the story mainly for comic effect.

6. Dee/Wangero wants the quilts as icons representing her ancestry, as works of art, but Mama gives them to Maggie who lovingly remembers the actual women who made them. The quilts for Maggie will not be symbols but a living heritage.

7. The major conflict in the story concerns the clash between two cultural heritages. Dee/Wangero has embraced her African ancestral roots, but Mama, who knows nothing of this culture, sees value only in her personal heritage. Most readers will think that Mama has the better understanding of family heritage since she gives the symbolic quilts to Maggie.

8. The title, "Everyday Use," could apply to the practical use of the artistically groomed yard as a living room, to Mama's real-life competence, to the bare-bones house, to the lovely benches and churn, and finally to the priceless quilts. So, if the theme involves learning to see the cultural value and beauty of everyday things, we see that the quilts go not to the exotic Dee/Wangero but to the very everyday Maggie.

## Ideas for Writing [p. 162]

You might want to ask all of your students to write briefly on the first prompt under "Ideas for Responsive Writing." This prewriting will serve to sharpen their understanding of point of view as they move to the more challenging critical writing assignments, all of which involve exploring point of view in one way or another.

## Sharpening the Conclusion [pp. 163–64]

The advice in this section is aimed at getting student writers to understand and create stress or emphasis—that is, to end their writing on a strong point. Even the best writers have to control the flow of their ideas in a way that will lead to a strong, emphatic closing. Writers can improve their conclusions in a number of ways:

    a.   trim the ending by cutting less important phrases and clauses;
    b.   shift the important ideas or points to the end;
    c.   break up long sentences and end with a relatively short one;
    d.   extract the best idea and isolate it in the last sentence—the clincher.

Sometimes these experiments lead to gimmicky, even irrelevant endings, but students will probably gain from the experience of manipulating the arrangement of their ideas and words. One more revision won't hurt them.

### Making Connections
→ Analyze the symbolic function of hand-stitched quilts in revealing theme in "Everyday Use" and Susan Glaspell's "Trifles."

### Audio
→ Interview with Alice Walker. 45 minutes. Available from American Audio Prose Library.

### Videos
→ *Alice Walker.* Biography of the author. 33 minutes, color. Available from Films for the Humanities & Sciences.
→ *Alice Walker: A Portrait in the First Person.* The author talks about her life and works. 28 minutes, color. Available from Films for the Humanities & Sciences.

### Websites
→ *Alice Walker the Official Website.* **Alicewalkersgarden.com**
→ *Voices from the Gap: Women Writers of Color.* Includes photographs and illustrations with a biography, bibliography, and links to interviews and essays.
**http://voices.cla.umn.edu/artistpages/walkeralice.php**


## Chapter 10   Writing About Setting and Atmosphere [pp. 165–81]

In this chapter we deliberately chose the word *atmosphere*, instead of *mood*, since *mood* is often used (perhaps mistakenly) to mean the same thing as *tone*, which is an altogether different concept in literary criticism. *Tone*, as we understand the term, is the attitude of the author toward the written work. Typically a *tone* might be amusing, light, warm, sympathetic, facetious, sarcastic, ironic, satirical, biting, scathing, or sentimental. But *atmosphere*, which is closely associated with the setting of a work, is created to stir feeling in the reader, as Poe does in "The Cask of Amontillado" by taking us beneath the ground into a dank chamber crumbling in decay and lined with moldering ancestral bones. Shirley Jackson creates a deceptive, ironically eerie atmosphere by setting her story of ritual execution on a sunny summer's day.

## Prereading Suggestion

Encourage students to visualize the three main characters, to imagine what they look and sound like. What do they wear? How do they walk? Some students may even draw sketches of the three men. Also ask which actors they would cast in the roles of Tub, Kenny, and Frank, should the story be filmed.

## Prewriting Exercise [pp. 176–77]

1. This prompt might be expanded to develop a responsive essay for this story. The different season would change a lot of the details: Tub would probably sweat profusely and have trouble breathing, for example. And the absence of hunting rifles would require a big change in the way the plot develops, although a fishing trip that includes a lot of drinking and going out on the water could still end disastrously. The primary character interactions would likely remain the same.

2. The first ten paragraphs encapsulate the relationships and personalities of the characters. Kenny drives far too fast, blares the horn, jumps the curb, and makes more than a token attempt to run over Tub. Kenny and Frank are an hour late to pick up Tub, letting him wait in the cold dawn, and then Frank snaps at Tub for complaining about it. Frank's irritability is further indicated by his insistence that Tub stop rubbing his hands together. We see Tub as a weakling, easily bullied by his mates and dropping items from his food stash as he stumbles out of the truck's way. All three men see nothing risky about driving into the countryside in freezing cold with a hole in the windshield, showing the poor judgment that ultimately ends in death.

3. The snow and cold provide an uncomfortable backdrop to the action from the very beginning of the story. The severe weather turns what might be mere foolishness into dangerous behavior. It also makes the men more touchy and irritable than they might be if they were comfortable. On a plot level, Frank and Tub's stops to get warm on the way to the hospital sign Kenny's death warrant.

4. a. An occasion like a hunting trip is often associated with bonding between masculine men, some type of expression of their natural instincts. The trip is also typically an escape from the demands of women and civilization. While Tub, Kenny, and Frank do some male bonding on the trip, it is fraught with cruelty and pettiness rather than manly virtue. They are not free of the influence of women (see 4.e.), and their uncivilized behavior has no natural nobility.

   b. The characters are distinct early on. Kenny is an unfunny practical joker, insensitive and crude; Tub is fat and impulsive and serves as the outsider for the others; Frank is irritable, morose, and distracted by his affair with the babysitter.

   c. The first indoor scene, in the farmer's house, reveals that the man asked Kenny to shoot the dog when Kenny knocked to ask whether they could hunt on his land. This revelation is important because by making killing the dog part of a joke, Kenny fooled Tub into thinking he himself was about to be shot. In a sense, Kenny's tomfoolery leads to his own murder. The second indoor scene is the tavern where Frank and Tub stop on the way to the hospital. This scene

37

includes the revelation that Frank is having an affair with the fifteen-year-old babysitter and intends to leave his wife. The scene ends on the macabre note of the two men extolling the virtues of friendship as their third friend lies in the snow bleeding to death outside. A further grotesquerie: the men carelessly leave the directions to the hospital behind at the tavern. The third indoor scene occurs at the roadhouse where they stop again. The revelation of this scene is that Tub has no glandular reason for being so fat: he just eats all the time, and even his wife doesn't know his secret.

d. Frank's ordering the pancakes for Tub is difficult to interpret. There is some element of cruelty in the way Frank prepares the pancakes and insists on Tub's gluttony. It could be that Frank enjoys encouraging someone else who has trouble curbing an out-of-control appetite. On the other hand, it may seem to Tub like an act of acceptance and permission to be himself.

e. Frank's babysitter girlfriend has clearly influenced him, at least superficially. We frequently hear him say things in terms that are out of character and sound vaguely like a fifteen-year-old's wisdom, yet indeed reflecting more empathy than Frank has had before. The fact that Roxanne has been able to affect him even this much indicates her power over him. Her wisdom has not gone very deep, as we see in scenes like the one where he glorifies friendship and then goes outside to berate his dying pal for thrashing around in pain. Frank and Tub are both guilt-ridden over the secrets they keep from their wives. The farmer's wife understands her husband's feelings about the dog better than he admits, and she is the one who gives the shortcut directions that might have saved Kenny's life.

f. Tub's sudden shooting of Kenny is quite shocking because it comes so fast and unexpectedly, even though we know that Tub has reason to resent Kenny. The men's occasional acts of thoughtlessness and cruelty to each other are shocking, such as Kenny and Frank's lack of concern when Tub gets lost at the creek and their driving off without him, making him run and jump in the back of the moving truck. The pancake scene is shocking in its strangeness and ambiguity. Finally, the last scene, in which Frank and Tub take the blankets off the dying Kenny and laugh about his final practical joke, is very shocking, though we are certainly prepared for their brutishness.

## Ideas for Writing [pp. 178–79]

Encourage students to read carefully and make notes on all of the writing suggestions before deciding which one to use for their essay. All of the topics will promote insights about the story.

## Improving Style: Sentence-Modeling Exercise [pp. 179–81]

Because sentence modeling may be new to your students, you can help them get the idea by writing one of the sample sentences on the board and marking the parallel elements. Also let them know that they need not imitate the sentence structure precisely but should try to come close enough to catch the cadence of the balance that makes the model sentences impressive. Suggest that students rewrite at least two sentences in their drafts to improve the style and balance.

## Making Connections
→ Discuss the idea of masculine folly in Faulkner's "Barn Burning," Wolff's "Hunters in the Snow," and Updike's "A & P."

## Audio
→ *Tobias Wolff interview with Kay Bonetti* (1985). 57 minutes. Available from American Audio Prose Library.

## Website
→ *Influences: An Interview with Tobias Wolff* by Travis Holland (2009).
**Fictionwritrsreview.com/interviews/influcences-an-interview-with-tobias-wolff**

# Chapter 11   Writing About Theme [pp. 182–98]

Students often have more difficulty in *stating* theme than in *understanding* theme. Many common literary themes can be expressed in familiar maxims (such as, "People who live in glass houses shouldn't throw stones" or "You should practice what you preach"), but in writing about literature students need to learn to phrase themes in a more mature and thoughtful manner. They usually need practice in order to master the technique.

Every time you begin the study of a literary work, you might try having your students write an in-class statement of the theme in a sentence or two. At the start of the semester, you can have them compose their theme statements after having discussed the selection, but later in the semester, have them write before the class discussion—in order to judge how well they are learning to understand and express the theme of a work on their own. Collect these impromptu writing samples and read them aloud to the class, asking the students to discuss the virtues and shortcomings of each one. At the end, reread the two or three that everyone agrees are the most effective. In these exercises, stress the importance of precise word choice and clear sentence structure.

## Prereading Activity
Ask students if they can give examples of narratives (stories, movies, TV programs) that combine humor with violence. What do they think of this mix? Why would a writer put these two elements in the same story?

Or you might ask students to think about the concept of "grace." What does the term mean to them? Supply them with a definition and ask if they can give examples of acts of grace.

## A GOOD MAN IS HARD TO FIND by Flannery O'Connor [pp. 183–94]
This is a difficult story for most students, partly because it has such realistic details combined with a fantastic plot and partly because it eludes any conception of "theme" or

"moral" within normal reading experience. One cannot say that the family gets shot due to their unrelieved horribleness, because their encounter with the escaped prisoners is such a coincidence. And The Misfit, Bobby Lee, and Hiram are hardly embodiments of moral enforcement.

Perhaps the best way to approach the story is through the responses it elicits. Most readers will respond with a mixture of humor and horror, and a discussion of where these reactions originate is fruitful. We can see that phrases like "a lady," "nice people," "a good man," and "a gentleman" are used in bizarre contexts, and in general what people say is not in direct relation to reality. For example, the waitress responds to June Star's rudeness by saying, "Ain't she cute?" and the children's response to the car accident is "a frenzy of delight." The Misfit is the most polite character, and only the monkey and the cat behave reasonably.

O'Connor herself provides a helpful discussion of the story in comments she made at a public reading of the story in 1963 (published as "The Element of Surprise in 'A Good Man Is Hard to Find'" in *Mystery and Manners: Occasional Prose*, ed. Sally and Robert Fitzgerald).

### *Figuring Out the Theme* [p. 194]
Leading questions on the story elements will vary; here are some possibilities.
1. Are good men hard to find? Why? What is a "good" man? Are there any in the story?
2. How important is it that this is a "journey" story? What kind of countryside is depicted? Why does the author include the scene about the Negro child standing at the door of a shack [p. 185]? What kind of place is the Tower restaurant? Why is the scene at the Tower included (pp. 186–87)?
3. What is the point of the epigram (quotation) at the beginning of the story? What might the dragon represent? Why don't the grandmother and The Misfit have names? How are they alike? Are they meant to be types or archetypes? Why does Bailey allow his mother and his children to boss him around? Is Red Sammy Butts a foil to The Misfit? What is the ironic meaning of the children's names, John Wesley and June Starr?
4. Is the cat the cause of the family's troubles? Is there any symbolism in its name (Pitty Sing)? What is symbolic about The Misfit's taking Bailey's shirt and picking up the grandmother's cat? Why are Hiram and Bobby Lee in the story?
5. How does the story divide in half? When does the satiric comedy turn into violence and death? What is the purpose and effect of all the foreshadowing? Is the encounter with The Misfit purely coincidental or inevitable?
6. When and why does the grandmother change her mind about The Misfit?
7. Why does the author have the grandmother tell the story about Edgar Atkins Teagarden? What is the meaning of the narrator's description of the grandmother's corpse?
8. Why does The Misfit shoot the grandmother? What is the significance of the last two things The Misfit says?

### Stating the Theme [p. 194]
Students will state the theme in various ways. Here are some possible responses:

> For some people only an inescapable threat of death can shatter their complaisance and force them to face their shortcomings and vulnerabilities.

> "A Good Man Is Hard to Find" dramatizes a world that is morally shallow and controlled by coincidence and violence.

> The story contrasts the superficial beliefs of the grandmother with The Misfit's more profound thoughts about Jesus, both of which are off-balance and deadly.

### Ideas for Writing [p. 196]
Use the responsive writing topics about the grandmother and her family as the basis for a critical analysis of either or both of these.

### Achieving Coherence [p. 197]
The use of "glosses" forces students to consider what they are saying at each stage of their paper. You may want to use the overhead projector or distribute a brief sample to demonstrate how to add glosses to a paper. This technique is a variation of outlining the first draft, a revising procedure that was explained in Chapter 3.

### Making Connections
→ How does O'Connor's use of violence in this story differ from the way William Faulkner ("Barn Burning") or Tobias Wolff ("Hunters in the Snow") uses violence?
→ Compare the chilling character of The Misfit with that of the creepy Arnold Friend in Oates's "Where Are You Going? Where Have You Been?" Is there something almost supernatural about them?

### Website
→ *Comforts of Home.* A site dedicated to Flannery O'Connor, containing biographical material; recent news about O'Connor and her works; and links to online essays, offline essays, and other sources. **www.mediaspecialist.org/index.html**

## Casebook: Joyce Carol Oates's "Where Are You Going, Where Have You Been?" [pp. 199–214]

This casebook provides materials for using secondary critical sources in writing about literature. You might begin by having students write a personal-response essay on Oates's story; its themes, symbolism, characters. Then ask them to incorporate ideas and quotations from at least three of the critical interpretations in the main text. (Refer to the opening pages of Chapter 5 for an example of revising a personal critique and turning it

41

into a source-based essay.) This limited approach to using secondary sources can be a valuable introduction to researched writing. You can be sure the analyses come from the students themselves, and students get practice in integrating and documenting sources on a small, manageable scale.

## WHERE ARE YOU GOING, WHERE HAVE YOU BEEN? [pp. 199–210]

Like "The Ransom of Red Chief" by O. Henry, this kidnap story has a disturbing twist: in this case, the victim halfway (or three-quarters?) wants to go. Connie's life at home is a fairly normal, middle-class white one. However, in her view it is insufferably boring and the people in it dullsville. Fueled by the pop music that infuses the story and her life, Connie has vague dreams of escape to a more exciting world. She escapes to tawdry teenaged hangouts and liaisons and invests them with romance through a transformation assisted by song lyrics. The thin line between reality and fantasy supports the motif of deceptions and illusions in the story.

After refusing to go to a terminally dull family picnic, Connie sits in the heat in a stupefied daydream and then listens for a hypnotic hour and a half to the Bobby King XYZ Sunday Jamboree. Then the bizarrely named Arnold Friend and Ellie Oscar fatefully drive up the lane. Connie's interaction with Friend is a drama of lies, hints, deceptions, suspicions, and finally threats. It has a shimmering air of unreality most of the time, with a repeated image of distracting reflections that fool the eye. Connie's state of mind is such that even though by the end of the story she knows that Friend is not one, that he has planned her abduction and will likely carry out his threats upon her family if she does not cooperate, the unknown looks better than the known. She voluntarily walks out to him.

In one sense, Connie acts heroically, saving her family by sacrificing herself. The heroism is tainted by the fact that she actually wants to leave her family, and her future looks bleak anyway. At least, with Arnold, she is going to "so much land that [she] had never seen before." He confuses her and seduces her with images from the popular songs that seem to be her sole connection to a better life, and she succumbs.

### Questions for Discussion and Writing

1. How is this story different from what you'd expect from a kidnap story? What is the victim's attitude toward being abducted?
2. What role does popular teen music play in the story? Go back through the story and make a list of the places it comes up. How does it affect Connie?
3. What kind of life does Connie have at the beginning of the story? What makes her happy and unhappy? Would you call her a normal middle-class teenager? Why or why not?
4. Could you interpret one theme of this story to be reality versus illusion? What different parts of the story fit the theme?

## Videos

➜ *Smooth Talk*. A dramatization of the story; with Treat Williams and Laura Dern. 92 minutes, color, 1985. Available from Vestron Video.

➜ *Joyce Carol Oates: American Appetites*. 30 minutes, color, 1990. Available from Filmic Archives.

## Audio

➜ *Joyce Carol Oates*. The author reads "Marya" and "Where Are You Going, Where Have You Been?" Available from American Audio Prose Library.

## Websites

➜ *Celestial Timepiece: A Joyce Carol Oates Home Page*. Offers extensive information and resources as well as a discussion forum.
**http://jco.usfaca.edu/**

➜ *Oates, Joyce Carol Forum Frigate*. A forum for discussing Oates and her works.
**http://carolinanavy.com/fleet2/f2/zauthors/Oates,JoyceCarolhall/ shakespeare1.html**

# ANTHOLOGY OF SHORT FICTION

The following brief analyses and possible responses to the questions in the main text may prove useful to you in teaching the stories included in this anthology and in formulating writing assignments derived from them.

**THE BIRTHMARK** by Nathaniel Hawthorne [pp. 215–26]

Hawthorne himself once wrote, "I am not quite sure that I entirely comprehend my own meaning in some of these blasted allegories." While "The Birthmark" is not as heavily allegorical as some of his works, we can certainly see the characters as representing concepts. Alymer is an archetypal hubristic scientist attempting to play God. The removal of the birthmark, he says, "will be my triumph, when I shall have corrected what Nature left imperfect, in her fairest work." Georgiana, of course, is that "fairest work," flawed by the birthmark, "that sole token of human imperfection," which signifies her "liability to sin, sorrow, decay, and death." Aminadab "represents man's physical nature," and serves as a foil for Alymer, who is "a type of the spiritual element." Students may need to be made aware that Hawthorne in this story uses the term "spiritual" not in a religious sense but to indicate Alymer's affinity for the occult, as he attempts through alchemy to "acquire a power above nature." It is Aminadab, the man of the flesh, who delivers the prescient warning to Alymer: "If she were my wife, I'd never part with that birth-mark." The story can certainly be seen as condemning the vaunting pride of Alymer, as he persists in his folly despite knowing the danger and, even more importantly, knowing that many of his previous experiments have failed (including the shocking one in which a flower, "lovely" like his wife, is blighted by his touch). Hawthorne's cautionary tale of man's attempt to surpass the laws of nature may bring to mind a number of questionable scientific advances: the development of the atomic bomb, germ warfare, and other weapons of mass destruction, as well as one currently relevant to the story, the controversy over cloning human cells.

## Possible Responses to *Questions for Discussion and Writing*

1. Responses will vary, but students may suggest that Alymer represents the intellectual, the spiritual, the superstitious in human nature. Aminidab clearly represents man's physical nature. Georgiana represents ethereal beauty as well as selfless devotion. Alymer is flawed by his egotism, his vaunting pride that makes him seek to play God and "correct what Nature left imperfect." Aminidab, being a foil for Alymer, is perhaps too incurious, too unquestioning, too much a creature of the senses. Georgiana, who seems to have no mind of her own, is flawed by an excessive devotion to her husband that borders on the demented.

2. The shape of the birthmark reminds us that it was placed there by the hand of God or of Nature and hence must not be tampered with.

3. The major conflict in the story involves Alymer's struggle to attain control over Nature, to achieve accomplishments on a level with the God head.

4.   Hawthorne's allegory stresses the folly of vaunting pride, of elevating science to the level of a religion, of considering himself capable of controlling Nature. Science today treads a fine line between being the salvation of humankind and of destroying it. Consider the advances in medicine, the marvels of engineering, the convenience of automobiles and air travel. Consider also the disastrous floods caused by damming rivers, the yearly highway death toll, the inventions of poison gas and the atom bomb.

5.   The story provides ample evidence to support the argument that Georgiana is complicit in her own death. She encourages Alymer in his "scientific" endeavors to produce a potion to remove her birthmark, even though she knows full well that all of his previous recorded experiments have failed. She tells him calmly, "I shall quaff whatever draught you bring me; but it will be on the same principle that would induce me to take a dose of poison, if offered by your hand." Her inordinate love of her husband borders on lunacy and proves her undoing.

### Additional Questions for Discussion and Writing
1.   Write an essay about Alymer's character as a mixture of "deep science" and superstition.
2.   What is the function of Aminadab? Explain how he functions as a foil to Alymer.
3.   Do you think Alymer is the victim of forces beyond his control?
4.   In January 2002, the President's Council on Bioethics selected this story for discussion in determining the ethical implications of human cloning. Go to the Council's website (www.bioethics.gov), click on Bioethics in Literature, and scroll down to the questions on "The Birthmark." Discuss what you think Hawthorne's position would be if he were a member of the President's Council on Bioethics.

### Audio
→ *The Birthmark*. 1 cassette, 63 minutes. Read by Walter Zimmerman. Distributed by Jimcin Recordings.

### Making Connections
→ Compare Alymer's obsession with that of Abner Snopes in Faulkner's *Barn Burning* or the narrator of *The Yellow Wallpaper*.


## THE CASK OF AMONTILLADO by Edgar Allan Poe [pp. 226–31]
Poe's stories are written not to express a theme but to produce an effect of horror on the reader. Often his stories depict the disintegration of a human psyche or, as is the case in "The Cask of Amontillado," the behavior of a man already mad. Setting is crucial in most Poe stories. The "supreme madness of the carnival season" is important in allowing the narrator to find his victim already drunk and costumed as a fool. The descent into the dank, moldering, bone-filled catacombs beneath the palazzo increases our horror as we realize Montresor's fiendish intentions. The narrator's skill in using reverse psychology is

one of Poe's most effective touches. Because Montresor plays on Fortunato's pride in judging wines, the victim hastens his own destruction.

## Possible Responses to *Questions for Discussion and Writing*

1. The first-person point of view is particularly effective because it allows Montresor to mask his diabolical plan behind lighthearted patter as he leads the ironically named Fortunato to meet his agonizing death. Montresor gradually allows us to perceive his diabolical intentions as we follow his passage with Fortunato through the eerie depths of the catacombs.

2. The nature of the insult is left to the reader's imagination, but it is entirely possible that there may have been no insult at all. His claim of a "thousand injuries of Fortunato" certainly bespeaks exaggeration, and Montresor is a person of such a duplicitous nature that he is quite capable of imagining a slight so that he can have an excuse to justify in his own mind the murder of his friend.

3. The setting is absolutely crucial for the building of suspense as Montresor leads the drunken Fortunato to his doom. Poe creates the ultimate in horror settings in the dank and chill, claustrophobic tunnel, its dripping ceiling festooned with nitre, like spiderwebs, with walls of granite "lined" with mounds of human bones—and ending in a crypt.

4. Montresor pretends that he wants Luchesi to inspect his keg of wine to verify whether it is indeed Amontillado, thus appealing to Fortunato's vanity as a wine expert. Thus Fortunato himself insists on going to Montresor's palazzo to judge the authenticity of the wine, unknowingly sealing his grim fate. Montresor, employing reverse psychology, has the added pleasure of trying to dissuade his drunken friend from going because he is suffering from a head cold, and "the vaults are insufferably damp." Several times during the course of their venture through the catacombs Montresor urges Fortunato to turn back, only to have the poor fool (who is in costume as a court jester) insist on pressing forward.

5. A character sketch of Montresor provides an excellent way of focusing on many elements of this story, which are enacted by or related to the protagonist.

## Additional Questions for Discussion and Writing

1. How does Poe maintain suspense until the very end?
2. Explain some of the many ironies in the story.
3. In what ways is this tale unlike many contemporary horror stories?
4. Rewrite this story as a play or film script. It already contains a lot of dialogue. Add stage directions as well as suggestions for casting, costumes, music, camera angles, lighting, and so forth.

## Making Connections

➜ How does Montresor's motive and method for revenge compare with Abner Snope's ("Barn Burning")?

## Audio
➔ *The Cask of Amontillado*. A reading of the work. Available from Caedmon Records and Spoken Arts Records.

## Videos
➔ *The Cask of Amontillado*. 19 minutes, color, 1979. Available from Films for the Humanities & Sciences and from Filmic Archives.
➔ *The Cask of Amontillado*. 29 minutes, b&w, 1965. American Short Story Classics Series. Available from Michigan Media.


## DÉSIRÉE'S BABY by Kate Chopin [pp. 231–35]
This story illustrates Chopin's remarkable economy in creating characters. In surprisingly few words she conveys a precise understanding of the personalities of both Désirée and her husband, Armand. She does it with small details like these: "When he frowned she trembled, but loved him. When he smiled, she asked no greater blessing of God" and, "'Armand,' she called to him, in a voice which must have stabbed him, if he was human. But he did not notice." A grasp of Armand's "imperious and exacting nature" and his patriarchal concern for his family name, "one of the oldest and proudest in Louisiana," reveals that he never deeply loved Désirée. He is quite willing to cast her off as unworthy when he thinks she has black ancestors: "he no longer loved her because of the unconscious injury she had brought upon his home and his name." This theme of woman as damaged goods if she fails to live up to male specifications is closely related to another message. By revealing the cruel and irrational effects of racial prejudice, Chopin presents a powerful plea for tolerance.

## Possible Responses to *Questions for Discussion and Writing*
1.  Désirée is a wife so submissive and so devoted to her husband that she cannot successfully defend herself from his untrue accusations concerning her race, nor does she find it possible to live without his love: "When he frowned she trembled, but loved him. When he smiled, she asked no greater blessing from God." Armand, on the other hand, is impetuous: he "fell in love, as if struck by a pistol shot." He is also ruthless with "an imperious and exacting nature," even in the running of the plantation: "His negroes had forgotten how to be gay, as they had been during the old master's easy-going and indulgent lifetime." He is quick to blame Désirée for the mixed blood of their child, even though she presents concrete evidence proving that she is white. Nor does he even respond to her goodbye when, her spirits crushed, she leaves the plantation with their child.
2.  Armand's family pride would be mortally wounded if it became known that he fathered a child who was not white, who had even a drop of Negro blood, so he jumps to the conclusion that his wife is the one responsible for the race of their child. Désirée, discovered "asleep in the shadow of the big stone pillar," remains shadowed even afterward by her husband's home: "The roof came down . . . black like a cowl,"

47

and "solemn oaks . . . shadowed it like a pall." But she is also shadowed emotionally by her domineering husband whose distant behavior after the baby comes "makes her miserable enough to die."

3. The story presents a strong condemnation of racial prejudice and also shows how unsuccessful a marital situation can be when one partner exercises all the power.

4. In paragraphs 42–44 we are led to believe that Désirée drowns herself and the baby to escape what, to her, was a fate worse than death—the loss of her husband's love and his rejection of their child. The imagery is deathlike: it is October and the sun is sinking, suggesting the dying of nature and the dying of the day. She does not go to her mother's plantation but, like Shakespeare's Ophelia, "disappeared" in "the deep, sluggish bayou; and she did not come back again."

5. We can only infer what Armand's reaction would be from everything we've learned about his behavior in the story. A more fair and just person would be aghast to discover that the Negro blood in his child came from him, not his wife, whom he blamed for it. But we can surmise that the "imperious" Armand might well retreat into denial and ignore the evidence.

6. There is ample evidence to support the claim that Désirée is held emotionally captive by her slavish devotion to her husband.

### Additional Questions for Discussion and Writing

1. What do you make of the stone pillar in the shadow of which Désirée is found sleeping (second and fourth paragraphs)? What does this image foreshadow?
2. Discuss how this story is a good example of situational irony.
3. Do you think Chopin misleads her readers into thinking that Désireé is responsible for the mixed race of the child? How and why?

### Making Connections

➔ How does Chopin's attitude toward marriage in this story—and in "The Story of an Hour"—compare with the views of marriage presented in other stories in this book: "The Chrysanthemums" by John Steinbeck, "The Day It Happened" by Rosario Morales, "The Bridegroom" by Ha Jin. Are Chopin's views outdated? Do other writers share her attitudes? Do you think writers like Chopin, who wrote over a century ago, would be pleased with the present state of marriage (including divorce)?

### THE STORY OF AN HOUR by Kate Chopin [pp. 236–37]

Brilliantly crafted to entice readers into empathizing with Mrs. Mallard, this brief work is a tour de force. Chopin makes it clear that the widow who rejoices in her new freedom did not consciously arrive at this perception. Instead, in a state of "suspension of intelligent thought," this "thing" came to her even as "she was striving to beat it back with her will—as powerless as her two white slender hands would have been." The ironic ending is also foreshadowed in the first line by the reference to Mrs. Mallard's "heart trouble," a trouble that acquires a double meaning as the story progresses. The major theme is the same as that of *The Awakening*—the constriction of a woman's life by marriage in the late nineteenth century.

## Possible Responses to *Questions for Discussion and Writing*
1. Mrs. Mallard's heart trouble is literally heart disease, but she also appears to suffer emotional "heart trouble" since she feels not lost but liberated upon hearing of her husband's death.
2. Many of the images suggest that her life experiences will be expanding: the open window, the open square, "trees all aquiver with spring life" (suggesting rebirth as nature comes back to life), "the delicious breath of rain" (water being symbolic of spiritual rebirth), someone singing, birds twittering, "patches of blue sky" (all positive, life-enhancing images)—except, at the end of the passage, the clouds piling up in the west, suggesting tragedy, even death, since every day dies in the west; these concluding dark images can be seen as foreshadowing her husband's death (or her own).
3. The "joy that kills" in the final line could mean that Mrs. Mallard dies from the joyous shock of seeing her husband alive or, more likely, the agonizing shock of seeing her dream of freedom vanish.
4. A feminist reading of the story might state the theme as a plea for equality in marriage instead of a union like the Mallard's in which one "powerful will" exerts control over the other person.
5. Some students may devise a claim that Mrs. Mallard is not a sympathetic character but is heartless, even cruel, since she is elated to hear the news of her husband's death. Others, though, may support a claim that she is a woman who was repressed in her marriage and thus is justifiably relieved to find herself free to live now as she chooses. There is evidence to support either claim.

## *Additional Questions for Discussion and Writing*
1. What do you think Louise Mallard's married life was like? Compose some diary entries in which Mrs. Mallard describes and comments on her relationship with Brently.
2. Find out about Kate Chopin's life and marriage. How autobiographical is this story?

## Making Connections
→ Compare Mrs. Mallard with Elisa in "The Chrysanthemums" by Steinbeck. What do these wives have in common? How do they differ?

## *Videos*
→ *The Joy That Kills*. 56 minutes, color. Available from Films for the Humanities & Sciences.
→ *Kate Chopin: Five Stories of an Hour*. Five versions of the story. 26 minutes, color. Available from Films for the Humanities & Sciences.

**THE YELLOW WALLPAPER** by Charlotte Perkins Gilman [pp. 238–49]
Gilman's story offers a good opportunity to read through the various lenses offered in
"Critical Approaches for Interpreting Literature." For example, it can be read in light of
Gilman's late first-wave feminism (historical), modern feminism (gender focus and
reader response), the autobiographical (biographical), and the "rest cure" of S. Weir
Mitchell, especially the effects of the drugs used as part of that treatment (psychological).
Invite students to work in groups to research each of the topics and then present their
readings of the story in light of those contexts and insights.

## Possible Responses to *Questions for Discussion and Writing*

1.  As is clear from John's dialogue, he treats his wife as a child, calling her, for
    example, "a blessed little goose." Thus the room, a former nursery, further
    infantilizes her. The bars, once meant to keep children safe, become her prison.
2.  The narrator wishes to write, to work, and to have "less opposition and more society
    and stimulus." The conversations between husband and wife trace the narrator's
    progression from passive wife, willing to be told what is best for her, to outright
    resistant rebel.
3.  Sunlight represents John's seemingly rational world and moonlight the narrator's
    romantic sensibilities. That John rejects her emotional realities is captured early on:
    "I even said so [that there was something strange about the house] to John one
    moonlight evening, but he said what I felt was a draft and shut the window." As the
    story proceeds, it is the moonlight that allows the narrator to fully explore the
    wallpaper and to escape, at least in her own mind, the oppression of John's rational
    world: "At night in any kind of light, in twilight, candlelight, and worst of all by
    moonlight, it becomes bars! The outside pattern I mean, and the woman behind it is
    as plain as can be."
4.  Near the middle of the story, the narrator, looking at the moving pattern in the paper,
    discovers that the "woman behind shakes it." Having first been driven to despair and
    frustration by the "artistic sin" of the "sprawling flamboyant patterns" in the paper,
    she begins to look beneath the system that oppresses her and assert herself against it.
5.  In moving the woman behind the paper outside, Gilman extends her critique beyond
    the relationship between John and the narrator to outline the expansive nature of
    sexism in her culture.

## *Making Connections*
→Compare the husband and wife relationships in "The Yellow Wallpaper," "The
Chrysanthemums," by John Steinbeck, and "The Story of an Hour" by Kate Chopin. Are
the dynamics of these marriages dated or still relevant?

## *Video*
→Search YouTube for scenes from the 1989 Masterpiece Theater production of "The
Yellow Wallpaper."

**HANDS** by Sherwood Anderson [pp. 249–53]

You may want to explain the story's context when your class begins to discuss "Hands." It comes from *Winesburg, Ohio*, a collection of twenty-three stories held together by a common small-town location. Characters from one story appear in the others, as George Willard appears in this one.

"Hands" is relevant today, as ever, when communities are roused to point accusing fingers at individuals whom they perceive as dangerous to young people. Like Adolph Myers/Wing Biddlebaum, these individuals might well be gifted eccentrics who have not mastered the codes of ordinary social behavior. The fact that even Wing never seems to understand what he was accused of (homosexual advances toward his students) certifies his innocence of such aggression. His actual sexual orientation is not really important, though students may find evidence in the comparison of Wing to "the finer sort of women" and in his dream of young men at his feet.

The action of the Pennsylvania men and its repercussions in Wing's life are the substantial issues of the story. The first rumor started in an enamored student's dreams, which the half-witted boy could not distinguish from reality, and the first action against Wing came from a saloonkeeper, whose view of human nature could understandably be negatively distorted. Wing finds himself in exile, ridiculed by the young people he loves and hiding his talents except from George Willard (who is the voice of broadmindedness in Winesburg in several stories).

## Possible Responses to *Questions for Discussion and Writing*

1.  Wing Biddlebaum's decaying house, perched "on the edge of a ravine," is similar to his precarious position in the little town where he lives. The field that has been "seeded for clover" but produces only weeds is symbolically like his successful teaching career, which he lost because of small-town gossip and ignorance. The image of the "cloud of dust that floated across the face of the dying sun" suggests the young people's lack of spirituality and human kindness as they needlessly hassle the old man. The whole scene leads into the earlier story of Wing's torment when he was called Adolph Meyer. The major theme of the story is implicit in that episode, as Anderson shows us the cruelty and ignorance that lie beneath the peaceful serenity of a small town in the heartland of America.

2.  Poetry often contains an element of the mystical seldom found in prose. And Wing Biddlebaum's hands are mystical; they seem not under his control: "The hands alarmed their owner" and earlier had caused tragedy to befall him.

3.  The men of the Pennsylvania town caused Adolph Meyer to flee and were even prepared to hang him because they thought he was homosexual. His touch "caressed" the children, and his voice was "soft and musical." The men should, of course, have questioned the first report since it came from a boy who was "halfwitted" and had only imagined the "strange hideous accusations." Anderson perhaps chose the town's saloonkeeper as the one who stirred up the confrontation because saloonkeepers in

that day were usually uneducated and were not themselves considered upstanding citizens.

4. Wing is trying to tell George not to waste his life in the backward town he happened to be born in. When he tells the young man he "must begin to dream," he means that he must use his imagination to figure out a way to enlarge his life experiences. Anderson has left the content of Wing's teachings vague in order to avoid limiting in any way the young man's chances of expanding his horizons.

5. The final image of Wing as a penitent receiving the host fits perfectly the role he has played throughout the story. He has been harassed (perhaps persecuted) for innocent behavior by small-minded people who wrongly perceive him as a threat. The tone at the end is solemn, even religious, as Wing Biddlebaum receives a benediction in his humble surroundings.

### Additional Questions for Discussion and Writing

1. The introduction to the stories in *Winesburg, Ohio* is titled "The Book of the Grotesques." Find out what the term *grotesque* means as a literary device. (Flannery O'Connor also used *grotesques* in her fiction.) Then discuss Anderson's use of the grotesque in "Hands."

2. Do you think Adolph Meyers's physical contact with his students was inappropriate? How would such contact be viewed in your community today?

3. What is the role of George Willard in this story?

### Making Connections

→ Compare Wing's life to that of Baowen in "The Bridegroom" by Ha Jin or of the speaker in the poem "Commitments" by Essex Hemphill. How did oppressive circumstances affect each of these men? What were their responses?


THE GRAVE by Katherine Anne Porter [pp. 253–58]

Porter's "The Grave" is a bildungsroman but from the perspective of a young girl rather than a young boy. At the beginning of the story, Miranda is an innocent preadolescent. She seems more male than female in appearance and behavior, given as she is to following her brother around in clothes identical to his and, like him, carrying a gun. But the skinning of the rabbit reveals the mystery of reproduction, redolent of sex, and including blood, suggestive of menstruation as well as birth. Miranda, without fully grasping the facts of human sexuality, makes the connection subconsciously: "She understood a little of the secret, formless intuitions in her own mind and body, which had been clearing up, taking form, so gradually she had not realized she was learning what she had to know." Paul swears her to secrecy, so she buries the image in her mind only to have it surface to her horror twenty years later, prompted by the "sweetness and corruption she had smelled that other day in the cemetery at home." She at once replaces the image with a pleasant one, the face of her brother, which allows her to avoid once more the prospect of giving birth, which Miranda (like Porter) has managed to avoid.

## Possible Responses to *Questions for Discussion and Writing*

1. This twist on the Adam and Eve story involves two siblings, Miranda and Paul, and thus removes the sexual element while retaining the gender tensions, issues of equality, and questions of social conformity versus independent thought. On their hunting trips, for example, "Miranda always followed at Paul's heels . . . obeying instructions. . . ." But, like Eve, Miranda is the more curious of the two and finds herself torn between obedience to social mores because of her "fine set of antennae" and her attraction to independent action.

2. Students will have varied personal associations with these symbols. For example, all are likely to identify with the curiosity the grave engenders in the characters, but, because of our modern and especially urban distance from the burial process, few will feel the comfort Miranda and Paul exhibit. More directed discussion of the symbolism can prepare students for the writing prompt in question 5, investigating lost or buried youth, lost or buried independence in marriage/femininity, buried memory. The dove, ring, and rabbits all link to love and the cycle of life, especially prefiguring Miranda's expected entry into a more traditionally feminine stage of marriage and motherhood.

3. As suggested by the symbols discussed in question 2, Miranda's experiences that day have generated reflection upon her own femininity and sexuality. While she is an experienced hunter, Miranda seems not to have associated the death it creates with the life of the animal, including its reproductive cycle. "The secret formless intuitions" cause her epiphany; death, life, and sexuality are merged as one memory that will return many years later in the Indian market. Students might enjoy speculating about Miranda's life between the grave experience and her memory of it years later. Has she married? What do her travels suggest about her life choices?

4. Students will begin their discussions of the themes of death, love, gender, and sexuality in their responses to questions 2 and 3. Other themes might include lost family wealth, community enforcement of gender norms, and sibling relationships.

5. You might want to save question 2 for small-group discussion in preparation for writing this essay.

## Making Connections

➜ Compare the symbolism of the gold ring that Miranda wears to the "heavy" gold ring in Adrienne Rich's poem "Aunt Jennifer's Tigers."

## Videos

➜ *Katherine Anne Porter.* Dramatizations combined with comments by Eudora Welty, Robert Penn Warren, and Joan Givner. 56 minutes, color. Available from Films for the Humanities & Sciences.

➜ *Katherine Anne Porter: The Eye of Memory.* Hosted by Joanne Woodward. 60 minutes, color, 1988. Available from Filmic Archives.

SPUNK by Zora Neale Hurston [pp. 258–62]

Hurston's story, which seems quite realistic at first, turns into a ghost story of sorts. The point of view is reflected through the dialogue of the observers in the small backwoods community, all of whom, along with Spunk Banks, are superstitious and attribute supernatural causes to Spunk's experiences. As a ghost, Joe Kanty has the courage he lacked when he was alive and mercilessly tormented by Spunk. Thus the title refers to Spunk Banks the man but also to the "spunk" (nerve, pluck, feistiness) that Joe Kanty exhibits as a ghost. In the last two paragraphs, the story becomes totally realistic again, as neighbors gather at Spunk Banks's wake to eat and drink and speculate on "who would be Lena's next." The story can be read as a cautionary tale against the kinds of sin that Spunk epitomizes—lust, pride, greed, blasphemy, deceit, lying, and adultery—or perhaps as a tribute to the quiet, retiring husband who gets his just revenge in the end.

If students have difficulty with the dialect in this story, you might suggest that they read the dialogue aloud. Giving sound to the unfamiliar words makes them easier to understand.

## Possible Responses to *Questions for Discussion and Writing*

1. Spunk is both literal and ironically figurative. It is the character's name, but it also highlights the character trait that he seems to embody and that Joe appears to lack. The irony is in (Joe's) spunk taking Spunk down and in Joe acting with the spunk that no one expects of him.
2. This southern black dialect is representative of many of the people with whom Hurston grew up and later studied as an anthropologist. It offers an authentic flavor of the community, especially in its often entertaining and comically exaggerating storytelling mode. The narrator's standard dialect highlights contrasting tones and perspectives.
3. Male braggadocio and posturing are at the heart of the story. All male characters are measured against a swaggering male norm (both physical and in conversation), and this becomes the plot of the story. Hurston seems to celebrate the conversational performance but to condemn the possible consequences.
4. Hurston's critique of the violent outcome of the plot appears in the final paragraphs where the narrator steps back to describe the aftermath of the deaths. She undercuts any mythologizing of Spunk through details such as the "dingy sheet," puts a less generous spin on the other men with their "coarse conjectures" and "guzzles of whiskey," and makes the whole plot pedestrian in the expectation that Lena will have another man sooner rather than later.
5. Before students write their essays, put them into small groups to generate lists of attitudes expressed toward Spunk in the conversations that take place before and after Joe's death.

## *Additional Questions for Discussion and Writing*

1. Discuss "Spunk" as a story about storytelling. How is Elijah an unreliable storyteller? How does Hurston distinguish between the third-person narrator's

reliable reporting and the men's unreliable stories? What point does this distinction convey?

2. What does this story say about courage and cowardice? Write an essay about the treatment and development of this theme.

3. One critic says "'Spunk' depicts a struggle among men over 'women-as-property' that continues even after the men's deaths." How do you respond to this claim?

## Making Connections
→ Compare the humor in "Spunk" with the humor in Eudora Welty's "Why I Live at the P.O."

## Video
→ *Zora Is My Name!* A tribute, with Ruby Dee and Louis Gossett, Jr. 90 minutes, color, 1989. Available from Filmic Archives.

BARN BURNING by William Faulkner [pp. 262–75]
To prepare for understanding "Barn Burning," urban students need to understand the seriousness of the crime, so they are encouraged to do some research into this vigilante practice. Furthermore, this story is best understood with a background in the historical setting—the U.S. South in the 1930s. The economic, political, and racial climate at that time and place should be discussed.

## Possible Responses to *Questions for Discussion and Writing*
1. The Snopes family life appears desperate and dreary, punctuated by violence, crime, and stealthy moves by night. The father and older brother are peas in a pod, always described in terms of their brutish similarity, while the mother and aunt are as tired and overworked as the two mules. The sisters seem to exist in perpetual "idle inertia," bovine and useless: one wonders, if the family is preserving them for marriage, who in the world is going to marry them? No one finds any joy in life. Sarty is the narrator and the only family member not paired with another, with an uncertain role in the family. The fact that Sarty, the aunt, and the sisters sleep on the floor is a telling one.

2. Abner says, "Stick to your own blood or you ain't going to have any blood to stick to you," in a primitive philosophy of in-group loyalty and out-group cruelty. The story's narrative often refers to unavoidable genetic predisposition, "old blood which he had not been permitted to choose for himself." Snopes "had in his blood an inherent vicious prodigality with material not his own," and the narrative asserts that his descendants would treat their automobiles with the same mindless cruelty as Abner inflicts on his gaunt mules. In spite of Abner's claim of sticking to his own blood, he actually repeatedly puts them in danger and ignores their needs.

3. Even the first scene, the court hearing on a barn burning, highlights the conflict Sarty feels. He has to remind himself that he is on his father's side because of family ties, yet he accidentally slips into realizing that his father's enemies are in the right. He knows that his father is a criminal who justly should be punished. He has insight into

55

the malignancy of his family life, and when he sees Major de Spain's mansion, his inklings of a better world are instantiated. He sees the landowner's beautiful, orderly, plentiful lifestyle as a haven of "peace and dignity," just what his own world is lacking. These two worlds struggle within Sarty all the way to the last two paragraphs, in which even as he runs away he tries to assert some honorable truth about his father.

4. Abner is portrayed as one-dimensional, often described as a silhouette: "something cut ruthlessly from tin, depthless, as though, sidewise to the sun, it would cast no shadow." His emotions lack nuance and range. A psychologist would label him as suffering from emotional numbing, often a consequence of repeated severe trauma (such as ghastly wartime experience). Perhaps Abner's years as a horse thief have been traumatic.

5. The ending of "Barn Burning" occurs at dawn in the springtime; both times connote fresh new beginnings and hopefulness. The birds are singing, and Sarty is breathing easier. He thinks that walking will cure being cold and stiff from a long night outside. Finally, the closing line, "He did not look back," suggests that Sarty's old life is behind him. For these reasons, we can say that "Barn Burning" has a happy ending.

## Making Connections

➔ Compare the men in Tobias Wolff's "Hunters in the Snow" to Abner Snopes, focusing especially on the themes of male vanity and violence.

## Video

➔ You can view the 1980 film of *Barn Burning*, starring Tommy Lee Jones, at **http://www.ovguide.com/barn-burning-9202a8c04000641f800000000900f5a5**

HILLS LIKE WHITE ELEPHANTS by Ernest Hemingway [pp. 275–79]
This story consists mainly of dialogue, which often seems trivial, even pointless. We learn practically all we know of the characters (which is really very little) through what they say. But the understatement is so subtle that we only gradually realize that beneath the small talk lies a very serious argument: the unnamed male speaker wants the woman (Jig) to have an abortion, which she resists. In the end, the man manipulates "the girl" (as Hemingway insists on calling her) to agree to the operation, although it appears that she is not completely swayed by his words. The speeches, if read carefully, do reveal a difference in personalities: the man seems literal-minded, irritable, unthinking; the woman seems more sensitive and emotional.

The description outside the dialogue is highly suggestive. The landscape seems to mirror the two choices that the woman faces: a dry, sterile landscape ("no shade and no trees") on one side of the train tracks and a peaceful fecundity ("fields of grain and trees along the banks of the Ebro") on the other side. The setting of a railroad junction serves to reinforce the crossroads motif.

**Possible Responses to *Questions for Discussion and Writing***

1.  The point of view is objective, consisting primarily of conversation with a brief description of the setting and an occasional indication of an action, almost like a stage direction. The reader is expected to figure out who the characters are, what is being discussed, and what possibilities might result from their discussion.

2.  The repetition of the number *two* and the parallel, nonintersecting lines all suggest that these are two separate people with different values and objectives who profess to love each other and are trying to resolve their problem, but it seems apparent that they may eventually end up going their separate ways.

3.  This story focuses on a male/female relationship in which the dominant male seeks to convince the reluctant woman to have an abortion. The abortion is the central issue in the story simply because the conflict would not exist if the woman were not pregnant. The lack of communication results from their both being firmly committed and unyielding in their opposing viewpoints. At the end, the woman insists, "I feel fine now," but we have no concrete reason to believe she has actually changed her mind. She may have just gotten tired of arguing.

4.  The white elephants in the title can be seen in two different ways, like the story itself. A white elephant in an Asian or African culture is a valuable creature that would be treasured by anyone who possessed it (as a desired baby might be). But a "white elephant," in a garage sale, for instance, is something unwanted that the possessor would like to get rid of (as an unwanted baby might be). The fetus that Jig carries is clearly wanted by her but unwanted by her lover.

5.  Hemingway leaves both questions unanswered, but either response can be reasonably argued. It seems sensible to speculate that if Jig gets an abortion, the two will probably remain lovers—at least for a while. But if she keeps the pregnancy, then the decision becomes more problematic. Will the man stay with her if she ignores his wishes? If so, how long? We know he does not want to become a father.

**Additional Questions for Discussion and Writing**

1.  Write the backstory for this episode: how old are these people? Where are they from? What do they do for a living? How did they meet? How long have they known each other? What kind of relationship have they had? What differences are there in age, experience, social status? What has led them to this point in their relationship?

2.  Why does the woman say they can't have the whole world, that they can't go anywhere they want, that "it isn't ours any more"? Who's taken it away, and why can't they ever get it back again?

**Making Connections**

→ Compare Jig to the young wife in Morales's "The Day It Happened" or to China in Boyle's "The Love of My Life." What similarities do you see in their ability (or lack of ability) to deal with their male lovers?

→ *An Introduction to Ernest Hemingway's Fiction.* Lecture. 45 minutes, color. Available from Filmic Archives.

SALVATION by Langston Hughes [pp. 279–81]
In preparation, discuss childhood episodes that remain vivid in memory and why. What is it about a certain story that makes it stand out in a child's mind and continue being told into adulthood? Like "Salvation," many such narratives have to do with turning points that are not quite understood by the child but become more meaningful in adulthood.

Hughes captures the liveliness of the revival meeting by including bits of conversation, whispered mutterings, the words of the preacher. Reading these passages aloud will illustrate the contributions of the dialogue.

## Possible Responses to *Questions for Discussion and Writing*
1. The child's point of view dominates the description, while the adult's point of view is evident less often—for example, in the last paragraph in which he obviously knows about what happened in his life after twelve.
2. Answers may vary somewhat, but he stands up "to save further trouble"—i.e., to please his aunt and gain the approval of the adults who have been hectoring him to stand up and be saved.
3. As the last sentence indicates, he cries because he has lost his faith; he disappointed his aunt and Jesus disappointed him. Westley, "swinging his knickerbockered legs and grinning down a me," seems much more aware (and accepting) of his dishonesty and is apparently not bothered by it; so it's doubtful that he cried later.
4. Hughes does not seem to reject religion as such but rather the social pressure that it involves.
5. The irony is that the young boy's "salvation" actually had the opposite effect—his fall away from Jesus—suggesting how the appearance of religion can so easily mimic the real thing. Note that he cried "for the last time in my life but one."

## *Making Connections*
→ Compare the young Langston with other young people who learn a hard lesson about life, especially about the adult world: Sarty in Faulkner's "Barn Burning" and Sylvia in Bambara's "The Lesson."

## *Video*
→ *Langston Hughes.* 60 minutes, color, 1988. Available from Filmic Archives

## *Website*
→ Resources for Reading Langston Hughes from the Academy of American Poets. Provides biography, background, questions, criticism, suggested reading, and links to other sources. **www.poets.org/page.php/prmID/323**

**THE CHRYSANTHEMUMS** by John Steinbeck [pp. 281–90]

Elisa Allen is good with flowers, like her mother before her, but she is vaguely anxious and unfulfilled. Elisa is strong and mature, at the height of her physical strength, but there is no appropriate outlet for her energies. She is like the Salinas Valley she lives in: a "closed pot," shut off by the fog from the sky and from the rest of the world. Her urge to fulfill her nature is directed into the chrysanthemums, which bloom profusely (in contrast to her own barrenness—she has no children).

The men in the story feel none of Elisa's unfulfillment. They take the opportunities of the male world for granted. Henry Allen has sold his cattle for a good price and is celebrating by taking his wife out to dinner. The itinerant repairman is temporarily down on his luck, but he recognizes an easy mark when he sees one. He flatters Elisa and hands her a line about chrysanthemums for a lady he knows down the road. Both men disappoint Elisa. Her husband's reward of a trip to town is just a concession to allow her to accompany him for his entertainment. After Elisa does her hair and puts on makeup and her prettiest dress, the only compliments that her husband can offer is that she looks "nice" and "strong" and "happy." And when Elisa sees that the tinker has cruelly discarded her chrysanthemum sprouts, she is too disheartened even to attend the prizefights (where she might get some satisfaction of seeing men hurt each other, as they have hurt her). At the end of the story, Elisa is "crying weakly—like an old woman"; her strength and energy have been completely depleted.

## Possible Responses to *Questions for Discussion and Writing*

1. The chrysanthemums can, of course, symbolize all of the ideas listed plus any more reasonable connections that your students can come up with.
2. Since the fog "sat like a lid on the mountains and made of the great alley a closed pot," we understand that Eliza is isolated "from all the rest of the world." The foothill ranch where she and Henry live is "bathed in cold pale sunshine," suggesting perhaps that any passion in her life has by now cooled and faded.
3. Eliza craves attention and acknowledgment of her sexuality from both men, but neither responds satisfactorily. As she talks to the tinker, "her breast swelled passionately"; "kneeling there, her hand went out toward his legs" and "her hesitant fingers almost touched the cloth." There is a clear undercurrent of desire in her actions. She later makes herself attractive for Henry, as she prepares for what appears to be like a date with him, but he ruins the romantic mood by complementing her appearance as "nice" and "strong" and happy"—not the way she hoped to be perceived. As a way to get some business, the tinker feigns interest in the chrysanthemums and concocts a story about taking a sprout to another of his customers down the road. (Eliza sees later that he has thrown the flower away but kept the pot.) Her husband manipulates Eliza by complimenting her on her "gift" with plants, hinting that she might be able to help run the farm and suggesting they go to Salinas for dinner and a movie.

4. See the previous answer.
5. Eliza would probably like to break some men's noses and bloody their chests—or see them hurt each other as they have hurt her. But she backs down and settles for wine with dinner.

### Additional Question for Discussion and Writing
➔ Two different ways of life are presented in this story. Identify and discuss them.

### Making Connections
➔ Compare Elisa and Tome Hayashi of "Seventeen Syllables" by Hisaye Yamamoto. How do these women cope with their less-than-satisfactory husbands? Would you say that they are strong women who refuse to be defeated? Explain.

### Video
➔ *The Chrysanthemums*. Film guide with purchase. 24 minutes, VHS. Available from Pyramid Film & Video.

### I STAND HERE IRONING by Tillie Olsen [pp. 290–96]
This story is an often bitter and despondent recounting of the trials of being poor and having children. Olsen's monologue hammers home emotionally wrenching scenes and makes the needs and wants of both mother and child painful to the reader. When the mother refuses to give a conventional "love overcomes adversity" story, the reader must live in poverty with the single mother, rather than gloss over the difficulties. Here is a long tale of missed opportunities, intimidating professionals, and the grievous insufficiency of life at the edge of poverty. It is clear that the living conditions have created spiritual and emotional deprivation as well. The mother gives up much of her life and aspirations in order to care for her children. It is no mystery to her. She tries to suppress her own feelings as she recounts the upbringing of her talented daughter, Emily, to the imaginary audience of a school counselor. The self-control is admirable, if incomplete. Olsen reflects the common experiences of millions of people, and the reverberations strengthen the tone and impact of the story.

Critic Robert Coles points out that the last words of the story "bring the reader back to the first words. . . . A working woman is making the best of *her* situation, even as she expects her daughter to do so. A mother shakes her fist at the universe, not excitedly, and with no great expectation of triumph, but out of a determination to assert her worth, her capabilities, however injured or curbed, her ability to see, to comprehend, and to imagine—and to assert too her daughter's—everyone's." And writer Amy Hempel says that "Olsen gives us the life of a family and of a generation, of the country during the Depression . . . . The story's dignity comes from the mother recounting the things she was unable to do *for her daughter*. . . . What she feels is not guilt but grief."

**Possible Responses to *Questions for Writing and Discussion***

1. When Emily is only eight months old, her mother has to leave her in the care of a woman downstairs "to whom she was no miracle at all." Then the mother has to leave her with her husband's parents. At age two Emily is sent to an ill-run nursery school. When she is four or five, "she had a new daddy to learn to love." She has the red measles and doesn't recover, so she has to go to a sterile and bureaucratic convalescent home for poor children and is there for eight months. She does not do well in school, she suffers from asthma, and she does not get along with her sister Susan. Her mother has four children now, besides Emily, who has to help raise the littler ones. Finally at high school age Emily displays talent as a comedian, and "suddenly she was Somebody," who appears to have a career possibility. Her growing up was difficult since there was never enough money, and she had to share her mother's love and attention with too many siblings, but she seems to have turned out well enough at the end, or seems to have adapted to her many disappointments by developing an at least superficially happy persona.

2. Ironing in this story seems to suggest the pressures in life that can flatten a person's attempts to succeed. It is an especially apt symbol of traditional women's work. The last line reinforces this idea as the mother seems to be hoping her daughter will cultivate her talents, will become aware "that she is more than this dress on the ironing board, helpless before the iron."

3. In that paragraph the mother recounts all the trials that Emily had to suffer in growing up and blames herself for some of those difficulties, at the same time that she makes reasonable excuses for her failings: "I was a young mother, I was a distracted mother"; "We were poor and could not afford for her the soil of easy growth." She seems to blame herself for some of those difficulties but, in fact, carefully outlines the external causes for what would appear to the social worker to be a mother's failures. The paragraph may be seen to function as expiation of the mother's guilt. If the paragraph had come earlier, it would have undercut the effectiveness of the mother's anguished accounting of all of Emily's problems.

4. The mother actually says, "Let her be," not "Let it be." She is, in effect, talking to herself, reassuring herself that Emily will be all right, even if she doesn't enjoy a stellar career: "So all that is in her will not bloom—but in how many does it? There is still enough left to live by." But she wants Emily not to be ground down by circumstances ("helpless before the iron") as she herself was while struggling to raise too many children with too little money.

*Additional Questions for Writing and Discussion*

1. Make a list of the major events of Emily's life. How would *you* sum up this life?
2. Ironing is emphasized in the title and mentioned several times in the story. Why?
3. What is the point of the next-to-last paragraph? Why is this paragraph needed? What would be the effect had it come earlier in the story?
4. Why does the mother say, "Let it be"? Do you think she is right to say this?

### Making Connections

➔ Examine the varieties of mother-daughter relationships in Tillie Olsen's "I Stand Here Ironing," Hisaye Yamamoto's "Seventeen Syllables," and Alice Walker's "Everyday Use." What connections can you see among the relationships and settings of the stories?

### Audio

➔ *I Stand Here Ironing.* 77 minutes, 1 cassette. Includes several selections. Available from American Audio Prose Library.

SEVENTEEN SYLLABLES by Hisaye Yamamoto [pp. 296–305]
From the beginning of "Seventeen Syllables," we are aware of a cultural conflict between Tome Hayashi and her teenaged daughter (who has such an American name), Rosie. Rosie pretends to admire her mother's haiku because she doesn't want to admit that she has not mastered Japanese while "English lay ready on the tongue." She also does not admit that the haiku she likes is a humorous, colloquial one. In the end, Tome realizes that Rosie's promise never to marry is just a dodge like these.

Parallel plots concern the two females moving steadily away from the father's control. As Ume Hanazono (her pen name), Tome creates a strong intellectual life and companions, excluding the conventional, inartistic husband. Rosie discovers her sexuality and thinks much more of Jesus Carrasco than of her father. Both women are veering toward danger.

Ume Hanazono's life ends when her husband destroys her haiku prize. In her unhappiness, Tome tells Rosie about her sad past and how her hormones landed her in America indebted to a slow-witted husband. Rosie, enrapt with sexual feelings herself, is not ready to learn from her mother's example. Her mother, no doubt envisioning her daughter's dreadful future, finds it difficult to comfort her.

### Possible Responses to *Questions for Discussion and Writing*

1. Rosie's mother would like to interest her daughter in *haiku*, but Rosie has no interest in language or poetry, only in a new boyfriend, Jesus, of whom her mother would not approve since she wants to protect her daughter from any premature sexual entanglements. The reason Rosie's mother is so concerned is made apparent at the conclusion of the story, giving it a nice unity.
2. Ume's (Tome's) literary success annoys her plodding, anti-intellectual husband by making him feel inferior. He expresses his anger by destroying her "best poem" prize right in front of the magazine editor who has delivered it, thus bringing her brief writing career to a shattering, abrupt end.
3. Rosie's feelings for Jesus are decidedly sexual: "Thus, kissed by Jesus, Rosie for the first time fell entirely victim to a helplessness delectable beyond speech." At first they have a friendly bantering relationship that soon turns flirtatious, culminating in her sneaking out to meet him after dark and receiving a kiss. Her feelings for him are important since the sexual awakening Rosie experiences with the kiss is the same

hormonal surge that led her mother to ruin her life with a pregnancy by a man from a higher social class who could not marry her.

4. The episodes about Rosie and the ones about her mother focus on their relationships with men: with Jesus, in Rosie's case; with her husband and Mr. Kuroda, in her mother's case.

5. During the visit to the Hayanos, we see the tension between Rosie's intellectual mother and her dull father, as he drags the family home while all but him are having a delightful time. We can also tell that he is jealous of his wife's ability to converse with Mr. Hayanos about *haiku*, a topic about which her husband is necessarily silent and resentful. Rosie is aware of the problem in her parents' marriage but decides to ignore it.

6. Rosie's mother knows full well the power of sexual desire and the enormous price young women often pay when they respond to it. Since she herself has paid a terrible price, she tries to warn her daughter, hoping to spare her a similar fate, but Rosie's "Yes, yes, I promise" comes too quickly, too glibly. It takes Tome a few moments before she can collect herself and comfort her daughter, fearing as she does that Rosie will most likely fall prey to the same compelling hormonal danger that Tome did at her daughter's age.

## Additional Questions for Discussion and Writing

1. What does Rosie mean when she says that she "lived for awhile with two women"? Have you ever felt like this about a parent or relative? Might anyone see *you* as two people at some point in your life?

2. In what ways is *haiku* the central metaphor of the story? What does it suggest about the difficulty of communicating in two different languages, and how does it comment on the role of women in a traditional society such as Japan's?

3. Who is the main character in the story—Rosie or her mother? Compare the story to Tillie Olsen's "I Stand Here Ironing" regarding this same point.

## Making Connections

➔ What are the young women attempting to escape in Yamamoto's "Seventeen Syllables" and Oates's "Where Are You Going, Where Have You Been?" or in Morales's "The Day It Happened"? Will their escapes be successful?

➔ Compare the sexual response and involvement of Rosie in "Seventeen Syllables" with that of China in Boyle's "The Love of My Life." What saves Rosie from China's fate?

## Video

➔ *Hot Summer Winds*. Written and directed by Emiko Omori. Based on "Seventeen Syllables" and "Yoneko's Earthquake." 1991. PBS American Playhouse series.

## THE DAY IT HAPPENED by Rosario Morales [pp. 305–8]

In "The Day It Happened" Rosario Morales presents a glimpse of spousal abuse set in a Puerto Rican enclave within a city in the United States. The narrator, a girl "almost thirteen," is, like Huck Finn, an innocent observer who reports the action without making moral judgments. She, along with her female relatives and neighbors, fears for Maria's safety since they all know she is pregnant and that her husband beats her on Saturday nights. But everyone makes excuses for him: "Ramon had to be out of his mind, that's what most of us thought. I mean you had to be so regularly mean to a person who adored you." Even the long-suffering wife, Maria, "excused his temper," and her mother, instead of confronting Ramon, simply keeps her daughter company when she is "too ashamed to go to church" because of her bruises. This society seems to accept female bullying as a male prerogative. They all expect Ramon to be furious if he catches his wife in the act of leaving him, but instead the macho male falls to his knees, weeps openly, and begs her not to go. To everyone's surprise, including the taxi driver, "Maria had to tell him to drive off." Your students will probably enjoy speculating on whether Maria will eventually return to Ramon—as well as whether she should or not.

## Responses to *Questions for Discussion and Writing*

1. The people in the neighborhood, even the women, seem to take wife beating for granted as a husband's right. Might Morales be saying something about gender and community norms among Puerto Rican immigrants?

2. Josie perhaps feels embarrassed by the beatings because female victims of spousal abuse are often encouraged to think that they have somehow brought it on themselves. Most readers will think she has nothing to be ashamed of; rather, that she should stand up for herself. Her mother, reared we presume in a male-dominated culture like the one in the story, would, most probably, be one of the people who taught her daughter that women should submit to their husbands because that's just the way it is.

3. The narrator, Mami, and the neighbor Olga are all fearful of Ramon's temper ("Someone needed to pray for Josie. It was five o'clock and Ramon was due home any minute"), so we can assume that Josie would be, too, since we know that he beats her regularly, yells at her for no good reason, and that "Saturday nights there was sure to be a fight." Even other macho males in the neighborhood don't approve of Ramon's behavior; he "was too much even for them." We also know that Josie is still crazy about Ramon, despite the beatings. The narrator says it's obvious that she adores him because of "the way she looked at him, boasted of his strength, his good job, his brains." And sadly, she even makes excuses for his violence: "He can't help himself," she reasons. "He doesn't mean it." So when she finally does gather the courage to leave him, we can be sure it's because of her pregnancy: "She was scared he would hurt the little baby growing inside of her and worried about the child growing up with Ramon for a father." Her final courage is inspirational.

4. Ramon undergoes a change that totally reverses his personality. He goes from swaggering arrogance to craven humility. Most readers would likely agree that his true personality may lie somewhere in between the two extremes, but because the machismo culture allows him to be a dominating bully, he takes advantage of the privilege and treats his loving, submissive wife abominably. Both behaviors come from an essentially weak personality.

64

5. Morales's story presents a convincing argument against spousal abuse, showing some of its causes as well as several of its debilitating effects on family life.

## Making Connections

→ Compare the strong Eliza Allen in Steinbeck's "The Chrysanthemums" with the weak wife in "The Day It Happened." How does each character fare at the end of her story?

## DEAD MEN'S PATH by Chinua Achebe [pp. 309–12]

This story dramatizes the collision between progress and tradition. Achebe has said that Africans live at "the crossroads of cultures," and this story presents some of his "fascination for the ritual and the life on the other arm of the crossroads."

At first reading this brief tale seems to be a straightforward account of the failure of a young, progressive schoolteacher to change the superstitious ways of an African village. But a closer look reveals the ironies in Achebe's presentation. The arrogance of the young headmaster, Michael Obi, is hinted at in the description of his wife, who has been "completely infected by his passion for 'modern methods,'" and in his own comment on the "grand opportunity we've got at last to show people how a school should be run."

The climax occurs in the meeting between the headmaster and the village priest. Although Obi has been "outspoken in his condemnation of the narrow views" of others, he is revealed in this scene as the one with narrow views. He listens "with a satisfied smile on his face" and refuses to bend "regulations." Ironically, the more experienced priest is willing to compromise: "Let the hawk perch and let the eagle perch." The outcome is inevitable, and Achebe drives home the irony in the last line of the state supervisor's unfavorable report, which criticizes "the misguided zeal of the new headmaster."

## Possible Responses to Questions for Discussion and Writing

1. The irony in the last sentence of that paragraph is that by the end of the story the views of the "older and less educated ones" have been proven correct. This irony is not apparent upon first reading, even though the whole story turns on it.
2. Obi's wife is clearly devoted to him. She has become "completely infected by his passion for 'modern methods'" and his disdain for the old ways. The choice of the verb "infected" suggests that she has almost been programmed by him. She is considerably self-centered and superficial, as she looks forward to becoming "the queen of the school" now that her husband is in charge. Her clichéd question to him ("a penny for your thoughts") is prompted by a "woman's magazine she read," but clearly not for intellectual stimulation. She is included in the story as a foil for her husband to exemplify his previous success in winning acceptance of his "modern methods," thus heightening the disastrous failure of his new ways at the end.
3. Headmaster Obi fails to bring "progress" to the school because he is arrogant and inflexible, refusing to compromise even though he's been told that "there was a big

row some time ago" when an attempt was made to close the path. He is given ample opportunity to understand why he failed when the government education officer's report states that "the tribal war situation developing between the school and the village" stems partly from "the misguided zeal of the new headmaster." But given the headmaster's character traits, one can easily believe that he will rationalize his failure and convince himself that it is the superstitious villagers who are at fault.

4. The central conflict in the story is between progress and tradition, with progress losing in this case because the protagonist is pigheaded and refuses to respect the villagers' viewpoint or to compromise his own inflexible "regulations."

## Making Connections

→ Compare the clash of old and new cultural practices in Achebe's "Dead Men's Path" and Walker's "Everyday Use."

### AN OUNCE OF CURE by Alice Munro [pp. 312–20]

Before reading this story, ask students to brainstorm memories of events in their teen years that at the time seemed tragic but that they now view as evidence of their inexperience and immaturity. If you have time, ask them to draw simple representations of these experiences and then get into groups and narrate the stories to one another.

## Possible Responses to *Questions for Discussion and Writing*

1. The first-person narrator in Munro's story recounts her experience with humor and self-deprecation from the perspective of a mature adult.
2. We know the narrator's parents are not social drinkers, so it's quite believable that her "disastrous ignorance" about alcohol contributed to the fiasco. In fact, she is generally socially and emotionally unprepared to prevent the disastrous aftermath of Martin's abandonment. The adult looking back recognizes her "own incommodious nature." Her mother tells the Berrymans that although her daughter "seemed to do well enough at school [she] was extremely backward—or perhaps eccentric—in [her] emotional behavior." This caused her mother to give up hope of having a normal daughter—and the girl's behavior seems to bear out this judgment.
3. Without an ability to stand outside and judge her experiences, the young narrator was unable to see the humor in the situation. However, by the time she tells us this story, we see that the narrator has become remarkably perceptive.
4. The mother's own "forthright and unemotional way" kept her from understanding that making her daughter's immaturity so public would deepen the girl's vulnerability to social ostracism. Scapegoating among teens is as common today as it was then, though the acts that lead to being excluded change over time.
5. She is jolted out of her obsession by recognizing "the terrible and fascinating reality of my disaster; it was *the way things happened*." She is released by "a glimpse of the shameless, marvelous, shattering absurdity with which the plots of life, though not of

fiction, are improvised"—which is followed by "an ounce of cure." That cure, of course, is her getting over Martin Hollingwood.

## Making Connections
→ Compare the handling of the retrospective point of view in this story and John Updike's "A&P."

## Audio
→ "Interview." 72 min. 1987. Available from American Audio Prose Library.

THE FAT GIRL by Andre Dubus [pp. 320–30]
This story's limited third-person point of view presents a detached almost clinical look at a young woman who lives most of her life trying to live up to other people's images of her. Her mother warns Louise that boys won't like her if she's fat, but her father's primary means of bestowing love and attention is to encourage her to eat all she wants. In college her roommate Carrie takes over and directs her dieting, and Louise loses almost seventy pounds. But the narrator points out that "she felt that somehow she had lost more than pounds of fat; that some time during her dieting she had lost herself too." Louise does earn the approval of her parents for losing weight, and she wins a husband, too: a "lean, tall, energetic man with the metabolism of a pencil sharpener" who (significantly) works for her father. Satisfying all these other people, however, does not satisfy Louise, who is sometimes "assaulted by the feeling that she had taken the wrong train and arrived at a place where no one knew her, and where she ought not be." So Louise does what she's always wanted to do—she eats. Her thin husband will leave her, of course, but it doesn't seem to bother her: she won't have to keep trying to please him by being someone (some "body") she never can be.

You might use postreading question 4—about the causes or reasons for overeating—as a preparation for reading the story and then return to discuss it afterward. The recent emphasis on obesity in America should give this story relevance and significance, even though it was written more than thirty years ago.

## Possible Responses to *Questions for Discussion and Writing*
1. She knew that they were arguing about how her physical image reflects on him and about his inability to accept her as a fat girl.
2. The central conflict seems to be between Louise's self-image and the image that others want her to have. It revolves around her sense of who she is—her identity— and the attempts of others to redefine her.
3. They are foils who stand for the normative values that Louise has to fight against. They also represent the social forces (peer pressure) that cause Louise discomfort and pain, even though they provide her with support and friendship.
4. The story doesn't seem to take a definite stance on the causes of overeating. It touches on most of the views: psychological, physical, moral, and social.

5. She is unhappy when she is thin. In the end, Louise seems at home with herself, even if it means her husband will leave her. The response to the writing prompt doesn't have to be in narrative form; it could be a first-person entry (or entries) in Louise's diary, a letter or an exchange of letters with another character (her mother or Carrie), or a third-person description by someone like a counselor or a therapist.

### Making Connections
→ Compare this story's messages about image and self-worth to those expressed in the poem "Barbie Doll" by Marge Piercy and the play *Beauty* by Jane Martin.


## WHAT WE TALK ABOUT WHEN WE TALK ABOUT LOVE by Raymond Carver
[pp. 330–38]
Though some readers find no fascination in listening to rich people get drunk and babble, Carver must be admired for reproducing so accurately the timbre of the event (or nonevent). As promised in the opening sentence, Mel does most of the talking in the story. Though he first asserts that spiritual love is the only real love (having been in the seminary but quitting for medical school), he very soon abandons that stance. The violence and suicide of Ed, Terri's old boyfriend, provoke Mel, and he says that those acts were not driven by love. Terri uselessly insists that they were, with Mel calling her "a romantic," further confusing the scene, while Laura and the narrator are so relativistic that they won't even condemn abusive relationships.

The narrator has some kind of definition of love, made obvious when he says of Laura, "In addition to being in love, we like each other and enjoy one another's company," as though the last two items were not included in the definition of love. The idea that love does not last tangles the issue further, with Terri claiming that Laura and the narrator are too newly wed to be experts and Mel being amazed that he used to love his first wife and now does not but loves Terri instead. The ideal of courtly love is suggested by Mel's ramble about knights—but so is the idea of not being injured. The tale of the old people who remain in love floats in and out.

As the story progresses, the effects of drunkenness come more and more into play, with the structure of the conversation becoming ever looser. At signs of sadness or conflict, the characters claim their love for each other, confounding the definition yet again. Toward the end, Mel segues into paternal love and is derailed by hatred for his ex-wife. Finally, the conversation, like the evening, fades into silence and darkness. The story delivers exactly what the title promises.

### Possible Responses to *Questions for Discussion and Writing*
1. The definitions and descriptions of love begin with spiritual love, move on to possessive or violent love, and then love as an absolute gets mentioned but not defined or explored. Next, the narrator, Nick, describes his friendship/love relationship with Laura, who says she knows what love is, but Terry points out that they haven't been together very long. Mel declares that "real love" is "physical love,

carnal love, sentimental love" but admits that it doesn't necessarily last. The characters never really arrive at a definition of love, perhaps because midway through the story they are well into their second bottle of gin.
2. This story can be distinguished from most short stories because it has no plot. Carver's stories are recognizable for their focus on conversation, often meandering and fairly pointless conversation.
3. The narrator is saying that their love is not simply carnal but based on friendship.
4. We are introduced to the four characters in the story and know that one of them, Mel, is a cardiologist; we are given the setting—Mel's sunny kitchen in which the four are sitting around a table drinking gin—and we know they all have come from other places to live in this locale—wherever that is.
5. This assignment should inspire any creative writers in your classes.

### Additional Questions for Discussion and Writing
1. Do the characters really talk about love? Or are they talking about jealousy, misunderstanding, and pain?
2. How does each couple represent a different stage of love?

### Making Connections
→ What type of love is evident at the beginning of the relationship between China and Jeremy in Boyle's "The Love of My Life"? How about the love described in Donne's poem "A Valediction: Forbidding Mourning" or Shakespeare's "Let Me Not to the Marriage of True Minds"? Do these kinds of love fit any of the categories described in Carver's story?


### THE LESSON by Toni Cade Bambara [pp. 339–45]
Bambara's "The Lesson" aptly teaches a lesson of its own: the unfairness of the distribution of wealth in a rich capitalist society—a society "in which some people can spend on a toy what it would cost to feed a family of six or seven" for a year. Sylvia, the feisty, street-smart narrator, knows all the rules of survival in her impoverished environment, but she doesn't quite grasp the lesson in socialist economics that Miss Moore is trying to teach the children by showing them the sailboat in F.A.O. Schwartz. The academically gifted Sugar gets the point at once, but Sylvia at the end of the story is only on the verge of understanding. Intuitively, she's angry; she just hasn't figured out yet who or what is making her furious. Her final line, "Ain't nobody gonna beat me at nuthin," suggests that she soon will get the message and direct her energy and ingenuity toward beating the system.

The story is saved from being overtly didactic by the colorful language and the astute portrayals of the youngsters, with their humorous nicknames and raucous banter. Sylvia, a smart kid with attitude, is the leader of the pack. Yet bright though she is, she misses the point of the lesson because her perceptions are colored by her antagonism toward all authority figures—especially the well-meaning Miss Moore, who represents

69

the establishment only in Sylvia's mind. This antagonism makes Sylvia a somewhat unreliable narrator, especially concerning the right-minded Miss Moore and the other adults. Sylvia starts out intending not to let Miss Moore get through to her. But there are places in the story where Sylvia is affected. One such moment occurs when she notices her own reaction: "'Unbelievable,' I hear myself say and am really stunned." After that, she talks to Miss Moore, hesitates before entering the store, and feels anger and irritation. Since the lesson Miss Moore is teaching is the lesson Bambara wants the readers to learn, Miss Moore is surely a more admirable person than Sylvia makes her out to be.

## Possible Responses to *Questions for Discussion and Writing*

1. Sylvia is a spirited survivor of the racism and poverty that define her community, a bright, verbal, and creative teenager who has learned to reject before she can be rejected and to mock before she can be mocked. Take, for example, her first reactions to Fifth Avenue: "Everybody dressed up in stockings. One lady in a fur coat, hot as it is. White folks crazy." This resourcefulness and potential make her the perfect narrator for the story because she is Miss Moore's perfect student for the lesson. She is a reliable but also entertaining narrator in her honest reporting of her strong thoughts and words. After all, this language and those views are her weapons of self-defense. She is not, however, reliable in revealing those things she cannot yet understand—that is, those things that Miss Moore is trying to get her to see about herself and her potential.

2. Miss Moore is first revealed through Sylvia's eyes as a troublesome outsider, a woman who had been to college, the woman who plots "boring-ass things" for the children. Readers who accept Sylvia's stereotypical view of this "lady" with "nappy hair and proper speech and no makeup" might expect her to be simply a teacher of the kind of cultural lessons that lead to black accommodation or acculturation, lessons about the things to be gained by aspiring to white norms. This is a conformity that the rebellious young Sylvia is not at all interested in pursuing. The adults, on the other hand, are suspicious of Miss Moore, even condescending, but they also sense some promise of opportunity in her influence. Sugar, who hasn't yet developed Sylvia's resistant stance, is more open to Miss Moore's persuasion.

3. While visiting the toy store, Sylvia experiences the familiar emotions of desire and shame, emotions that trigger her resistant pride. In her confused adolescence, this pride leads to a desire to act out, to "punch somebody in the mouth." Eventually, though, left by Miss Moore to discover the lesson for herself, Sylvia begins to articulate a more conscious if not fully understood resentment of her exclusion: "Who are these people that spend that much for performing clowns. . . . What kinda work they do and how they live and how come we aint in on it?" As the group leaves the store, the hard work of Miss Moore's lesson leaves Sylvia with "a headache for thinkin so hard."

4. The last line of the story, "But ain't nobody gonna beat me at nuthin," captures the hope that Miss Moore has succeeded in her lesson, that the spirited, clever girl she sees when she looks at Sylvia has begun to resee her community and her place in the

larger world and that Sylvia will bring her spunk and energy to bear on changing her life, a promise that is underscored by her shift from focusing on the money as the source of some immediate desire (the path taken by Sugar at the end of the story) to a focus on her mind as a place for deeper satisfaction (a need to "think this day through").

5.  If students write this essay, you will want to concentrate a significant part of class discussion on question 1, especially on Sylvia as the naïve but clever narrator of the story.

## Additional Questions for Discussion and Writing

1.  Briefly describe each of Sylvia's friends. How do nicknames help characterize the ones who have them?
2.  In what ways is this a story about borders, both literal and figurative? Pick out examples and explain them.

## Making Connections

→ Compare Sylvia with other young people who learn a hard lesson about life, especially about the adult world: Sarty in Faulkner's "Barn Burning" and young Langston in Hughes's "Salvation."

## Audio

→ *An Interview with Toni Cade Bambara and Kay Bonetti.* 90 minutes. The author discusses her writing style. Available from Audio Prose Library.

## THE LOVE OF MY LIFE by T. Coraghessan Boyle [pp. 345–57]

This compelling story presents a psychological challenge—trying to understand how two young people could be so bright academically yet so ignorant in conducting their personal lives. Since Boyle tells us that the plot is based on an actual incident, the questions are even more pressing. "What were you *thinking*, for Christ's sake?" the girl's father demands, and we as readers also want to know why this tragedy happened to these nice, smart, well-meaning, ambitious kids. How could they go off on a week's outing together and forget their contraceptives? Why doesn't China tell her parents, with whom she has a good relationship? Boyle, who has convincingly embellished the journalistic account of the incident, gives us a clue at the outset in describing China's attitude about sex: "She kept thinking of the way it was in the movies, . . . [with] the music fading away . . . and everything . . . glowing as if it had been sprayed with liquid gold." Remember Madame Bovary who fell prey to similar illusions depicted in the romance novels of her day. And we get another clue later when China tells Jeremy, *"I will never, never be like those breeders that bring their puffed-up, squalling little red-faced babies to class."*

But equally puzzling is China's denial. She is unable to deal with her pregnancy, even though Jeremy prods her repeatedly to go to a clinic. Her paralysis leads to the grim, bloody birth and the disposal of "that thing," that "mistake clothed in blood and mucus," as Jeremy calls it, and the sad rift between the lovers as they are imprisoned. The rift yawns when we are told that China is going to testify against him at the trial. Boyle is making a number of points in this story, one of which is the implication that parents shouldn't trust their children implicitly with adult freedoms. He is, surely, enlisting our sympathy for unwed teenaged mothers. And he is also showing us powerfully the hazard of confusing illusion with reality.

## Possible Responses to *Questions for Discussion and Writing*

1. Both of these young people are so in the grip of their hormones ("their hips joined in the slow, triumphant sashay of love") with few restrictions on their sexual behavior and so sheltered from any financial or social worries that they seem almost to be living in a dream world. By the end of the story that golden world has vanished, replaced by the hardships and restrictions of prison. No more "Swiss-chocolate almond ice cream" or "hot chocolate laced with Jack Daniels." Now China considers her life "ruined beyond any hope of redemption," Jeremy has "lost everything—his walk, his smile" and looks "like a refugee, like a ghost." Instead of cuddling, the two are quarreling, and China is prepared to testify in court against Jeremy.

   They are to blame for what happened to them, although some might cut them some slack because their indulgent parents spoiled them and gave them too little parental supervision. But it was not a lack of supervision that caused the tragedy: it was forgetting the contraceptives—"a mistake," Jeremy calls it—compounded by China's refusal to tell her parents that she is pregnant.

2. China's adamant refusal to deal with her pregnancy is puzzling, but we are told early on that she thinks of sex "the way it was in the movies" with "everything in the frame glowing as if it had been sprayed with liquid gold." She also cares a great deal about her reputation for being smart. Even though she has already been accepted at the university of her choice, she is still "hitting the books" because, she says, "it'll kill me if people like Kerry Sharp or Jalapy Seegrand finish ahead of me." Neither can she bear the thought of being in the same category with "*those breeders*" at her school who become accidentally pregnant. Since an unwanted pregnancy is not in keeping with her self-image, she slips into denial.

3. There is no way to justify China's adamant refusal to deal with her pregnancy then later agreeing to testify against Jeremy in court for getting rid of the baby, but it may be possible to understand why she behaves this way. She sobs to Jeremy over the phone, "I want to see our daughter's *grave*," as if she has an emotional attachment to the baby. When "imprisoned like some fairy-tale princess in her parents' house," she is undoubtedly being heavily influenced by both her lawyer and her parents to claim that Jeremy "acted alone" in disposing of the body, so we can assume that she finally gives in to the pressure.

4. Jeremy feels he has done nothing wrong because he has tried his best to get China to get rid of the pregnancy ("'Go to a clinic,' he told her for the hundredth time"), but she adamantly refuses, even refuses to discuss it. He does as she tells him: gets a motel room, stays with her during the bloody birth, follows her instruction to "get rid

of it. Just get rid of it," and returns her to her dorm room. Later, as the two are being sent off to separate cells, his last words to her are "You told me to get rid of it." So, in his estimation, he has done what he thought was required of him by "the love of his life."

5. Creative writing prompt.

### Additional Questions for Discussion and Writing

1. Why does China behave the way she does? Write a first-person account of this story from her point of view—perhaps in the form a diary entry or a letter to her parents.
2. What role do the parents of China and Jeremy play in this tragic story? Would you put some of the blame on them?
3. If you were a defense attorney, how would you defend China? Jeremy?

### Making Connections

➜ Compare the young couple's response to an unplanned pregnancy in this story with that of the couple in Hemingway's "Hills Like White Elephants."

### GERALDO NO LAST NAME by Sandra Cisneros [pp. 357–58]

This brief sketch from *The House on Mango Street* demonstrates the power of Cisneros's evocative elliptical style. In less than two pages, the author captures the isolation and pathos of the life (and death) of an illegal immigrant. The young man has almost no identity, just a first name. He means nothing to the police or to the hospital workers. The sorry facts surrounding Geraldo's meager existence and insignificant death are revealed through the eyes and reactions of Marin as conveyed and augmented by the unnamed narrator (who is actually Esperanza, Marin's friend and the narrator and main character of *The House on Mango Street*). The narrator punctuates the account with pointed remarks and questions: "Ain't it a shame," "But what difference does it make?" "How does she explain?" "What does it matter?" The narrator also points out that the police and the doctors know very little about the conditions of Geraldo's life: "How could they?" she asks. These comments force the reader to think about the place in American society that people like Geraldo occupy—where does he fit in?—and about the insensitivity and racism of officials who deal with nameless, undocumented workers. In the final paragraph the narrator expresses the respect for Geraldo that no one else in this country has shown and that no one in his home country can: "His name was Geraldo. And his home is in another country."

### Possible Responses to Questions for Discussion and Writing

1. These few details capture the sad state of too many inner-city emergency rooms, which are notoriously understaffed and where highly paid specialists are hard to come by. The poor and the undocumented, by implication, are less likely to receive necessary and life-saving treatments.

2. The "they" are the hospital staff and police who are grilling Marin about Geraldo, a young man whose life and circumstances seem foreign to their own experience. Marin, whose life at least intersects with Geraldo's, is expected to be a mediator, because her questioners fail to distinguish between the lives of Marin and Geraldo— that is, between native and immigrant Hispanics.
3. Cisneros shifts to the point of view of Geraldo's Latin American family in the final paragraph, capturing the fact that Geraldo is alienated not just from those around him in the United States but also from those he left in his home country (who will "wonder, shrug, remember"). He becomes a kind of "unknown soldier."
4. Students might begin this assignment by working in small groups to generate a list of things Marin knows and doesn't know about Geraldo and another list of things the narrator knows or implies about both Marin and Geraldo.
5. Questions 1–5 will help students draw the broad outline of Geraldo's life.

### Additional Questions for Discussion and Writing
1. How does this selection differ from a conventional short story? Would you even call it a short story? What would you call it?
2. What is Marin's reaction to Geraldo's death? Is she annoyed that she has to be involved? Does she care for him more than she wants to admit?

### Making Connections
➜ Compare this story with Erdrich's "The Red Convertible" or Anderson's "Hands." What do these stories have to say about the effects of alienation?

### Video
➜ *Sandra Cisneros*. Interviewed by Dorothy Allison. 60 minutes, 1996. Available from Facets Multi-Media: www.facets.org


THE RED CONVERTIBLE by Louise Erdrich [pp. 358–65]
This story is one of fourteen related stories that make up Erdrich's first novel, *Love Medicine* (1984), which chronicles the lives of two families on a North Dakota reservation between 1934 and 1984. "The Red Convertible" takes place in 1974, when Henry Junior comes back to the Chippewa Indian reservation after more than three years in Vietnam. The first-person narrator—Henry's youngest brother, Lyman—uses the past tense to describe the finality of what happened to his brother and the red Oldsmobile convertible they once shared.

After an opening frame of four paragraphs, the story is told as a flashback, beginning with background on the two brothers and their pleasure in the car and then moving to Henry's return from Vietnam and his disorientation. When Henry fixes the convertible, he momentarily regains some of his former spirit, and the brothers get behind the wheel again, trying to recapture the carefree innocence of their youth. But Henry's inner turmoil, like that of the flooded river they park alongside, drives him to self-destruction. In the last paragraph, Lyman describes how he drove the car into the river after he couldn't rescue Henry, and the terrible irony of his opening remarks—"Now Henry owns the whole car, and . . . Lyman walks everywhere he goes"—is finally made clear.

Erdrich's use of symbolism (the convertible, the open highway, the river) is natural and unobtrusive. The story's episodic structure is loose and comfortable, like the relationship between the brothers; and the laconic, understated presentation of the narrator makes his emotional loss even more poignant and credible.

## Possible Responses to *Questions for Discussion and Writing*

1. The red convertible stands as a symbol of the relationship between the two brothers, reflecting their individual and collective moments of "repose" and struggle. The car runs flawlessly through the months the pair travel the country; Lyman puts the car "up on blocks" while Henry is away at war. When Henry returns with posttraumatic stress, Lyman batters the car to match the frail brother's psychic state. Henry repairs it in a gesture of love for his brother; in their final drive, Henry realizes the impossibility of returning to his prewar self, and Lyman sends the car into the water in recognition of the end of their shared lives.

2. The picture, taken during a fleeting postwar moment of peace and brotherly connection, becomes too painful for Lyman to live with day to day, reminding him of the cost of the war to Henry and to him. Thus it stands as a symbol of the loss outlined by the story as a whole. Lyman seems hopeful at the moment the picture was taken ("Just the way he said it made me think he could be coming around"). This suggests that the picture becomes painful only later, when he rediscovers it and finds he cannot even find joy in remembering this rare moment of calm.

3. Lyman runs the car into the river to return it to his brother, as he has tried to do in the past, and to bring light and understanding to his terrible loss.

4. The discussion of questions 1–4 will provide a number of ideas for this essay.

5. Students might use the condition of the convertible (question 1) as a guide to outlining their response to this prompt.

## *Additional Questions for Writing and Discussion*

1. What do you think happened to Henry in Vietnam that changed him?

2. Describe the effect of the first paragraph when it is reread after finishing the story.

3. What do the episodes of travel (the place under the willows where they rested, taking Suzy home to Alaska) add to the story?

## *Making Connections*

→ Analyze the narrator of this story. Is he reliable? Compare him to other first-person narrators (Sammy in "A & P," Sylvia in "The Lesson," or Cheng in "The Bridegroom").

→ Interview with Erdrich and her husband, Michael Dorris, about the centrality of a Native American identity to their work. 1 cassette, 50 minutes. Available from American Audio Prose Library.

## THE BRIDEGROOM by Ha Jin [pp. 365–78]

Ha Jin has rare empathy for people striving to balance the past and the future while caught on the cusp of change. In this story he explores the clash of humanitarian feelings and bureaucratic intervention. The story's protagonist, who has been taught that "homosexuality . . . originated in Western capitalism and bourgeois lifestyle," is unable to credit his own sympathy for his son-in-law. In his contributor's note to *The Best American Short Stories 2000*, Ha Jin makes this comment about the story's inception:

> "The Bridegroom" was willed into existence. By that, I mean I didn't have the story in my mind originally. For several years I was writing a collection of short stories, all set in a city in Manchuria. To make the collection broad in scope, I needed stories of different styles and of different subject matter. Since homosexuality was a relatively rare and challenging topic, I chose to create a story out of the articles and books I could gather about it. The story was very hard to write and probably took me a year to finish.

> I wanted a narrator who is compassionate but prejudiced at the same time. To my mind, this might be a good way to make the voice convincing and authentic and to give some depth to the story.

At some point in the discussion of this story, you might want to inform students that the Chinese have stopped classifying homosexuality as a mental illness. In April of 2001, the Chinese Psychiatric Association issued new guidelines, which say that homosexual behavior is not considered abnormal. This is a remarkable turnaround for China's mental-health establishment, which had long opposed the World Health Organization's standards calling for acceptance of homosexuality. You might ask students if this information changes their understanding and appreciation of Ha Jin's story.

## Possible Responses to *Questions for Discussion and Writing*

1. The author of the story has the broader experience and modern understanding of homosexuality that the first-person narrator lacks. The narrator offers Jin the opportunity to outline the causes for prejudice against homosexuals, in particular the consequences of inexperience, cultural taboo, and conflicting personal agendas. Jin casts doubt on Cheng's views in a variety of ways, from the snippets of reported dialogue among the gay men ("At last we men have a place for ourselves") to the obvious conflict between the flesh-and-blood man Cheng admires and the stereotype he sees when he casts Baowen as an other, a homosexual.

2. Cheng goes through a sequence of strongly conflicted feelings about Baowen. Before he knows of his homosexuality, Cheng is grateful that Baowen marries Beina but is suspicious that he will cheat on her because she is not conventionally attractive. He develops a fondness for Baowen and is protective of his relationship with Beina. While Cheng is initially unable to reconcile his handsome, kung fu–fighting son-in-law with his own naïve notions of what homosexuals must be like, Cheng spends the remainder of the story vacillating between complete rejection ("All this talk sickened me. I felt ashamed of my so-called son-in-law") and compassion based on his honest reactions to the real man in front of him ("For some reason his faced turned rather sweet—charming and enticing, as though it were a mysterious female face"). In the end, however, his loyalty to and fear of the factory culture requires that he reject Baowen to protect himself and his family ("If I lost my job, who would protect Beina?").
3. Long Fuhai betrays Baowen for the same reasons Cheng must ultimately reject his son-in-law: a fully internalized fear of the power of the Communist political process. Like Baowen, Long Fuhai cannot have a trusting, loving relationship (of the kind Cheng wishes for Beina and Baowen) because of these fears and the self-loathing the cultural taboo against homosexuality creates in both Long Fuhai and Baowen.
4. Despite Cheng's conflicted feelings, and a clear sense of Baowen being "a good fellow," his fear proves stronger than his own instincts as the story closes, with no clear evidence that he can escape the power of the state. That he is right to fear its power is evidenced earlier in the story when the more educated and equally sympathetic psychiatrist tortures Baowen: "I have no choice but to follow the regulations."
5. As someone who has firsthand experience of both American and Chinese life, Jin has a comparative understanding of the complex implications of cultural taboos as well as the consequences of conflicting personal and political agendas.

## Additional Questions for Discussion and Writing
1. How do you assess Jin's narrator, Old Cheng? Is he a reliable narrator?
2. When did you figure out that Baowen was gay? Was it before Cheng found out? If so, why were you able to figure it out before he did?
3. Why does Beina marry Baowen? Is she as uninformed and naïve as Cheng? Why does she say she's going to wait for Baowen, even though she knows he's gay?

## Making Connections
→ Compare the importance of cultural influences in this story with those operating in "Seventeen Syllables" by Hisaye Yamamoto.
→ Compare Ha Jin's treatment of Baowen to Sherwood Anderson's portrayal of Wing Biddlebaum in "Hands." Which depiction is more sympathetic?

**SECONDHAND WORLD** by Katherine Min [pp. 378–79]

Despite this story's brevity, it fully illustrates one of Min's core artistic beliefs, "Fiction is the elegant lie that leads to the truth," in part because it gets "much closer to the emotional truth." The length also allows for a fuller classroom explication than is generally the case with fiction, including a quick read-aloud before discussion begins.

### Possible Responses to *Questions for Discussion and Writing*

1. After students have explained the timing of their grasp of the riddle, discuss the clues Min provides to our understanding of her theme: while details provide temporary distraction and even comfort, they do not provide deeper understanding and long-term solutions.

2. Min has said in interviews that she is "tempermentally suited to be a poet," because "I love words and sounds and cutting to elemental transcendence. But I'm too undisciplined to actually think too hard about meter and rhyme schemes. And I'm sort of attached to character. And to some sort of event or story. (I wouldn't venture as far as plot, because I don't that often in my work.) But my prose writing is lyrical (that kiss of death word), and I would say that short stories, with their possibility of perfection and handheld craftsmanship, are still more comfortable for me than novels." Add these insights to the discussion of her craft.

3. The opening paragraph reflects both the necessary sterility of the burn unit and Isa's escape into its seemingly safe medical objectivity and detachment.

4. This question could be used as a prewriting activity.

### Making Connections

→Compare Min's handling of the theme of grief and death to Anne Sexton's approach in her poem "The Starry Night." Include differences between genres in your analysis.

### Video

→Visit the Burn Survivor Resource Center page and watch one of the "Featured Stories."

**EVACUATION ORDER NO. 19** by Julie Otsuka [pp. 380–88]

Otsuka's story offers a good opportunity to link close reading skills, reader response, and historical context. The discussion and writing questions begin by asking students to study the author's use of the fiction writer's toolbox. They then move to an exploration of readers' personal knowledge and emotional responses and end by excavating the historical events behind the story and how they were represented by popular culture and the media (as opposed to the intimate view offered by the story).

### Possible Responses to *Questions for Discussion and Writing*

1. The time between the mother reading the notice about the evacuation and the family's removal is ten to eleven days. The extent of a reader's ability to understand the mother's actions is partly determined by his or her familiarity with the events of

the Japanese internment. Even those who know about Execution Order No. 19, however, are struck by the collision of the slow pace of the story against the sudden and demanding dismantling of a home and way of life.

2. Choosing to identify the characters by their role in the family rather than by name focuses attention on the family unit and on the fact that their individual experiences represent the larger group of Japanese Americans affected by these events.

3. Students should be able to brainstorm a long list of traits and events to link these characters with both their American and Japanese cultures, though the characters' lives are primarily linked to mainstream American culture at the time: the mother's white gloves when she leaves her home, the son's baseball glove and *Joe Palooka* comics, the daughter's love of Audubon's *Birds of America*. And the family as a whole shares the period's popular music as a soundtrack of their days. Small details, however, remind us of the influence of the parents' heritage: the bonsai tree, the ivory chopsticks, and the rice balls stuffed with picked plums. Until the war and the father's arrest, these elements of their lives are seamlessly woven into a family's everyday life.

4. Ask students to write out their answers to this question and then compare the scenes they have selected. For example, the mother's more complex nature might best be captured in the scene where she throws out *The Gleaners* or when she breaks down in the night and finally allows herself to feel the impact of the events. The son's youth is captured in his teasing of his sister or his need for comfort in the night. And many scenes remind us that the daughter is a girl at once still a child but moving toward adult independence that will now be taken away from her.

5. Students will have strong responses to the white-dog scene. One way to approach it is to study the placement of the scene in the story. Another is to study the mother's actions throughout the scene and to link it to her breakdown later that evening.

6. This website offers access to a number of additional cartoons and editorials that provide valuable comparisons.

## Making Connections
→Compare the impact of the slow unfolding of events in "Execution Order No. 19" and in "The Lottery" by Shirley Jackson. What similar and contrasting goals did the authors have for this approach?

## Website
→Visit the PBS site *Children of the Camps*: **www.pbs.org/childofcamp/index.html.** Included are a description of a documentary on the topic and an extended timeline of the Japanese internment.

**THIS IS WHAT IT MEANS TO SAY PHOENIX, ARIZONA** by Sherman Alexie [pp. 388–97]

The protagonist of this story, Victor, is engaged in a quest to recover his inheritance (which is mainly an old pickup truck that his father left him). He must also come to terms with who he is and where he fits in the world. Victor is in conflict with himself and his surroundings: he is angry at his father, who deserted him and his mother; he is discouraged by the poverty, drunkenness, and isolation of reservation life; he clashes with the tribal elders and blames white society for his problems. Victor has given up hope. His companion, Thomas Builds-a-Fire, is a perfect foil for Victor. Thomas is comfortable with himself and his society; he has embraced the ways of his Native American heritage and is not troubled by the problems of his life. Thomas tries in vain to share his views with Victor—and the rest of the tribe. But Victor doesn't want anything to do with the old ways: "The only thing [Victor] shared with anybody was a bottle and broken dreams." In beating up on Thomas and shunning his friendship, Victor expresses his contempt for his Indian past, which has amounted to nothing for him and his people, and demonstrates how deeply troubled he is by the things that diminish his life. By the end of the story, Thomas has helped Victor recover the truck, but Victor must still find his own peace and identity. In splitting up the ashes of Victor's father, the two young men acknowledge their bond, but what each plans to do with his share of the ashes marks the fundamental difference between them. Ever hopeful, Thomas will take his share and spread them on the water, allowing the spirit of Victor's father to rise. Predictably, Victor is more resigned and pessimistic: he might do the same thing but likens the act to "cleaning the attic" and "letting things go after they've stopped having any use." But he does agree to stop once and listen to one of Thomas's stories. Is that the hopeful beginning of Victor's renewal?

## Possible Responses to *Questions for Discussion and Writing*

1. If his stories are any indication, Thomas spends a lot of time thinking about Victor and his father. This past is too painful for Victor, and the relationship with his father is one that he would rather not confront.

2. Thomas has a strong sense of the connections between individuals and their tribe. In addition, his traditional Indian sense of time transcends Western (linear and narrative) separations among the past, present, and future. This informs his storytelling. For example, at seven, Thomas predicts not just Victor's father's leaving but his motives for it. The emotionally confused and vulnerable Victor, on the other hand, resists these traditional notions, especially the seemingly pointless telling of "the same damn stories over and over again." To hear the stories would require that Victor confront the reasons for his father's leaving as well as his conflicted relationship with Thomas. For others in the tribe, Thomas's stories remind them of what they have lost and the futility of hope.

3. To prepare for this assignment, place students in small groups to select three or four key conversations between Thomas and Victor and to analyze Victor's attitudes toward his father, Thomas, and himself in each.

4. Alexie explores a number of broad themes—love, betrayal, and friendship, for example—all in the context of the loss of native traditions, roles, and values (storytelling, warriors, strong family, and tribal bonds).
5. As part of this assignment, ask students to rewrite one of the main scenes in the story using first-person narration.

## Additional Questions for Discussion and Writing
1. What does the title mean? What does "This" refer to?
2. What do the flashbacks to the two men's childhood add to the story? What purpose do they serve?
3. What's the point of Thomas's conversation with Cathy, the Olympic gymnast?
4. Why can't Victor be friends with Thomas when they get back to the reservation? Why can he be friends with Thomas when they are traveling to Phoenix?
5. Alexie has said that "humor is an essential part of [Indian] culture." Examine the humor in the story and explain how it helps to develop the story's main themes.
6. Watch the movie *Smoke Signals*, which is based on this story; compare the story to the film treatment.

## Making Connections
→ How does this story compare with Louise Erdrich's "The Red Convertible" in its depiction of reservation Indians?

## Video
→ *Smoke Signals* (1998). 88 minutes, color. Directed by Chris Eyre. VHS and DVD. Available from Amazon.com and other sources.

# A PORTFOLIO OF SCIENCE FICTION STORIES

Students are familiar with science fiction stories of various types: ask for favorites from movies and TV as well as from print media. What do they like (or not like) about this genre? Do they distinguish between different subgenres within this type of fiction? As a specific point of reference, ask students if they are familiar with examples of dystopian literature—that is, accounts of a future world in which present tendencies are carried out to their intensely unpleasant culminations. Some of them will probably know *1984, Brave New World, Fahrenheit 451, The Handmaid's Tale*, or the movies *Blade Runner, Brazil,* and *Wall-E*. All of the selections in this portfolio are dystopian in one way or another.

**THERE WILL COME SOFT RAINS** by Ray Bradbury [pp. 398–403]
One of Bradbury's most famous stories, "There Will Come Soft Rains" was written in an era (the early 1950s) when there was great concern about the devastating effects of nuclear weapons. The atomic bombings of Hiroshima and Nagasaki occurred only six years earlier, and this story offers haunting, cautionary images of the desolation of those events. The central irony of Bradbury's narrative is that humans in the story were destroyed by their own technology, much of which was intended to protect and improve their lives. And even though this technology survived the demise of its human inventors, it is destroyed by the forces of nature, which ultimately triumph over all other powers.

## Possible Responses to *Questions for Discussion and Writing*
1. Sara Teasdale's poem expresses the theme that nature is indifferent to human beings. The last four lines recapitulate the effects of the story's ending. And the recitation by a mechanical voice, amidst all the chaos and destruction, adds another layer of irony to the theme of the futility of human effort. Written as a critical response to World War I, the poem is an even more trenchant comment on the lunacy of nuclear war.
2. Brainstorming in groups or as a class will help students to develop and support one of these statements.
3. The words "soft" and "softness" (along with several mentions of "silence") contrast with the frantic action of the story.
4. The house outlives the people who designed and created it. The devices that were meant to protect and support the human inhabitants are useless—against both the nuclear explosion that killed the people and the forces of nature (fire, wind, rain) that destroy the house.
5. Answers will vary. As the penultimate story in the collection, it is possibly meant as a warning that humanity cannot escape its own destructive tendencies, not even by going to Mars. People who are capable of traveling to another planet cannot preserve the planet they live on.

**THE ONES WHO WALK AWAY FROM OMELAS** by Ursula K. Le Guin
[pp. 403–8]
In her novels and short stories, Ursula K. Le Guinn uses speculative fiction to critique contemporary civilization; she is especially concerned about social justice and equality. In this philosophical look at how a utopia works, the author creates a complex civilization, envisioned with detail and authority. She suggests that however carefully one may construct a utopia, human beings will be unhappy with it. Le Guin admits sex, drugs, and music to paradise and shows that even these ingredients will not keep the peace. At the story's center is the psychomyth of the scapegoat; Le Guin takes this notion—that the well-being of some depends on the suffering of others—and pursues it to the extreme. The suffering of the child makes the utopia possible, but it also evokes guilt in some—a reaction that causes them to walk away. Le Guin says she began writing the story with the word *Omelas* in mind. It came, she says, from a road sign: Salem (Oregon) backward. She goes on: "Salem equals schelomo equals salaam equals Peace. Melas. O melas. Homme hélas."

As preparation for reading the story, ask students to ponder or discuss this question: Is a society with universal peace, plenty, and contentment possible?

## Possible Responses to *Questions for Discussion and Writing*

1. The narrator of the story is an individual ("I") from a different society than the one portrayed as Omelas. He is addressing a "you" from his own society. There are hints that he is making up Omelas as he goes along—for instance, he changes his mind about details. While the narrator obviously has complaints about his own society, the closing of the story indicates that he doesn't believe an ideal society like Omelas can exist without a very dark side. Whether the narrator would be one who walks away is an open question.

2. Ideas about who is the protagonist and who the antagonist will vary. One might say that the ones who walk away from Omelas are the heroes (protagonists), and the corrupt structure of Omelas is the antagonist. Perhaps the people who remain in Omelas and reap the rewards of its underlying cruelty are the antagonists.

3. The story seems to be a fable, especially with the suggestion that the narrator is fabricating it as he goes along. It is being told to make a point. The point might be that peace, plenty, and contentment always have a price in distress, deprivation, and misery. This may be too cynical a point of view for many students to accept. Another moral might be that we should be aware of whether our happiness is based on someone else's misery.

4. Modern American society enjoys many luxuries that are the products of people's suffering and exploitation—for example, expensive blue jeans made in sweatshops in China or cheap childcare performed by victims of human trafficking. Omelas can be seen as an allegory about such situations.

5. Creative writing prompt. Suggest students use first-person pronouns: *I* or *we*. Or write from the point of view of a reporter who has interviewed several people who walked away from Omelas.

### Making Connections

→Compare Le Guin's use of the scapegoat theme with that of Shirley Jackson in "The Lottery."

→Compare the use of fantasy in this story and in Hawthorne's "The Birthmark."

**SPEECH SOUNDS** by Octavia E. Butler [pp. 408–17]]

Using surprisingly few descriptive details, Butler lets us know that the story is set in the future after some terrible disaster. Our two main clues are that the roads are full of potholes, and it takes a full day to journey twenty miles. We discover that there are few cars, the bus runs only occasionally, and there are "blocks of burned, abandoned buildings, empty lots, and wrecked or stripped cars." But most devastating is the revelation that, having lost the ability to speak or use language, people are behaving like animals. Not only are people unable to express their thoughts and feelings, but they also resent those few who have not lost the power of speech. The main character, a woman named Valerie Rye, is in constant danger from rampaging males but survives thanks to a forty-five automatic that she conceals in her pocket. This cautionary tale makes us aware of the importance of civil behavior, of the risk of allowing rudeness to go unchecked, and of the need for people to respect each other through courteous speech. The story ends with Rye contemplating what it will mean to be a teacher to the children—to educate them in using a skill that may no longer be of any use, that others will envy enough to murder them.

### Possible Responses to *Questions for Discussion and Writing*

1. Clues in the first two paragraphs that the story is set in the future following some disaster of major proportions are these: it is "a day's journey one way" to travel twenty miles; the bus is lurching over potholes on a major thoroughfare; Rye, the main character, "had expected trouble sooner or later in her journey"; and the two young men having an argument are employing "mock punches" and gestures instead of "lost curses."

2. Rye's name symbol is "a large golden stalk of wheat," since she apparently could not find a symbol featuring a stalk of rye, another nourishing grain. Both grains are used in making bread, universally considered "the staff of life," which suits Rye's role as a nurturer, as she rescues the children at the end. Obsidian, as the story explains, is "a smooth, glassy black rock." Its sheen and hardness suggest the character's relative cleanliness and strength. He is like a rock to Rye, someone she can cling to, until he is blasted to oblivion by a bullet.

3. The children's ability to speak gives the story a hopeful ending; Rye now has someone to care for, to teach, and to care about. She is no longer forced to contemplate suicide from loneliness; and there is even hope that the disease may have run its course, perhaps allowing civilization to be reestablished.

4.  This cautionary tale makes us aware of the importance of civil behavior, of the risk of allowing rudeness to go unchecked, and of the need for people to respect each other through courteous speech.
5.  There is ample evidence—the quarreling, confusion, and fear depicted in the story—to support the claim that language and human speech are necessary for the maintenance of a civil society.

### Additional Questions for Discussion and Writing
1.  How far into the future is this story set? What do you think happened to cause the destruction and the loss of speech? What possible causes are mentioned in the story?

2.  What is a "dystopia"? Look up the term and write an analysis of "Speech Sounds" as an example of a dystopian tale.

### Making Connections
→ Compare Valerie Rye with the strong Eliza Allen in Steinbeck's "The Chrysanthemums." Try to determine what makes Valerie a survivor at the end of her story whereas Eliza is defeated by so little at the end of hers.


### THE YEAR OF SILENCE by Kevin Brockmeier [pp. 417–27]
The author says that in his midtwenties be became unusually sensitive to noise. He resented cars that drove by his apartment with their stereos thumping; he was disturbed by police helicopters that flew overhead when he was trying to sleep; he was even bothered by the hum of his refrigerator. He says he remembers wishing he could "harness the momentary quiet that sometimes came over a room at parties and apply it where it was really needed—to the many engines of the world."

The structure of the story is built around the process of taking away something from a community bit by bit and then returning it in the same way. Brockmeier says that when he finished the story he realized he had been building the narrative "in small discrete chunks of incident"—and that's when he divided the story into short numbered sections.

### Possible responses to Questions for Discussion and Writing
1.  At first the silence had various salubrious effects; the citizens felt the silence was natural and helped them to get to know themselves better: see sections 12 through 15. But when the sound started to come back, "It turned out that in spite of everything the silence had brought us, there was a hidden longing for sound in the city" (section 21). And, "A consensus slowly gathered among us. We had given up something important, we believed: the fire, the vigor that came with the lack of ease" (section 22).
2.  The sections mark out the gradual elimination of sound (incident by incident) and its gradual return.
3.  The first-person plural point of view makes the story seem close up and personal, but

85

it also lends some authority to the events by not limiting the observations and conclusions to those of a single person. This style of narration implies consensus, that everyone in the city attests to what happened.

4. The people seem very advanced technologically and mechanically. Many of the inventions are developed quickly and effectively.
5. Answers will vary.
6. In Morse code, the message is L I S T E N  W E L L.

### Sample Student Paper: Comparing Dystopias [pp. 428–30]

Ask students to write their responses to the interpretations offered in this essay. Identify one more point of comparison that the author missed or left out—and one point of difference that he overlooked. Also, ask how much the use of secondary sources contributed to the discussion. Were they necessary?

# A PORTFOLIO OF HUMOROUS AND SATIRICAL STORIES

**WHY I LIVE AT THE P.O.** by Eudora Welty [pp. 431–40]
This delightful story, which was Welty's first published work, first appeared in the *Atlantic Monthly* in April 1941. The plot consists largely of a battle of words related by a first-person narrator in the humorous hyperbole of the Southern idiom. Welty reproduces this colorful language with consummate skill. Critics have written about the story basically from two perspectives, both focusing on Sister, the narrator. One group thinks Sister truly is unfairly treated, "the only sane person in a childish, neurotic, bizarre family," one who shows "unerring good sense and admirable mastery over the reality in which she finds herself." She is honest about her dislike for Stella-Rondo, who often seems to be a troublemaker. She lies about Sister's behavior with Uncle Rondo and eventually turns the family against her. The family does treat Sister badly (Mama even slaps her), even though she's the only one in the house doing any work. Uncle Rondo sets off firecrackers in her bedroom and finally prompts her to move out of the house.

Other critics, however, see Sister as primarily at fault for the rift in the family. These writers point out her exaggerated self-pity and "ironic self-exposure as a petty and jealous sibling." She leaves the family to save her pride, spitefully taking with her a number of items that the others will miss: the electric fan, the pillow (right from behind Papa-Daddy), the radio, the sewing machine motor, the thermometer, and the "great big piano lamp." The last sentence in the story makes clear her unwillingness to compromise or even to listen to other viewpoints.

Welty herself has commented on the story, suggesting that Sister will move back home once she gets over being mad. "I was trying to show how," she says, "in these tiny little places such as where they come from, the only entertainment that people have is dramatizing the family situation, which they do fully knowing what they are doing. They're having a good time. . . . It's a Southern kind of exaggeration."

## Possible Responses to *Questions for Discussion and Writing*

1. Sister's bids for sympathy are so exaggerated that we laugh: she makes green-tomato pickle because "Somebody had to do it"; "Stella-Rondo hadn't done a thing but turn her against me . . . while I stood there helpless over the hot stove." Among our favorite expressions are "She like to made her drop dead for a second"; "Do you think it wise to disport with ketchup in Stella-Rondo's flesh-colored kimono?"; Uncle Rondo "piecing on the ham"; Stella-Rondo "had a conniption fit"; "kiss my foot"; and "Jaypan came within a very narrow limit of drowning."

2. The racial slur shows that Sister and probably her whole family are uneducated bigots—despite Sister's having gone to the "Normal School" and Papa-Daddy's being a leading citizen of the tiny, jerkwater town. Welty shows the racial prejudice that was endemic at that time in that place, just as Twain did in *Adventures of Huckleberry Finn*. The last sentence in the story also shows us that Sister is closed-minded, unwilling even to listen to the other side of the argument.

3. Stella-Rondo is just as snippy and rude as Sister. When Sister implies that Shirley-T is not adopted (but illegitimate), Stella-Rondo commands Sister in no uncertain terms to "make no future reference to my adopted child whatsoever." She twists Sister's words about Papa-Daddy and lies about Sister's appraisal of Uncle Rondo in the flesh-colored kimono (if we can believe Sister's report of what she had actually said). Mama takes Stella-Rondo's side in the domestic dispute because she clings to the romantic view of her family as happy and doesn't want to believe that her daughter has a child born out of wedlock, which was still very much a shameful thing at the time this story was set.

4. Sister's statement is ironic because she, too, is "cutting off her nose to spite her face" by leaving her comfortable home and moving into the small space at the back of the post office. She tells us three times how happy she is and how much she likes it there, even though there's "not much mail," so she has little to do and almost nobody to talk to. From what we've seen of Sister in the story, we can be fairly sure she wouldn't really be happy living all alone.

5. Critics have written from both of these perspectives. See discussion earlier.

### Audio

→ *Eudora Welty*. 1 hr. CD. The author reads six stories, including "Why I Live at the P.O." Available from Caedmon Records and Harper Audio.

→ *On Story Telling*. 53 minutes, 1961. Available from Audio Prose Library.

**A & P** by John Updike [pp. 440–45]

"A & P" is a frequently anthologized story, perhaps because of the strong first-person point of view. The narrator, a 19-year-old male, lets us in on his stream of thoughts unabashedly. Students may see how this point of view is different from an objective one. The mixed tenses (past and present) reflect the way someone might really tell a story out loud.

The narrator is certainly a disaffected youth, with something negative to say about everything from pineapple juice to Tony Martin. He obviously thinks his job, the people he works with, and the shoppers are beneath him. The fact that he's stuck in a dead-end job, taking orders from a boss he doesn't respect and being careful not to upset his parents, may contribute to his snide attitude. Thus, when he quits, he is not leaving behind a beloved career.

Women in particular come under Sammy's critical scrutiny, and the only female that seems to pass is Queenie (though parts of the other girls with her are magnanimously okayed). The fact that she ignores his dubious heroism, perhaps, is what pushes him to insist on quitting. It is interesting to ponder whether Updike was creating a chauvinist monster on purpose or whether he thought Sammy really was a small-town hero. Your students may be divided on the issue.

Adventurous students might also be interested in reading "A & P Revisited" by Greg Johnson, a contemporary retelling of Updike's story that hilariously transforms

Queenie and her companions into UZI-toting, leather-jacketed terrorists. It's included in a collection of Johnson's stories *A Friendly Deceit* (John Hopkins UP, 1992).

## Possible Responses to *Questions for Discussion and Writing*

1. Sammy exhibits a nonchalant attitude toward his job. The ease with which he quits it certainly shows this, along with his disdain for the usual customers, whom he describes as bums, "sheep pushing their carts down the aisle," "houseslaves in pin curlers," "scared pigs in a chute." He has little affinity, either, for his coworkers. Stoksie, a young man about Sammy's age, already has "two babies chalked up on his fuselage" (a reference to the practice of fighter pilots in World War II, who would proudly affix images of enemy planes they had shot down in air battles on the fuselages of their planes). Sammy observes in what sounds a bit like a sneer, "I forgot to say he thinks he's going to be manager some sunny day." He employs a clever bit of wordplay when he says that the lecherous butcher, while watching the young women go by, is "sizing up their joints." Lengel, the manager, who doesn't even rate a "Mr." before his name, is described as "pretty dreary," with "that sad Sunday-school-superintendent stare." At the end after Sammy quits, his attitude changes. Now dejected, Lengel "begins to look very patient and old and gray."

2. Sammy quits his job as a protest against his boss's rebuke of the three young women in their skimpy bathing suits: "So I say 'I quit' to Lengel quick enough for them to hear, hoping they'll stop and watch me, their unsuspected hero." Sammy sees his gesture as an act of heroism on his part, but since it's evident that he's bored with his job and wants out of it anyway, he has made no sacrifice. The young women simply hurry out without giving him a second look, eager to get away from the embarrassing situation. He walks out, looking for "my girls," but they are long gone.

3. We have no way of knowing whether the world will be hard on Sammy hereafter. We do know that his parents will be disappointed, perhaps angry, that he has quit his job for little or no reason. His "stomach kind of fell," so perhaps he's having second thoughts already and thinking the job maybe wasn't so bad after all. But he's young and has a supportive family (his mom irons his shirts and his parents are friends of his ex-boss; perhaps they'll help him find another job). But he's definitely feeling let down because he thought he was making a gallant gesture and nobody even noticed.

4. There's no doubt that Sammy, the first-person narrator, is sexist. He objectifies the young women, focusing in detail on their bodies as they walk through the store. But the real clincher is his observation that "you never know for sure how girls' minds work (do you really think it's a mind in there or just a little buzz like a bee in a glass jar?)." And his observation about "the plump one in plaid, that I liked better from the back—a really sweet can" is majorly offensive, as is his referring to one of the three as "Big Tall Goony-Goony." But the story itself is not sexist. The story clearly reveals Sammy's sexist behavior as adolescent and even laughable.

5. This writing assignment will help students to grasp the importance of point of view in fiction, as well as in understanding how human beings respond to social

interactions in real life, depending upon their own attitudes and position in a social setting.

## Additional Questions for Discussion and Writing

1. Why do you think the story is written in mixed past and present tense?
2. Can Sammy's decision to quit be seen as a positive one? Explain how it might be interpreted as a gesture to break with conformity, to be independent, and to do the right thing.
3. What do you think of Sammy's use of detail, especially in describing people? What do the figures of speech he uses indicate about his character?

## Making Connections

➜ Compare Sammy to Jake in Dagoberto Gilb's "Love in L.A." What do these characters have in common?

## Audio

➜ *John Updike*. The author reads six stories. 169 minutes. Available from American Audio Prose Library.
➜ Interview. 1980. Available from American Audio Prose Library.


## HAPPY ENDINGS by Margaret Atwood [pp. 445–48]

Atwood's modern parable of life's many possible twists and turns can be read in any number of ways: as a clever feminist transgression of the romantic fairy tale, as the experienced writer's parody of pedestrian writers of formulaic genres, as a middle-aged person's ironic summary of the battle between free will and fate.

The opening story, version A, introduces the conventional elements of the happy modern relationship: love, jobs, "a charming house," "two children," a "challenging sex life," "worthwhile friends," "fun vacations," the ability to retire, "stimulating and challenging" hobbies, and a timely and apparently quiet death. From there Atwood offers up five prequels, sequels, and variations that add texture, depth, and complication.

First come the human variables. Love doesn't always happen as expected: in version B, a prequel, "Mary falls in love with John, but John doesn't fall in love with Mary." And sex may be merely a "selfish pleasure and ego gratification" that, in this case, ends in Mary's suicide, a tragedy. In version C, a sequel, John, now married to Madge, has achieved his "respectable job and is getting ahead in his field," but, sadly, the younger love interest, Mary, "isn't impressed by him," leading to tragedy number two, a murder/suicide and an indirect feminist recognition of the varied ways in which women and men face obstacles to their "happily ever after" version of their lives.

Versions D and E shift outside the relationship to natural disaster and illness, events beyond human control that Atwood satirically frames as choices: "If you like, it can be 'Madge,' 'cancer,' 'guilty and confused,' and 'bird watching.'" Finally in F, Atwood brings forward her parody of formula fiction, making "John a revolutionary and Mary a counterespionage agent" but reminding the would-be author that "you'll still end up with A" and a reminder to the persistent romantic and the optimistic young reader that all stories share one "authentic ending," "John and Mary die. John and Mary die. John and Mary die."

Finally, all readers are led to the moral of the story, that a plot (what happens) is really only interesting in light of interesting cause and effect, the "How and Why." Questions 1 and 2 should help students to tease out Atwood's central themes and to engage them in responding to her views.

## Possible Responses to *Questions for Discussion and Writing*

1.  Version A defines classic romance and the dream life; version B explores male sexual exploitation and a female one-sided love, an inequality that leads the insecure Mary to build her life around her need for John to the exclusion of everything else; version C explores the love that erupts from a male midlife crisis, when all of John's past successes with classic romance and the American Dream fade in the face of "his hair falling out" and Mary's attraction to the younger man with "a motorcycle and a fabulous record collection"; version D returns to "true love" but the good life is literally destroyed by a "tidal wave," which, in version E, is further complicated by Fred and/or Madge's cancer and death. Version F brings all the versions into thematic focus: romance and the good life are, finally, a matter of random good luck; gendered notions of love, romance, and the successful life interfere with genuine love, mutual and respectful; good love stories focus on the complexities of human relationships, not the easy and superficial clichés.

2.  This refrain succinctly captures Atwood's sarcastic view of romantic expectations, in life and literature, that compel resistant readers to succumb to the narrative appeal of the genre. After exploring the elements of romance and the dream life in version A, you might use this refrain to explore students' reactions to Atwood's critiques of what are likely to be very real and immediate goals and ideals in students' lives.

3.  As in her use of the refrain discussed in question 2, Atwood's repetition of "John and Mary die" captures the fundamental truth and simplicity of this key life "plot" event—a reality that reader and writer alike must face.

4.  As Atwood makes explicit in version F, version A concentrates on the "what" alone, but subsequent versions add the more interesting "how" and "why." These particular phrases allow Atwood to critique the sexist nature of John and Mary's relationship, concentrating on the effects on Mary. Ask students to identify and compare key phrases in version C, where Atwood highlights the effects of gender roles on men in romantic relationships.

5.  Before assigning this essay, but after class discussion of questions 1 through 4, you might allow student groups to brainstorm in response to Atwood's quotation, focusing on how it reinforces or challenges any conclusions the class arrived at during discussion and whether it conforms to their own experiences and preferences.

**MY KID'S DOG** by Ron Hansen [pp. 448–51]

"My Kid's Dog" derives its humor partly from the slapstick situation—clueless daddy caught with a suspiciously dead family pet on his hands—and partly from the point of view, that of the daddy himself. This point of view is completely limited to the narrator, whose monologue tells us more about him than he probably realizes. However, the very fact that he can tell a joke on himself, involving Sparky's posthumous revenge, lends the narrator some likeability.

As a prereading exercise, you can ask your students to reminisce about family pets (their own or other families'). Did the whole family feel the same way about the pet? What was each person's relationship with the animal? What family strengths and weaknesses were brought out by taking care of the pet's needs?

## Possible Responses to *Questions for Discussion and Writing*

1.  The dog's name is Sparky, but the father calls it by at least eight different names. This purposeful lack of memory for the right name reflects that the narrator is not close to the dog, doesn't deal with him much, and doesn't believe that he is really worth much note.
2.  The narrator might be described as egocentric, well-off, spoiled, easily slighted, put-upon, sexist, superior, deluded, and educated, among many other descriptive terms. Exactly how much of this he means to reveal in his monologue is not certain. For example, his use of high-flown language ("an inventory of my progeny," "a condition of plenitude," "a sojourner on this earth") could be interpreted as self-mocking, mismatched to the silly domestic situation being described.
3.  Middle-class suburban life in this story is superficial and stereotyped—for example, each family member's activities are sex- and age-typed to a ridiculous extent. The relationships among the members are portrayed as weak and mutually exploitive, which may be the serious point Hansen is making. His mention in the headnote of "a more nuanced view of evil" may be applied to the spiritual emptiness of this apparently normal happy family.
4.  Most students will not think that the narrator changes over the course of the story. In fact, at the end the status quo is even reinstated down to the inclusion of a new family dog. The narrator appears to like himself the way he is and to think that his situation is humorous: no soul-searching is required.

## Videos

→ Ron Hansen reads "My Kid's Dog" and reveals the model for the main character at **http://vimeo.com/14916705.**

→ Hansen can be seen accepting an award as a Catholic fiction writer and talking about his work at **www.youtube.com/watch?v=H2niMvpyIUA.**

**NUIT OF THE LIVING DEAD** by David Sedaris [pp. 452–57]

David Sedaris has made a career out of the humor to be found in human nature by the alert and self-aware outsider, in this case, by an American living in France—and by a man who is willing to admit his fear of the dark and who is more interested in saving than hunting down a mouse. One approach to discussing the story is to identify the many kinds of outsiders in the story (including the ones just mentioned but also the burglar as "a Gypsy, a drifter, and, on two occasions, an Arab," as well as the spooks and zombies and the foreign tourists—a nice doubling of the American acting as a local in what he now thinks of as "my willage").

As question 6 suggests, this story also offers an ironic look at pop culture through an interesting mix of common and sophisticated allusions. Ask students to search for these references, which might include the title; the classic circulating story of the burglar ("I heard the story from four people, and each time it happened in a different place"); the cowboy shootout ("a flashlight in each hand, holding them low, like pistols"); the familiar plot elements of the classic horror story (the innocent stranger who happens onto the scene of the crime and, of course, all the props in the Sedaris kitchen).

Finally, you might begin your discussion of the style of Sedaris's humor by doing a close reading of the opening line of the story: what, exactly, does Sedaris find "strange"?

## Possible Responses to *Questions for Discussion and Writing*

1. Sedaris is both sympathetic and empathetic. While the events are cast in ironic terms, Sedaris is shown from the start as an advocate for the mice in his house. His goal is to spare the cute critters from death in his partner Hugh's attic traps and more immediately, on this night, to free a caught mouse. The irony deepens when he must save the mouse from suffering the effects of Sedaris's own good intentions. All of this, of course, counters the straw-stalker image of Sedaris that emerges from his description of his house when the van of tourists visits.

2. Sedaris tells three primary stories: the story of the dying mouse; the digression into the oft-recited village story about the burglar who dies in the chimney; and his interactions with the tourists who stop for directions. There are also secondary digressions (the Camembert-eating contest, the history of the Visible Man), but the mouse and the visitor stories converge as the immediate real-time narrative and become the occasion for Sedaris's more central purpose of reflecting on storytelling and genre—from the oral tradition of community gossip (the burglar story) to the effects of ghost and horror (and especially zombie) stories on people's real-life fears and actions (and thus the title of the story). Students will recognize the "telephone game" nature of the burglar story and will likely have friends and relatives who, like Sedaris, have found themselves caught in hopeless do-gooder actions or in their fear of the dark.

3. Exaggeration and interestingly juxtaposed images begin early: for example, "I think a death by starvation might command the headlines, for, oh six years." They also arise from his anthropomorphic readings of the hurt mouse's feelings ("He would

93

run down the stairs and into the yard, free from the house that now held such bitter memories," and the mouse "popped back to the surface and was using his good hand to claw at the sides of the bucket"). But such methods cluster, for the most part, in the description of the kitchen after Sedaris and the tourist enter: the organs of the Visible Man being stalked by the "large taxidermied chicken," the "meat hooks hanging from the clotted black interior" of the chimney, and the "meat cleaver lying for no apparent reason upon a photograph of our neighbor's grandchild."

4. As Sedaris introduces the theme of ghost and horror stories in paragraph 12, he creates the humor by mixing images of horror (ghosts, Nazis, death, pus-covered nightgowns) with especially informal phrasing ("to lurch out of the gate," zombies who "come a-callin"). In paragraph 13, he further contains the images of horror through the introduction of pedestrian domestic tasks ("writing letters, cleaning the oven, replacing missing buttons"—but not doing laundry out of fear of missing "shuffling footsteps of the living dead").

5. This writing prompt would be a logical follow-up to the discussion about the outsider suggested earlier and should be made more successful by the close attention to detail in questions 3 and 4.

6. The French *nuit* (night) adds depth to the classic horror film *Night of the Living Dead*, placing immediate emphasis on the long-term emotional side effects of such films and setting up his clever parody of the usual plot and typical images of the genre.

# A PORTFOLIO OF GRAPHIC FICTION STORIES

Many of your students will have read graphic fiction in its varied contemporary forms, but it is well worth spending a few minutes on the distinct qualities of the genre and teaching the specific reading strategies that will increase their appreciation for and understanding of the stories. One way to do this is to assign Hollis Margaret Rudiger's brief article "Reading Lessons: Graphic Novels 101" (*The Horn Book Magazine*, 82 [2006]: 126–35.) The article is available on the *Horn Book* website: **http://archive.hbook.com/pdf/articles/mar06_rudiger.pdf.** Rudiger demonstrates visual reading techniques using *Daisy Kutter: The Last Train* by Kuzu Kibuishi. She includes each of the elements mentioned in the textbook: the panel or bubble/box, the gutter or space between the panels, and the size and arrangement of these elements.

## TIME FLIES by Art Spiegelman [pp. 458–66]

One way to prepare students for the historical realities of the holocaust as they play out in the story is to assign sections of the University of South Florida's "A Teacher's Guide to the Holocaust": **http://fcit.usf.edu/holocaust/timeline/timeline.htm.** Class discussion might then include a comparison of their own more general knowledge with the specific historical and social events explored on the site. This experience of the gap between personal experience and historical events is at the heart of Art's exploration of his father's and his own stories in "Time Flies."

## Possible Responses to *Questions for Discussion and Writing*

1. This story includes many of the major themes of *Maus* as a whole: father/son relationships, the effects of the holocaust on survivors and their children (especially survivor's guilt), and the complexities of creating art that intersects with the author's personal life. The central visual cues of the story are Art's body as it grows and reduces in response to his emotions and thoughts and the recurrent piles of dead mice bodies that populate his emotional everyday life. In the fifth panel, for example, Art is burdened by the weight of both broader history (the bodies of the mice/Jews killed in the holocaust) and personal history (his mother's suicide and his own tendency toward depression).

2. "Time Flies" moves between the life of the father, Vladek, and the son, Art. As an artist at work on the story of his father's experiences in the German camps, both times seem equally present and vivid in his imagination. The parallels in the second and third panels, for example, focus a reader's attention on the similarities and contrasts between the deaths that dominate his father's story and the births of his own life, both of his child and his book.

3. The opening panel is a good example of the effects of showing the mask. As he works at drawing his book, Art is weighed down by his many identities. The top two panels on p. 462 show the effects of the shift from schematic to mask: in the first panel Art is fully in character as a Jewish child; in the next we are reminded that the child is imagined, a mask, and that his struggles with his past come from the "ghost"

of his father's history. Spiegelman having drawn his holocaust story as an animal fable has been the focus of much critical attention. Additional questions about the masks and figures might include these: Why show Jews as mice and Germans as cats? Can a schematically drawn "cartoon" be a respectful investigation of such a horrific historical event?

4.  Art struggles with the question of whether or not he should be writing his father's story, about his "credentials" for telling a holocaust tale and the reception it might receive. Beckett's existential claim about meaning and the effects of writing perfectly suits Art's own paradoxical relationship with his book: he has both a desire to escape his history, that is to remain silent, and a need to explore and therefore come to some understanding and peace or "absolution."

5.  Pavel provides Art with a contrasting version of the holocaust survivor, which allows Art a more complex critique of his father's responses to the war: to see Vladek as both an individual and a survivor. Pavel's love of stray cats and dogs provides some of the most overt irony in the story. The fifth and eighth panels on p. 462 call attention to Art's own use of animals as symbols and to the fact that we are at that very moment reading a book about the author writing the book we are reading.

6.  The references to the film and popular culture industries on p. 461 provide a good start for this writing exercise.

## Additional Questions for Discussion and Writing

1.  Write an analysis of the title as a double entendre. How do the panels on p. 460 expand on this figure of speech?
2.  Reread the panels on pp. 463–65. What are Pavel's goals in this therapy session? Does he succeed? Why is learning about the job of the cutter so helpful to Art?

## Making Connections

→Compare the effects of generational barriers on parent/child relationships in "Time Flies" and Tillie Olsen's "I Stand Here Ironing." Does it matter that one story is told by the child and the other by the parent?

## Video

→ Spiegelman's recent book *MetaMaus: A Look Inside a Modern Classic* (2011) includes a DVD with selections from his interviews with his father and other research materials used in creating *Maus*.

FUN HOME by Alison Bechdel [pp. 466–76]

Like "Time Flies," "Fun Home" is autobiographical and thus in many ways about the relationship between memory and time. Further, both Spiegelman and Bechdel are especially interested in how parent/child relationships shape art. Before reading "Fun Home," ask students to reflect on their own ability to remember specific interactions with their parents when they were children and how time has changed their feelings about and attitudes toward those memories. Follow up with discussion of how those experiences might have shaped their current talents and career goals.

## Possible Responses to *Questions for Discussion and Writing*

1. The last panel is a perfect visual representation of the isolation and alienation within the Bechdel family. Compare that panel with the unusually domestic scene in the final panel on p. 468. What complex mix of nostalgia and regret or even anger is captured by both?

2. Students might find their experience with Google Maps or Google Earth helpful in analyzing the way that Bechdel moves from the satellite view of her hometown in the first panel on p. 467 to the close-up shot of her father in the car. Ask students to analyze Bechdel's motives for these constantly shifting points of view.

3. The movement on p. 469 captures another shift in point of view, having us first stand with the young Alison, optimistically gazing through the camera lens at a sunrise, but finally panning out so we watch her as she walks through the polluted creek. Like many of the shifts in the story, this represents the tensions between a child's hopeful nature and an adult's realistic and more ironic knowledge. Ask students to trace their own feelings about these shifts in tone and their own experiences with moving from innocence to experience.

4. It captures the paradox of Alison having inherited her creative sensibility at the expense of a loving and supportive family experience. Further, it traces the honing of her art away from the aesthetics of her father, who repressed his daughter's budding talents by inserting his own art into hers.

5. "Fun Home" is largely about Bechdel's relationship with her father, but the blending of voices on the tape shows how both parents lived caught up in their individual artistic passions, regardless of the effect on their children. Also, though graphic fiction is largely visual, these panels engage another sense, playing the soundtrack of Alison's home.

6. Students might begin in groups, brainstorming the qualities of parenting in the story into columns of positive, negative, and those that are both.

## *Additional Questions for Discussion and Writing*

1. Look closely at the first panel and analyze the use of boxed commentary. Why are the boxes on the right and left separated as they are?

2. Locate instances of direct irony in the story. Begin with the final panel on p. 469.

## *Making Connections*

→ Both Spiegelman and Bechdel make references to famous writers and books. Locate these allusions and write about their effect on your reading of the stories.

### Video

→Bechdel recorded a YouTube video about her creative process, including what she terms the necessary "visual research" for capturing authentic historical detail and accurate body language for characters. "Alison Bechdel—Creating Fun Home: A Family Tragicomic": **www.youtube.com/watch?v=cumLU3UpcGY**


THE VEGETABLE by Marjane Satrapi [pp. 476–86]

Satrapi and French graphic artist Vincent Paronnaud made a film version of *Persepolis* in 2007. It received an Oscar nomination for best animated film and won the Jury Prize at the Cannes Film Festival. After reading and discussing the story, you might show the section of the film that covers "The Vegetable" period of her life or stream one of the many movie trailers available on the web. The tone and style of the graphic versus animated versions of the story are strikingly different and could lead to lively discussion as well as to writing topics.

### Possible Responses to *Questions for Discussion and Writing*

1. The opening panels, on Satrapi's responses to her growing adolescent body, capture a universal teen experience. The peer pressure to experiment with drugs and competition among girls for boyfriends are also typical. Atypical, however, is her physical separation from her parents as she goes through these struggles and especially her alienation from her Iranian identity in a foreign country.

2. While Satrapi chose to hide her identity from her friends, and even to suppress her own feelings about that identity, when her friends openly construct their own distorted versions of who she is and why she isn't open about herself, she erupts into a declaration of family and national pride. The result is an erasure of the guilt she's experienced.

3. Ask students to identify panels that would support the view that her style captures a child's point of view. A good example is the vegetable panel (p. 480) where she draws a literal representation of her parents' figurative metaphor. Then ask them to contrast this with the "super hero" panels such as the first panel (p. 477) or the last panel on p. 484.

4. The discussion of this question might begin with brainstorming what students know about Iran and the Iranian Revolution in 1979. Because this is likely to generate few historically or culturally specific responses, they can then discuss what more specific details they learned from the story itself about Iran and how Satrapi and her family experienced the revolution.

5. Group discussion of the style and tone of these two panels provides students with a good starting point for the essay.

## Additional Questions for Discussion and Writing

1. Describe Satrapi's self-constructed physical transformation on p. 478. What does she mean when she says, "It was beginning to look like something"?
2. Explain Satrapi's and Momo's contrasting views of death. How does this interaction prepare us for her final decision to break away from these friends?

## Making Connections

→ Revisit Spiegelman's last panel on p. 460 and Satrapi's last panel on p. 482. What similar goals do these panels achieve despite their differences in tone?

# PART III  WRITING ABOUT POETRY

## Chapter 12  How Do I Read Poetry? [pp. 488–91]

This brief chapter is a general presentation, an overview of terminology so that your students will have a base to work from. These concepts will all be more fully explained in the chapters following. Be sure to call to the attention of your students the useful "Critical Questions for Reading Poetry" list at the end of this chapter.

One excellent way to introduce your students to the study of poetry is to dazzle them with its sound. If you read poetry well (or if you know someone who does), a prepared reading can help students hear the pleasures of the form. Another excellent choice is to play recorded poetry for the same purpose. Or, if you write poetry or have colleagues who do, you can arrange for a live poetry reading and, possibly, a discussion of why people write poetry and why it's important and valuable in our technological world.

### *Activities for Creative and Critical Thinking*

You can help your students to enhance their appreciation for poetry and integrate their reading and writing skills by using some of the following projects:

- Find a song lyric that you think deserves to be called poetry. Write a short essay about this lyric that explains its poetic merits.
- Listen to some recent examples of rap and compose a short rap lyric of your own, one that tells a story.
- Record several different people reading the same poem aloud. Then write an analysis of these oral readings, focusing on the different interpretations that various readers give to the poem.
- Write a parody of any poem in this book. Do it in either prose or verse, but make it follow the structure of the original as closely as possible.
- Rewrite a lyric poem as an essay or a story. Assume the point of view of the persona in the poem; try to express the persona's feelings and ideas in prose. Don't just transcribe the poem into prose; try to capture the tone and message in your own words.
- Write a background commentary on the situation and emotions of the speaker in a poem. What circumstances and/or motives led this person to say what he or she says in the poem?
- Write an imaginary journal entry for the speaker of a particular poem.
- Write a letter to a poet, telling the author what you think of his or her poetry. Or ask questions about a specific poem. If the poet is still alive, send your letter to her or him.

# Chapter 13   Writing About Persona and Tone

[pp. 492–510]

Encourage students to use the term *persona* or *the speaker* (instead of "the poet says") for the sake of accuracy. Sometimes poets do speak in their own voices, but often they do not. And when they do not, the persona frequently is voicing ideas and attitudes that are the opposite of those espoused by the poet. Tone is sometimes of little importance in a poem, but when tone is important, it can be crucial. To miss an ironic tone is to miss the meaning of the poem.

## *Who Is Speaking?* [p. 492]

As an introductory writing experiment, ask students to adopt a persona and write in the "voice" of that persona. For instance, have them write as a parent to a son or daughter at college who keeps asking for more money (or who wants to drop out of school or has gotten in trouble with campus security). You can make the writing prompt as detailed or as general as you think it needs to be. You can also direct the writers not to identify their personas explicitly in the text and then have other students (in small groups or pairs) try to figure out who is writing. Ask them how they determined the identity of the writer (persona)—i.e., what clues were provided in the text?

## *What Is Tone?* [p. 493]

In this chapter we focus on verbal irony, since it's the main form of irony appearing in poetry. Because students frequently fail to pick up on irony, you may want to direct their attention to the other kinds—situational irony and dramatic irony—discussed in the glossary [pp. 1095–96].

To get at tone in written discourse, you can vary the earlier writing activity and direct your students to write more than one version of the same text—i.e., a letter from an angry, frustrated parent and one from an easygoing or permissive parent. Ask your students to discuss what changes in word choice and sentence structure occur as the tone changes.

A brief experiment involves asking your students to rewrite just a few lines of a poem to alter the tone. How many words have to be changed? Can one alteration change the tone? Insist that students find precise adjectives to describe the different tones they have created. Or ask your students to rewrite the titles of poems to suggest a different tone. What happens when we change "My Papa's Waltz" to "My Daddy's Dance" or "The Old Man's Rock 'n' Roll"? Can "The Ruined Maid" be retitled "The Fallen Woman"? Why didn't Hardy call his poem that?

## *Describing Tone* [p. 493]

You might want to add these to the list of adjectives that can describe tone: *angry, austere, bombastic, breezy, colloquial, comic, confessional, dreamlike, earthy, erudite, facetious, irreverent, nostalgic, ominous, pompous, prurient, sardonic, sensuous.*

### Asking Questions About the Speaker in *"My Papa's Waltz"* [pp. 499–500]
There is a good deal of disagreement about the tone of this poem. Individual responses to these questions will vary a lot, depending on personal experience and taste. Encourage students to be honest, and allow for a variety of opinions.

### Considering the Speaker in *"The Sins of the Father"* [p. 501]
Answers to some of the questions many vary.
1. The use of first-person pronouns ("my" and "I") along with the details from the past suggests that the speaker and the poet are the same person. The topic and the speaker's response seem authentic—at least based on an actual incident.
2. At first he's worried that his daughter thinks she is responsible for being teased and that she thus feels alienated and unwanted. He's heartbroken and upset for her—and then angry and vengeful ("makes me want someone / to pay").
3. His realization comes in line 8: "It makes me think—O Christ, it makes / me think of things I haven't thought about / in years." The feelings change from anger to disbelief and self-recrimination and finally to regret and helplessness.
4. The father takes on his daughter's guilt: he contributed to the practice of bullying and it's come back to haunt him. He failed to break the cycle of bullying.
5. Answers will vary: some may agree that there's nothing the father can do; others may feel that he should do something (talk to her, try to build up her self-confidence, buy her some new clothes).
6. The title comes from the biblical warning that the sins of the father are visited on the children (Exodus 20:5, Deuteronomy 5:9). As a onetime bully, the father does indeed blame himself for what happened to his daughter.

### Describing the Tone in *"The Ruined Maid"* [pp. 501–2]
Responses to these questions will vary, of course.
1. An innocent young woman from rural England (probably Hardy's home of Dorset) encounters a friend ('Melia) who has run away to London. The unnamed young woman questions 'Melia about her fancy clothes and citified ways.
2. "Maid" means an unmarried young woman, a virgin. This last meaning is crucial to the ironic tone and the idea of lost innocence. Hardy does not mean a female servant.
3. One definition for the noun *ruin* is "physical, moral, economic, or social collapse." The poet's almost cynical point turns on the fact that 'Melia's supposed moral collapse is accompanied by physical, economic, and social improvement.
4. 'Melia is probably a well-paid prostitute or a "kept woman." The bracelets, feathers, gown, and painted face (lines 13–14) suggest her occupation, as does her "lively" lifestyle (line 20) and her tendency to "strut" (line 22). In current American slang we might call her a "party girl" or a "call girl."
5. The opening tone of the questioner's lines is one of amazement and disbelief; by the end of the poem she is speaking with admiration and envy.

6. 'Melia seems proud, proper, cool, and even condescending. One critic has said she speaks with "cheerful irony" about her "ruin." Certainly she does not act ashamed.
7. The use of "ain't" in the final line might be taken as a slip into her former vernacular speech, suggesting that her urban polish does not run deep. But it is also possible to see 'Melia reverting to the ungrammatical language intentionally, with obvious relish, to emphasize the difference between her and her former friend. This interpretation reads the last line as a final mocking jab at her friend's excessive naiveté.
8. Hardy's tone is ironic, mocking, even sarcastic and cynical. The still innocent maid is poor, gullible, and confused; the ruined maid is self-possessed, attractive, and well fixed. This ironic reversal denies the traditional wisdom about the "wages of sin."

Stanley Renner provides some interesting social background and commentary on this poem in his article "William Acton, the Truth about Prostitution, and Hardy's Not-So-Ruined Maid," *Victorian Poetry* 30.1 (Spring 1992): 19–28.

### Describing the Tone in "The Unknown Citizen" [pp. 502–3]
1. Creative writing prompt. Could be done in groups or even as a class.
2. He is identified by number—no name is given.
3. The speaker (persona) is a representative of the state, some bureaucrat who helps to keep track of the masses. The persona uses the plural to identify with the state that he or she works for and to cover any personal responsibility for the opinions and conditions expressed or implied.
4. The name is comical, as is the rhyme.
5. The capitalization suggests that these concepts have become personified and are paramount in the society portrayed in the poem; they are impersonal entities that have become much more important than individual persons, who remain numbers.
6. The persona praises the Unknown Citizen for his conformity. Auden himself is critical of the Unknown Citizen and would surely deplore the ideas expressed by the speaker in the poem.
7. The poem is satirical. The tone of the satire is sometimes humorous, but overall, Auden takes a relentlessly critical approach in exposing the conformist, dehumanized society that the speaker represents and supports.

### Discovering Tone in "Go, Lovely Rose" [p. 503]
1. It appears that the woman has rebuffed the speaker in some way, refusing to see him or receive his attention.
2. The rose is a traditional symbol of romantic love, as well as of beauty that does not last long.
3. "Uncommended" means, literally, unsung; thus she is unnoticed and hence unpraised.

4. "Wastes" in line 2 strikes a slightly harsh note, with overtones of pining away in love sickness. Both lines have an edge to them. Is it too much reality to suggest that she is wasting her life while her body is wasting away, anticipating the "die" of line 16? The "shuns" in line 7 suggests a deliberate, almost obstinate avoidance of life's pleasures.
5. The last imperative in the sequence of polite commands—go, tell, bid, *die*—startles us a little. But in the time period when the poem was written, the word *die* carried a double entendre: it also meant to experience sexual orgasm.
6. No, poems at this time were usually sung.
7. Cajoling, charming, graceful, but quietly insistent, perhaps. There also seems to be just a touch of hostility or resentment lurking beneath the effortless charm of the speaker's words. The "then die" shocks us into focusing on the specter of age and death that *carpe diem* (seize the day) poems usually raise in their arguments for sexual pleasure. Contrast the tone of the speaker of this "invitation to love" lyric with that of the speaker of Andrew Marvell's "To His Coy Mistress" [p. 570], who seems more passionate and urgent in his entreaties.

### Discovering Tone in "One Perfect Rose" [p. 503–4]
1. Personal writing prompt, which might make a good basis (or introduction) for Critical Writing Idea 3.
2. They both use the rose as a symbol of love, and they both employ a twist or turn in tone to make their points.
3. Parker's poem exploits the tonal shift to create a humorous, down-to-earth comment on romantic love (and romantic love poems).
4. The apostrophe changes the two-syllable word to a one-syllable word that fits the iambic meter of the line. But the poet may also be mocking the artificial language of many love lyrics, which seem to resort frequently to this linguistic device—thus giving her own poem a quaint, old-fashioned touch.
5. An amulet is a magical charm, ornament, or signifier.
6. It changes from traditionally romantic to openly materialistic. The single word "limousine" upsets all our expectations—in both rhythm and diction—and throws the whole stanza into another gear.
7. The total effect is parody. The tone is humorous and iconoclastic, as the writer slyly undercuts the established tradition of romantic idealism in poetry.

### Analyzing the Student Response [p. 510]
In order to allow students to exercise their critical-thinking skills, we have deliberately included a sample student paper that argues for a questionable interpretation. You might want to emphasize that this is a personal-response paper, not a reviewed and revised critical essay.
1. The student states what he takes to be Housman's theme in the final paragraph of the essay. But surely Housman intended the poem to convey a broader meaning than the student settles for.

2. The student identifies Housman as the speaker in the poem in the fourth paragraph ("Housman tries to convince us . . ."). The speaker seems to be a detached (but not necessarily impartial) observer who could indeed be the poet.
3. The student fails to identify tone in the poem, which makes the analysis go off the track. Most readers think the speaker's tone is ironic. Who in his or her right mind would want to die young just in order to avoid seeing sports records broken? Although the student's opening sentence seems to use the same irony, he somehow misses the irony in the poem itself.
4. The student says that Housman "tries to convince us that it is best to die young," but he has missed the gentle irony of the line, "Smart lad to slip betimes away." Yes, those "Eyes the shady night has shut / Cannot see the record cut," but who would willingly choose to have that happen? To say, as the student does, that the poet thus "applauds the athlete's death" is to take seriously a message that—at best—might be intended to offer some comfort, to find some positive note in the tragedy.
5. The student allows his own experience as an athlete to color his understanding of the poem. He clearly agrees with the poet that sports records are not worth dying for, but he fails to see that Housman was being ironic. In the last paragraph, the student says that the poet "seems to think that setting records and living in the limelight are all that athletes are looking for in their lives." If that's true, then the poem is a sarcastic indictment of the overemphasis on the importance of winning. Most readers don't interpret it that way. The poet, if able to respond, might say that the student makes some perceptive comments about the poem but unfortunately misses the point.

# Chapter 14   Writing About Poetic Language [pp. 511–28]

Cultivating in your students a sensitivity to the literal and connotative meanings of words is crucial to their understanding and appreciation of poetry. We believe that the best way to go about making them responsive to the language of poetry is through close examination of numerous poems in class. Requiring students to learn definitions of the standard terms used in discussing poetry (*metaphor*, *personification*, *paradox*) may be counterproductive if your students already harbor negative feelings toward poetry. The important thing is for them to be able to *recognize* a metaphor and to grasp its meaning, not necessarily to be able to *define* one.

### *Examining Poetic Language* [p. 519]
1. The poem establishes its comparison by contrasting the temperate loveliness of the beloved with the "rough winds," the too-hot sun, the fading sun, and the shadow of death. The poem is a tribute that immortalizes "thy eternal summer," i.e., the unfading loveliness of the beloved.
2. Students should have fun with this assignment as they learn a great deal from it about the importance of rhyme and meter, as well as word choice. If any group feels intimidated by trying to write a serious poem as good as Shakespeare's, allow them to write a humorous version. Read the completed poems aloud to the class and ask them to discuss the effectiveness of the word choice and imagery. If some have

attempted parodies, you might want to ask them to read Shakespeare's own parody, "My Mistress' Eyes Are Nothing Like the Sun" [p. 584 in the anthology].

3. The poem compares the questing of one's soul for meaning to the patient construction of a spider's web. The soul is personified. When your students substitute synonyms, they will become aware of the perfection of Whitman's word choice. You may want to put them in groups after they have written their versions in order to discuss how changing the words distorts the meaning, alters the images, and destroys the meter. Encourage them especially to see that "ductile" ("till the ductile anchor hold") is a key word in understanding Whitman's search for a belief that is flexible, not a rule-bound creed.

4. *Metaphors*: the turtle is identified with or described in terms of several different objects, without the use of *like* or *as*. The images used to convey the point or subject of the implied comparison are often quite striking. It might be worth the time to explore the visual pictures these images put across.

  l.2: "a barely mobile hard roll" and "a four-oared helmet"
  l.4: "rowing toward the grasses. . . ." (the turtle's locomotion = rowing)
  l.8: "stuck up to the axle" (identified as a car or truck, linking back to "mobile" and "dragging a packing case" in previous lines)
  l.10–11: "convert / Her shell into a serving dish"
  l.13: "change her load of pottery [echoing "serving dish"] to wings"

*Simile*: ". . . like dragging / a packing-case places" (l.5–6)

*Personification*: use of personal pronouns *she* and *her*: "her modest hopes" (l.7); "never imagining some lottery" (l.13); "Her only levity is patience / The sport of truly chastened things" (l.14–15)

*Assonance*:

  l.2–3: barely . . . hard, mobile . . . roll . . . four-oared, afford
  l.4: rowing . . . toward
  l.5–6: track . . . graceless . . . dragging . . . packing-case places
  l.6: almost . . . slope
  l.7: modest hopes
  l.11: dish . . . lives

*Alliteration*:

  l.6: packing-case places
  l.11–14: luck-level . . . lottery, load, levity
  l.10–11: She skirts . . . shell . . . serving . . . She

*Internal rhyme*: four-oared, afford (l.2–3); ditch, which (l.10); lottery, pottery (l.12–13); wings, things (l.12, 15)

"August" begins with a striking visual image: the blackberries hanging swollen in the woods. It continues with a tactile image (ripped arms) and one of taste (cramming the black honey of the berries into the mouth).

The poem ends with two unusual metaphors: "this thick paw of my life darting among" the leaves, and the leaves described as "black bells." The last line—

"this happy tongue"—returns to the taste image, combined with the personification that "happy" suggests.

There are also a number of *-ing* words, which suggest movement and engagement: *reaching, thinking, cramming, darting.* The mention of the "dark creeks that run by" adds to this sense of movement.

5. In a general sense, the extended metaphor compares life to weaving a tapestry. A more particular meaning comes to light when students consider the nature of a tapestry, which frequently has a detailed, coherent pattern and may also tell a story. The persona in the poem tries to weave lasting meaning and pattern into his life span, only to find this task impossible. He takes several tactics, such as not looking behind him and tying new knots as they unravel, unsuccessfully. These tactics represent different ways of living—being future oriented and present oriented, respectively. His efforts to make a sensible narrative of both the past and the future are futile, and, as we see in the last lines, these efforts also ruin present experience. The extended metaphor suggests that trying to control our lives so that they acquire lasting meaningfulness is ill fated.

6. The central paradox in "My Son My Executioner" was nicely stated in a popular Bob Dylan song: "He not busy being born is busy dying." The new child promises an immortality of sorts (since he will probably live longer than his parents and hold them in his memory) while at the same time reminding his parents that they are themselves getting older, moving toward death.

## Choosing Vivid, Descriptive Terms [p. 521]
After students complete the exercise on improving sentences from their earlier papers, you might put them in groups to discuss each other's changes. Ask whether the changed or added words constitute an improvement. If not, ask them to think of another wording.

## Sample Student Paper [pp. 522–26]
The second draft of the sample student paper was marked (as shown in the text) by the instructor. The final draft includes the changes the student, Sonya Weaver, made in response to those comments, plus some of her own revisions and corrections.

After reading and discussing Donne's poem [pp. 586–87 in the Anthology of Poetry], you might want to read Sonya's second draft aloud (as the class follows in their books). Ask them how they would have revised the marked passages. Then let them compare their changes with those Sonya made in the final draft. Discuss which revisions are better and why. Be sure that your students have pen and paper when they work on their suggested revisions. And try to allow time for them to devise good sentences.

# Chapter 15   Writing About Poetic Form [pp. 529–51]

Some readers are not much interested in the mechanics of poetry; they may even think that looking at the details of form will rob a poem of its beauty and mystery. Although this attitude can be a rationalization for wanting to avoid the hard work of reading poetry, it's true that form is most meaningful when related to content and discussed in context. Having students memorize the structure and rhyme scheme of a Shakespearean sonnet doesn't work as well as asking them to explain how the form of a particular sonnet contributes to its overall impression.

### Exercise on Poetic Form [p. 531]

In this exercise, students are asked to arrange the lyrics of a song in lines on a page. If you use this as an individual exercise, you may ask students to write answers to the questions in the assignment. As a small-group activity, the exercise could be completed by four or five students listening to a tape or CD and deciding on the arrangement together. In this way, the questions will be answered in the course of the group's discussion. If more than one group works on the same song, it would be profitable to compare the two arrangements and ask each group to justify its decisions.

### Experimenting with Poetic Forms [pp. 538–39]

1.  "We Real Cool" has a jazzy, syncopated rhythm created by the placement of the subject, "We," at the end of the lines and by the shortness of the words and sentences. These two factors encourage a reading with unusual pauses, as in musical syncopation. The placement of "We" also functions to emphasize the word, perhaps stressing the egotism of the persona.
2.  The alliteration of *s* sounds in "Eight O'Clock" suggests the evil hiss of a snake or the discouraging hiss of air going out of a balloon or tire, both negative in effect. The variety of *o* and *ou* sounds (assonance) produces an ominous resonance, like the tolling of the bell that will mean the prisoner's doom. The repeated *k* sound in the second stanza is sharp and harsh, like the prisoner's fate and the sound of the gallows as the trap falls. Objectively, the poem tells the brief story of a prisoner who is listening to the town's church clock strike the hours until eight, which will be the time of his hanging. An objective account, of course, leaves out the subjective elements—the poetic effects and appeals created by alliteration, personification (the steeple in stanza 1 and the clock in stanza 2), and other devices.
3.  This is a very demanding exercise, and some students will not see the differences in stanza use. In general the quatrains are coterminous with sentence units; the stanzas point out these syntactic structures. Some authors, like Donne and Cummings, play against the traditional expectations in surprising, even devilish, ways.
4.  Tell students that they may add words as they rewrite the lines. There are no exact right answers, but here are our rewrites:
    a.  Because he served the greater community in everything he did.
    b.  He worked in a factory until the day he retired, except when he was in the war.

c. How pretty a town anyone lived in, with the sound of bells floating up and down.

d. The little men and small women didn't care for anyone at all.

## *Ideas for Writing* [pp. 540–42]

The Ideas for Expressive Writing involve creative composition. They can replace or supplement a critical paper on poetic form.

Topics 1 and 4 under Ideas for Critical Writing combine analytical writing with a comparison-and-contrast format, while topics 2 and 5 are typical analyses, requiring the writer to separate the elements of the poem and, ideally, to argue how they work together to support or create the poem's meaning. Topic 3 calls for applying the principles of deconstruction—or, rather, to consider how the poet deconstructs the sonnet form for his own purposes; it's a speculative topic that should appeal to students who prefer a less conventional topic.

## *Exercise 1:* Distinguishing Among Synonyms [p. 542]

a. *Renowned* and *famous* both mean widely known and honored; *famous* is used in reference to all pursuits, while *renowned* usually refers to intellectual or artistic fame. *Notorious* also means widely known, but the reputation is likely to be a negative one.

b. An *indifferent* parent is neither especially good nor especially bad; a *detached* parent is objective, not ruled by emotions; and an *unconcerned* parent is free of worry.

c. To *condone* an action is to overlook the degree of wrongness or inappropriateness. *Excuse* is most often used to mean pardon for social errors, like sneezing or being late. To *forgive* involves letting go any bad feelings or resentment one may have about a wrong action.

d. *Steal* is the most general word, meaning to take someone else's property without permission. *Pilfer* means to steal in small quantities and repeatedly, as, for example, your roommate might pilfer your beer supply. In the context of stealing, *robbery* usually means directly stealing from a person by using threats of violence or actual violence, whereas *burglary* involves breaking into a place intending to take something unlawfully, and *ransacking* involves a search for things to steal. *Looting* is stealing on a bigger scale, like plunder that takes place in war or a riot.

e. An *apparent* error seems to be real but may or may not be. A *visible* error may be perceived by the eye. An *egregious* error is obviously bad.

## *Exercise 2:* Words with Similar Sound or Spelling [pp. 542–43]

a. apprise—to inform; appraise—to evaluate
b. anecdote—a little story; antidote—a remedy
c. elicit—bring out; illicit—not legitimate
d. martial—pertaining to war; marital—pertaining to marriage
e. statue—sculpture; statute—rule or law

f.   human—a person; humane—kind, merciful, compassionate
g.   lose—misplace, fail to win (verb); loose—not tight or dense (adjective)
h.   idol—a worshipped symbol; idle—inactive, without a job
i.   accept—approve, receive, take in; except—exclude, omit
j.   simple—easy, uncomplicated; simplistic—ignoring complications or complexities, oversimplified
k.   beside—next to; besides—in addition to, except
l.   weather—atmospheric conditions; whether—if
m.   incidence—rate of occurrence; incident—event or happening
n.   angle—a figure in geometry, a position or vantage point; angel—a celestial being

### Exercise 3: Precise Adjective Form [p. 543]
a.   An intelligible essay is merely understandable; an intelligent one is logical and thoughtful.
b.   A hateful sibling is malicious; a hated sibling is intensely disliked, deserving or not.
c.   A likely roommate is probable or promising; a likable roommate is pleasant.
d.   An informed speaker knows the subject well; an informative speaker is enlightening.
e.   A workable thesis is practical; a working thesis is temporarily adopted until it proves practical or impractical.

### Exercise 4: Malapropisms [p. 543]
a.   superficial          d. examinations
b.   pinnacle             e. rude
c.   refuse

### Exercise 5: Words that Fit Context [pp. 543–44]
a.   *Stubbornness* has a negative connotation of being unreasonable or bullheaded; replace with *tenacity* or *steadfastness*.
b.   *Poignantly* suggests something moving or touching; replace with *obviously*. *Sympathize with* implies compassion or understanding; replace with *support*.
c.   *Displeasure* is not strong enough for shouting; a better choice would be *rage* or *frustration*.

### Sample Student Paper on Poetic Form [pp. 544–47]
This student paper, about 500 words long, is a good example of how poetic form can be discussed along with a poem's meaning. It's rare to see an analysis of poetic form without any interpretation of the work's meaning. Curvey's essay relates the attitude of the speaker to the images in the poem and then to its form. The last sentences sum up the relationship nicely: "The continuity and inner logic of the sonnet reflect the speaker's appraisal of the woman, as being both conventional and unique, a person with a wholeness and unity all her own. Though influenced by the demands of custom, she

remains splendidly herself." In other words, the poem both follows traditional sonnet form and also violates it to maintain its meaning.

One device that may not be obvious to your students is the use of repetition to maintain the focus of the paper. The first paragraph says that the speaker *admires* the woman, and the first sentences of paragraphs 2 and 3 also use the words *admire* and *admiration*, while paragraph 4 begins with a cognate, *compliment*. In this way, the reader is reminded in each paragraph to focus on the positive characteristics suggested by images in the poem: flexibility, strength, integrity, self-esteem, generosity, and love.

You might point out that whenever students encounter a poem with a familiar or common form, such as this sonnet of fourteen lines, they need to examine it to see whether it follows the conventions of that form and if not, which conventions are broken. This analysis may help illuminate the poem's meaning, as we see in the Curvey essay.

### Sample Published Essay on Poetic Form [pp. 548–51]
Both you and your students should enjoy this well-written and insightful critical article by David Huddle, explaining how the sound fits the sense of Robert Hayden's "Those Winter Sundays." The essay is remarkable in being free from jargon and is addressed directly to its readers. It can serve as a model for student writing and teaches a great deal about the functions of poetic form in the bargain.

# Casebook: The Poetry of Langston Hughes [pp. 552–63]

THE NEGRO SPEAKS OF RIVERS by Langston Hughes [p. 554]
The key to this poem is understanding who the speaker is (the "I"). Because of the various time periods, we know that it cannot be one person, though the title says "The Negro." Therefore, "The Negro" must stand for the whole race. The traditional symbolic meanings of the river are those of rebirth (as in baptism) and of the journey of life. Perhaps in this case, Hughes was writing about the journey of a whole race. The poem embraces a sense of racial history as soul deepening.

### Questions for Discussion and Writing
1. Do some research on the proper names used in the poem. Who is W. E. B. Du Bois, and why is the poem dedicated to him? What do the place names have in common?
2. Look carefully at the experiences listed in stanza 2. Could they just as effectively be listed in another order? Why or why not? Why are these specific activities listed?
3. What is a soul that "has grown deep like the rivers"? What do you associate with rivers? What symbolic meaning do rivers frequently have?

### Making Connections
→ Compare and contrast "Harlem," "Theme for English B," and "The Negro Speaks of Rivers." What conclusions can you come to about the importance of a poem's narrator?

**MOTHER TO SON** by Langston Hughes [p. 554]

This poem is a fine example of an extended metaphor: the implied comparison between life's progress and climbing a stair carries through the entire poem. "Mother to Son" consists of one long stanza, but asking your students to divide it into stanzas will produce a discussion of the three basic parts of the poem. The first section describes the mother's hard life; the second section suggests the growth and discovery she has nonetheless experienced; and the third section attempts to persuade the son to persist toward his own goals. The image of the "crystal stair" standing for an easy life may be unfamiliar to your students, but visualizing it will convey the meaning clearly.

### Questions for Discussion and Writing
1. Break the poem into three stanzas. Explain why you divided the lines as you did.
2. How is the relationship between the mother and son here traditional? Is it unconventional in any sense? What does the mother want the son to do and why?
3. What do you think of Hughes's use of dialect in the poem? Did you find it distracting? What function does the dialect serve?

### Making Connections
→ Compare this poem to "The Street" by Octavio Paz, which also uses an extended metaphor to make a point about human existence. Which do you prefer? Why?

### HARLEM (A DREAM DEFERRED) by Langston Hughes [p. 556]

The "dream deferred" in the poem is, of course, the same dream that the Rev. Martin Luther King later made the centerpiece of his famous "I Have a Dream" speech: the dream of equality in American society. The poem suggests through metaphor the psychological damage of unrealized hopes—of promises given to African Americans and not fulfilled, going all the way back to the forty acres and a mule promised to each black family following the Civil War. The simple structure, the spare diction, the scabrous similes, and the stunning last line all mesh perfectly to produce a poem of remarkable power and portent. Read it aloud for full effect.

Lorraine Hansberry used a phrase from this poem for the title of her play "A Raisin in the Sun," which appears in the Anthology of Drama.

### Questions for Discussion and Writing
1. What is the "dream deferred" mentioned in the opening line?
2. What effect do all the visual images describe?
3. How do these consequences culminate in the meaning of the final line?
4. Examine the similes Hughes employs to evoke the effects of the deferred dream and write an essay discussing the social implications these images convey.

## Making Connections

→ Compare Hughes's feelings about living in a racist country to those expressed by Claude McKay in "America" and Countee Cullen in "Incident."

## THEME FOR ENGLISH B by Langston Hughes [pp. 556–57]

Students enjoy this poem because they've probably received an assignment like the one the English teacher gives here. The contrast between the English teacher's assumptions and the student writer's is clear. In his theme, the student experiments with different ways to describe himself: the details of his physical situation, his likes and dislikes, the difference in race between him and his classmates and teacher, his citizenship, and so on. It seems that he stops in relief when he reaches the bottom of the page.

## Questions for Discussion and Writing

1. What would you write if you had the assignment that the speaker's teacher gives the class? How would you decide what to include?
2. What is the student's attitude toward the assignment? How can you tell?
3. The teacher says, "And let that page come out of you—then, it will be true." What do you think she means by this? What ideas about writing does she probably hold?
4. Do you think the racial difference is an important part of this poem? Or do you think the main point is about how the teacher and the student look at things differently?

## Considering the Poems [p. 558]

1. The traditional symbolic meanings of the river are those of rebirth (as in baptism) and of the journey of life. The rivers named are the historical origins of the speaker's race, from Africa to the southern United States. The poem endorses the idea of a racial memory in which the collective past is part of the present individual's consciousness.
2. This poem is a fine example of an extended metaphor: the implied comparison between life's progress and climbing a stair carries through the entire poem. The speaker is the mother, who has had a hard life in comparison to a "crystal stair," which brings forth images of ease and wealth. The image also reminds us of Disney fairy tale castles, not attainable in real life.
3. The mood of "The Weary Blues" could be described as distressed, sad, tired, slow—most apt of all, weary. Each stanza refers to weariness, and even the inanimate objects like the piano stool, songs, stars, and moon are tired. Your students will be able to recognize the pathos Bloom refers to; however, the joy of the crooner is more difficult to see. Perhaps the words *mellow, lazy, musical fool*, and the fact that the musician sleeps soundly bring out the fulfillment he finds in his music.

4. Students might discuss initial responses to "Saturday Night" such as, "That's not poetry," or just, "That's a weird poem." Cullen's comments suggest that such a colloquial style and low-life subject matter are not appropriate to poetry. Students may agree or disagree. You might ask them to point out other poems they have studied that contain elements Cullen would disdain.

5. The similes are drying up (like a raisin), festering like a sore, rotting like meat, crusting over (again, like a sore), sagging like a load, and finally exploding (like a bomb). Students may explore how each of these images suggests a different response to oppression. You might ask them to think about one of their own problems in terms of these similes to help them see the differences.

6. In the student's theme, he experiments with different ways to define himself: the details of his physical situations, his likes and dislikes, the difference in race between him and his classmates and teacher, his citizenship, and so on. It seems that he stops in relief when he reaches the bottom of the page. He does not appear to find any of the approaches to self-definition satisfactory or complete.

### Audio
➜ *The Poetry of Langston Hughes.* 2 cassettes. Performed by Ruby Dee and Ossie Davis. Available from Caedmon/Harper Audio
➜ *Langston Hughes Reads.* 50 minutes, 1 cassette. Hughes reads some of his most memorable poems. Available from Filmic Archives

### Website
➜ Resources for Reading Langston Hughes from the Academy of American Poets. Provides biography, background, questions, criticism, suggested reading, and links to other sources. **www.poets.org/page.php/prmID/323**

## The Art of Poetry: Art Insert [pp. 564–80]

This section provides an opportunity for students to study the ways that meaning can be conveyed through different media. The poems relate directly to the art in varying ways. The opening poem by Lisel Mueller gives a response to Edward Hopper's paintings—and to art in general. To help students enter into the dialogue between poet and painter, suggest that they write down their reactions to each reproduction in some detail before reading the accompanying poem(s). Then ask them to compare their reactions to the poet's. Here are some questions that may help them: Did reading the poem illuminate or alter your response to the painting in any way? Do you think you could understand the poems without reference to the paintings? Why does the poet choose to emphasize certain details in the painting and ignore others? Why do you think the poet chose to write about the painting? Is the poet interpreting the painting, making some judgment about it, or using it to comment on some common theme?

## AMERICAN LITERATURE by Lisel Mueller [p. 564]

Understanding two sets of images illuminates the meaning of the poem. First, Edward Hopper's paintings are aptly described in terms like "vacancies," "black spaces," "scoured and bleached," "skull-white," "nothing grows / except absence," "a room / stripped like a hospital bed," "bereft interiors." These images can easily be perceived in *Nighthawks* and in other Hopper paintings, which are easily viewed on the Internet. Basically, these are empty, minimally populated places, whose pasts we can only guess at.

On the other hand are the images of what the poets and storytellers bring with them: baggage, dowsing rods, dog-eared books, uneasy family photographs, lumpy beds, starting fires. The images are so at odds that Hopper's paintscapes emerge as blank pages for the writers to fill with their messy memories and emotional luggage.

## NIGHTHAWKS by Samuel Yellen [p. 565]

Edward Hopper's *Nighthawks* is familiar to many who have never had much interest in American art. The painting has entered into popular culture as almost an emblem of urban loneliness and alienation, despite the fact that a couple appears to be smoking, snacking, and drinking coffee together. Yellen's poem lets us see what the stark tone of the painting stems from: the setting, "on the corner of Empty and Blank"; the time, "the night's most desolate hour"; and the generic nature of the café, "Al's Coffee Cup or Hamburger Tower." The lone figure seated with his back to us seems to fit this setting and is described by Yellen as a lucky survivor of Russian roulette. Playing that suicidal game smacks of a jaded, reckless nature, of a folly engaged in by someone who places little value on his own life. In stanzas 4 and 5, Yellen envisions that the couple finishing their coffee have been "Not long ago together in a darkened room" in a heated sexual encounter in which "flesh beat and ground / on ravaged flesh." No romance here, apparently, for "they found / No local habitation and no name." The phrasing suggests a paid encounter in a briefly rented room with no names exchanged. The final stanza appears to counsel us to be grateful that we "are none of these!" But the overly dramatic apostrophe, "Oh," may signal that we should read that verse ironically, and the closing lines also seem overblown. Should we really be "complacent" and seeking only pleasure and self-satisfaction? Your students may want to argue the point.

## INVENTING MY PARENTS by Susan Ludvigson [p. 566]

As the title suggests, Ludvigson's poem imagines her parents as the couple depicted at the counter in Hopper's painting. Instead of Yellen's alienated pair in a stark, bleak setting, she envisions her charming, sophisticated parents drinking coffee in a "bright café" (l.1). This poet's positive impression of the setting invites us to view the scene in the painting as warm, almost homey. The details she gives us about her parents' conversation tell us a great deal about the two of them and their relationship. We can safely assume, for instance, that they are young. They have a five-month-old daughter, and they contemplate how the Second World War "will change them" (line 3); perhaps he could even be drafted (the painting is dated 1942). They are also quite literary and well educated. They discuss modernist writers of the 1930s: Ernest Hemingway, who wrote about war; Sinclair Lewis, who wrote about small-town USA; Kay Boyle, who wrote pacifist fiction; F. Scott Fitzgerald, who wrote about the American Dream (about which the couple disagree in l.6). At the end of the poem, the husband recites a line from John Donne's "The Canonization." We see the mother as highly imaginative in her fanciful vision of the American Dream (lines 7–11) and intellectual, as "her face is lit by ideas" (line 13). The father is clearly animated, genial, and agreeable: his gestures "are a Frenchman's. When he concedes / a point, he shrugs, an elaborate lift / of the shoulders, his hands and smile / declaring an open mind" (lines 14–17). He genuinely listens to his wife and near the end recites the line from Donne to make her laugh, "light / as summer rain when it begins" (lines 27–28).

## MUSÉE DES BEAUX ARTS by W. H. Auden [p. 567]
A reproduction of Brueghel's painting *The Fall of Icarus* appears above the poem; as you can see, many of the details mentioned in the poem are in the painting. Other paintings referred to are Brueghel's *Nativity* and *The Martyrdom of St. Stephen*. The poem takes up the "human position" of mythic events, saying that even as a miracle or tragedy is in progress, for most people everyday life is continuing as usual. The sense of historical relativity is reinforced by the mundane specific details, and whether or not so-called earthshaking events really are that momentous is called into question.

## NOT MY BEST SIDE by U. A. Fanthorpe [p. 568]
The painting *St. George and the Dragon* is a serious one: the style and subject matter reflect characteristics of fifteenth-century Italian painting. In contrast, Fanthorpe's poem interprets the painting in contemporary style and content, and this contrast is the source of humor. Each stanza comes from the point of view of a main character in the painting—the dragon, the fair maiden, and Sir George. Instead of the traditional demon, innocent victim, and hero, the characters are all self-preoccupied and quite insensitive to one another. Each one has worldly goals far from the realm of fable and fairy tale.

## THE STARRY NIGHT by Anne Sexton [p. 569]
Anne Sexton's attraction to *The Starry Night* and Vincent van Gogh can be explained at least partly by her similarity to the painter. Sexton was also plagued with deep depressions and hospitalizations. She made suicide attempts throughout her life and succeeded in 1974, poisoning herself with carbon monoxide in her garage after a poetry reading. Unlike Van Gogh, Sexton was immensely successful in her lifetime, earning many awards and fellowships including the Pulitzer Prize. In the refrain of her poem, we hear echoed Van Gogh's last words to his brother Theo. Dying in Theo's arms, from a self-inflicted gunshot, the painter said, "I wish I could pass away like this."

## MATISSE: "THE RED STUDIO" by W. D. Snodgrass [pp. 570–71]
In Matisse's painting *The Red Studio*, the most detailed objects are his paintings, which include identifiable images from Matisse's work. The furniture of the studio is barely

outlined but visible, and the rest of the room is an almost flat red background, which caught the imagination of the poet, who interprets the redness as a force engulfing the artist himself. Though Snodgrass suggests that the force is destructive, annihilating the artist as a person, not all viewers of the painting see it as menacing. (Hughes saw "images of comfort, refuge, and balanced satisfaction.") It may be that Snodgrass imposes his own view, that the creative process consumes the artist. Another view might be that the artist's creations are the most vivid expressions of his or her identity, leading to a different interpretation of the same painting. Relating these views to Lisel Mueller's poem at the beginning of the section will help students grasp the subjectivity of responses to art.

BEAUTY AND SADNESS by Cathy Song [p. 572]
This poem describes—and celebrates—the artistic process of Kitagawa Utamaro, a Japanese color-print artist, best known for his portrayals of women. He produced more than 2,000 prints plus a number of paintings and illustrated books (many of them with erotic images). His book *Insects* (1788) reveals his keen observation of nature—and is alluded to in lines 25–30 of the poem. Utamaro's women are idealized, with tall, slender bodies, long necks, and small shoulders. In fact, his women look more like fashion models from today's magazines than typical Japanese women of the late eighteenth century.

The speaker in the poem claims that one can feel the "invisible presence" of the artist in his prints. The imagery in the poem is striking, and most of the images of the women recall actual prints that Utamaro produced. (If you can, you may want to bring in more examples of Utamaro's prints.) The poem develops a contrast between the artist and his subjects: he is "quick" and "nimble"; they crouch like cats, are poised like vases, and maintain stillness. He is "dwarfed and bespectacled"; they are "slender, erect and tall." As the title indicates, the women's beauty is accompanied by sadness: the speaker mentions "their moments of melancholy" (line 28) and their vulnerable faces (lines 35–36), which the artist catches and transposes onto the delicate "skinlike" paper. The artist's eye is also "inconsolable" (lines 40–41). Could this shared emotion be the key to the relationship between artist and subject? Are his prints a way of transcending that sadness?

# The Art of Poetry: Questions for Discussion [pp. 573–76]

## Possible Responses

Mueller [p.573]
1. The images related to Hopper's paintings include vacancies, blank spaces, light scoured and bleached, something missing, and a bed after the patient has died. Many of Hopper's paintings display such images.

117

2. The images of poets and storytellers include baggage, dowsing rods, dog-eared books, lumpy beds, uneasy family photographs. These all suggest a hard-lived, full life. (A dowsing-rod is used to find water under the ground—perhaps in this poem, a search for meaning.) In fact, the contrast in the images Hopper uses and the poets' use could be expressed as empty versus full or dead versus living.

**Yellen [p. 573]**

1. The details capturing the tone include empty, bleak, desolate, hunched, Russian roulette, and no local habitation and no name.
2. The man was at least once desperate and suicidal enough to play Russian roulette.
3. The last stanza is ironic if readers see themselves partly in the *Nighthawks* characters. However, readers whose pleasures really do please will not find the last stanza ironic.

**Ludvigson [p. 574]**

1. Ludvigson's view of *Nighthawks* creates a tone of love and also includes a child's existence in stanza 2.
2. The couples are having a smart, literary conversation, implying that they are educated.
3. The mother seems engaged in life and sensitive, while the father is shown as expressive and enthusiastic. Their conversation and actions support these ideas.
4. The two poets bring their personal history to their interpretations, just as Mueller suggests in her poem. Each student's response, as well, is a reflection of his or her personal experience, though most people agree on some version of Yellen's vision. Few people have gone utterly without the experience of desolation and aimlessness that Yellen sees in *Nighthawks*.

**Auden [p. 574]**

1. The two types of events are everyday ones and unusual, even tragic, ones.
2. The examples of unnoticed suffering include the aged people waiting for religious signs, martyrdom, torture, and the fall of Icarus.
3. Research on the story of Icarus and its meaning will help students understand the poem and its different twist on the story's usual meaning.
4. In "Out, Out—" the characters "turned to their affairs" after seeing a boy's hand cut off and his subsequent death. This reaction is consistent with those in Auden's poem. Students may see the poems as too cynical to be accurate or as truthful points of view on people's reactions to other's suffering.

**Fanthorpe [pp. 574–75]**

1. Answers will vary—many readers may find the poem humorous at the point where they realize that stanza 1 comes from the dragon's point of view. In fact, the poem's humor comes from the unexpected points of view of the scene's characters.
2. The speakers are the dragon, then the maiden, and then St. George. Each speaker is quite self-absorbed, and each seems to have a main goal of self-aggrandizement. How students would cast a film version will vary by taste and time, we assume.
3. The story of St. George and the dragon is much more disturbing than the poem implies. For example, it involves the sacrifice of a young maiden to the dragon each

day, until the final maiden, who is the king's daughter depicted in the painting. Furthermore, in contrast with the poem, St. George does *not* win the maiden after slaying the dragon. This type of research helps your students understand the various interpretations possible in art.

4. The form of the poem is free verse, which makes sense because each stanza is meant to sound conversational, not poetic.

**Sexton [p. 575]**

1. Students can cite many details involving depression, loneliness, and death in the poem.

2. The quotation seems to contradict the poem, in that Van Gogh paints the stars to seek religion, while Sexton sees the painting as a depiction of despairing death.

3. Sexton's poem adds a lot to Van Gogh's painting. She envisions motivation and characterization ("the old unseen serpent") that many viewers would not see.

**Snodgrass [pp. 575–76]**

1. It seems as though the studio has somehow consumed the artist, leaving only the objects. Besides, the objects that are works of art are colorful, while other furnishings of the studio are crude outlines, almost unreal.

2. Students will be able to identify by title many of the paintings in *The Red Studio*, as well as some of Matisse's style, which is not bound by physical realism.

3. Many students may see the painting as Hughes did, a creative sanctuary, but view the poem quite differently, with the studio being more depleting.

4. Students may brainstorm about these personal settings—perhaps a bedroom at home, some natural spot, some workplace? Perhaps some feel that in these settings, they lose track of time, reality, and concerns with self. This loss of self when fully absorbed in some activity may be what the poem suggests.

**Song [p. 576]**

1. Song uses images like porcelain vases (easily broken), iridescent insects, and moths and the delicacy of the paper they are painted upon. All of these suggest fragile, fleeting loveliness.

2. Stanzas 2 and 3 most directly describe this specific painting, while stanza 1 describes Utamaro's paintings in general, and stanza 4 focuses more on the painter himself. Students looking at other Utamaro paintings should see their similarity to *Two Women Fixing Their Hair*.

3. Students may see the women's beauty as sad because of its fleetingness, lack of reality, effortful artificiality, or the total aim of pleasing men.

4. Line 34 probably refers to the bare knee of the girl in the foreground, a body part that would never be seen in full attire among these girls.

5. Stanza 4 suggests that Utamaro, instead of exploiting these girls, was actually providing them with the only immortality they would achieve.

6. Research on the painter will illuminate the last stanza in particular. It may also explain his choice of subject matter in general.

# Poetry and Art: Ideas for Writing [pp. 577–78]

1. The poets use the empty spaces to populate with their own inner preoccupations and personal pasts. For instance, the persons in *Nighthawks* seem to reflect the loneliness and alienation of the artist.

2. Nonliteral meanings of "starting fires" include making trouble, delinquency, destruction, disturbance, creating controversy, and compulsive crime. Students will have various ideas about how these relate to the act of writing poetry.

3. Students will vary in the stories they create about the people in the painting.

4. Flick Webb is somewhat like the nighthawks in that he seems without feeling, without pleasure, and without care for his own life. However, at least Webb used to be a big success at something, while we get the feeling the nighthawks never were.

5. Ludvigson envisions a completely different and more meaningful sexual bond for her parents—far from the raw, urgent union of the couple in Yellen's poem, as "Mouth burned mouth, flesh beat and ground / On ravaged flesh" (lines 18–19). In Ludvigson's poem, the sexual relationship is only suggested by their pleasure in "being alone together" (line 23) while "savoring / the fragrant night" (lines 22–23), and in the father's humorous injunction from Donne, "For God's sake / hold your tongue, and let me love" (lines 25–26).

6. Ludvigson's is a much rarer interpretation of the painting than Yellen's. Each student's response is a reflection of his or her personal experience, though most people agree on some version of Yellen's vision. Few people have gone utterly without the experience of desolation and aimlessness that Yellen sees in *Nighthawks*.

7. In the visual arrangement of the painting, "Everything turns away quite leisurely from the disaster." The artist does place the white legs of the drowning Icarus in the corner (not the center) of the work and makes them quite small in contrast with other features of the landscape. Students may find it difficult to find their own reactions to the painting after reading the poem because the poem is a compelling interpretation.

8. With so many images available on the Internet, students could share the picture they choose and their written reflections with the whole class, electronically. Focus class discussion on which reflections students found most compelling and why.

9. The fifteenth century saw more naturalistic styles than in the past, with more realistic depiction of light and shadow, space and anatomy. The dragon refers to this trend when complaining about his and the horse's unrealistic depiction in stanza 1.

10. This humorous exercise should be fun. You may want students to share their poems in small groups or over the Internet.

11. From the details generated in answering question 1 about Sexton's poem on page 575, students need to identify which are images, which ones metaphors and similes, and which ones connotative language.

12. In looking at a bigger painting, some students may see the religious hope reflected in the epigraph rather than the despair of the poem.

13. When students write about a painting themselves, they probably find that they study details more than they otherwise would. They also may note that their own experience influences their writing about the painting.

14. Research on these images will help students see Snodgrass's view of the red studio as consuming and obliterating the artist as a person.
15. The closest place to view a Matisse will vary by your school's locale—a museum would be best, but some students may need to view art books in the library or the Internet instead of actual paintings.
16. The early focus of the poem is on the women and a sympathetic view of their plight. However, the last stanza finds the figure of the painter behind the images as also sympathetic.
17. See question 1 about Song's poem on page 576. Students may note that the imagery related to the girls is never human.
18. Song sees the women as objects of sympathy. However, do all students see the painting the same way? Some, for example, may immediately focus on the technical aspects of the drawing or the interesting use of color. Some may consider the apparent luxury of the setting rather than its harsh demands.

**Sample Student Paper** [pp. 578–80]
Discuss how this essay could be turned into a critical analysis of Sexton's poem.

# ANTHOLOGY OF POETRY

**THEY FLEE FROM ME** by Sir Thomas Wyatt [p. 581]
This is a lover's complaint, a popular subgenre in Renaissance poetry, but it is a sophisticated and highly individual variation. The speaker laments that his former success with women has declined. He speaks of these women as if they had been tame animals that used to eat from his hand. But they are no longer tame; they flee at his approach. The metaphor of the hunt becomes clear when we know that hunting dogs "range" as they search for game, that "seek" is a command given to such dogs, and that "change" refers to an animal met by chance (which the dogs pursue instead of the quarry). Thus, the women have altered from tame animals to hunters themselves. In the second stanza the speaker erotically evokes a woman he particularly remembers, one who makes the advances and "catches" him in her arms. The speaker insists, in the last stanza, that this delightful occurrence was not a dream. He was presumably prepared to surrender—and be faithful to her—but the woman was not. She tames him and then forsakes him. He is free to do likewise, but his final question reveals that he is peeved and slightly confused by the role reversal: he wonders, since she treats him in this fickle fashion, how should he treat her?

## Possible Responses to *Questions for Discussion and Writing*
1. He seems bewitched, bothered, and bewildered by her. Unlike the other ladies in the courtly love game, who were "gentle, tame, and meek," this woman came on strong and then dumped him—and he's not sure why.
2. She comes to him, dressed in something sheer and sexy ("after a pleasant guise" means in an attractive costume or appearance), lets the gown fall to the floor, puts her arms around him, kisses him, and asks, "How do you like this?" She's self-assured and comfortable with her sexuality. Some people (including the speaker?) might call her a brazen hussy for the way she behaves.
3. He suggests that he was too conventional, too gentle and reserved; she was too bold for him, and he didn't know how to deal with it. He also throws in the old charge that women are fickle (see "new-fangleness" in line 19). But the truth is that he's getting older and not as successful in the wooing game as he used to be. (The first stanza indicates he once had them eating out of his hand—but no more.) The last line of the poem might be paraphrased this way: I'd like to know what she wanted from me.

## *Additional Questions for Discussion and Writing*
1. How do the old loves (stanza 1) relate to the attitudes expressed in the rest of the poem?
2. According to the speaker, the woman's way of "forsaking" is "a strange fashion" (line 17). What does he mean? Can you link "fashion" with "new-fangleness," which the *Oxford English Dictionary* defines as "(objectionable) modernness or novelty"?

### Making Connections

→ Compare the complaint of the lover in this poem with the ones expressed in "To His Coy Mistress" and "Go, Lovely Rose."


## WHEN IN DISGRACE WITH FORTUNE AND MEN'S EYES (Sonnet 29) by William Shakespeare [p. 582]

This sonnet departs from the usual Shakespearean structure of three quatrains and a couplet: the last six lines form a unit (a sestet). In the first eight lines the speaker cites circumstances when self-doubts overwhelm him; in the next four lines the speaker observes that the remembrance of the loved one ("thee"), which seems to occur at random ("haply" means "by chance"), lifts the speaker's spirits. The famous simile that ends the poem indicates that the speaker's joy is like the return of the lark's song at the beginning of the day. The lark's burst of joy suggests that heaven—called "deaf" in line 3—has suddenly become keener of hearing. The last two lines, comprising a separate sentence, sum up the ideas expressed in the lark simile (lines 9–12), suggesting that the speaker's spirit is genuinely restored by the memory of "thy love."

Students might profit from paraphrasing the poem, as several words that sound familiar had different meanings than they have today. "Featured," for instance, meaning "alike in features," would be paraphrased as "looking like." And "scope" could mean either accomplishments or breadth of understanding or knowledge.

### Possible Responses to *Questions for Discussion and Writing*

1. In the highly romantic and idealized world of Renaissance love poetry, the sentiment that "love conquers all" is readily accepted. The central contrast (or tension) in this poem is between the speaker's public misfortunes and his personal treasures, and there is simply no contest: "sweet love" wins every time, at least in poetry.

2. The speaker posits a time when he will be down on his luck: alone, despondent, frustrated, envious of those around him, even suicidal (line 9).

3. It would change an erotic love poem into a religious statement about the insufficiency of material wealth. This interpretation does not fit in easily with the rest of the 154 poems in Shakespeare's sonnet cycle, which focus on human love and passion.

### Making Connections

→ Compare this sonnet's portrayal of love as a solace against the harshness of the world with Matthew Arnold's explication of that same idea in "Dover Beach."


## LET ME NOT TO THE MARRIAGE OF TRUE MINDS (Sonnet 116) by William Shakespeare [p. 582]

This sonnet deals with the theme of love's stability and permanence. It treats its subject in a formal, rhetorical fashion. After the opening exhortation, which echoes the traditional marriage ceremony, the speaker goes on to explain his position by defining love, first negatively (lines 2–4), then positively (lines 5–8), and then negatively again (lines 9–12). The poem's argument is wholly contained in the three quatrains, and the final couplet is more like a challenge to the reader to deny the consequences of the airtight logic of the preceding lines. But the final comment is personal ("upon me") just as the opening exhortation is personal ("Let me"), providing a subjective frame for the rather academic or universal definition of love that comes between.

The abstract concepts of time and space are applied to the investigation of love, but the language moves from the abstract ("alteration") to a concrete image based on navigation. This complex metaphor compares love to a kind of sea-mark (like the North Star), which is proof against storms (line 6). The image of the third quatrain represents "rosy lips and cheeks" as coming within the "compass" (restricted space or area) of Time's bending sickle. "Bending" of line 10 and "alters" of line 11 tie up the last negative definition with the first one by recalling the "alters" of line 3 and the "bends" of line 4.

## Possible Responses to *Questions for Discussion and Writing*

1. The opening lines echo this sentence from the traditional marriage ceremony: "If any person can show just cause why this couple may not be joined together, let him speak now or forever hold his peace."

2. Often called "platonic love," this form of love emphasizes the spiritual over the sensual (or physical); it is often seen as a "higher" form of love. John Donne's poem "A Valediction: Forbidding Mourning" [p. 568] is a supreme expression of this kind of attachment. It might be interesting to have students compare their descriptions of this kind of love.

3. The two comparisons involve nautical navigation (a "bark" is a term for a small sailing ship). Love is like a landmark (perhaps a lighthouse) or fixed star (the North Star) that keeps a lost or irresolute soul ("a wandering bark") on course. These metaphors develop the theme of love's constancy and steadiness. They are similar to the compass metaphor that Donne uses in "A Valediction: Forbidding Mourning," in which the beloved is the fixed leg of the compass that keeps the absent lover constant and faithful.

### *Making Connections*

➜ Compare the qualities of love expressed in this sonnet with those that John Donne evokes in "A Valediction: Forbidding Mourning."

THAT TIME OF YEAR THOU MAYST IN ME BEHOLD (Sonnet 73) by William Shakespeare [p. 583]
This sonnet explores the connections among mortality, death, and love. The time frame becomes increasingly shorter, moving (in the three quatrains) from a season to a part of one day to a moment of recognition. The bold and complicated metaphors picture the

aging speaker as a winter-ravaged tree, the twilight moving into night, and a feeble fire choking on the ashes of its own expended fuel. The common link to the three quatrains (autumn, sunset, a dying fire) is diminution or dying. The couplet may need explication.

## Possible Responses to *Questions for Discussion and Writing*
1. The speaker presents himself as getting older: he's in the autumn of life and moving into the cold and dark of winter.
2. The first quatrain describes the approach of winter as the dying leaves drift to the ground. The second quatrain presents images of falling night, and the third quatrain develops an image of a dying fire whose embers are being extinguished by its own ashes. They all suggest loss of light and heat (and waning life).
3. The last two lines might be difficult to explain, but the idea is that the speaker's lover (the "thou" of the poem) realizes that the time for love (and sex) is growing shorter and that it would be a good idea to take advantage of the time that's left. The cliché "make hay while the sun shines" is not a bad summary of the idea expressed in the final couplet.

## *Additional Questions for Discussion and Writing*
1. How is a body like boughs, and how are bare boughs like a ruined choir loft?
2. Does love always grow stronger between people as they get older? Write a brief response to this sonnet, exploring the relationship between love and aging.

## *Making Connections*
➜ How do this poem's thoughts and feelings about love and aging compare with those expressed in "Sailing to Byzantium" by William Butler Yeats?


## MY MISTRESS' EYES ARE NOTHING LIKE THE SUN (Sonnet 130) by William Shakespeare [p. 584]
In Shakespeare's day it was fashionable for poets to imitate the sonnets of Petrarch, the Italian poet whose praise of his beloved Laura started the rage for sonnet writing. The result of all the imitation was a surplus of Petrarchan conceits (or elaborate comparisons). In Sonnet 130, Shakespeare, who often drew on Petrarchan conventions himself, pokes fun at poets who thoughtlessly use the exaggerated figures of speech. Shakespeare is confident that his readers have read numerous imitations of Petrarch, and he turns their clichés to his own uses. The last line is a bit difficult because the words *she* and *compare* are both nominals. It might be paraphrased this way: I think my love is as rare as any woman ("she") who is misrepresented ("belied") through false comparisons ("false compare").

It may be helpful to point out that in Shakespeare's time the term *mistress* meant "beloved" or "chosen one" and had not yet acquired the connotations of illicit lover or kept woman that contemporary usage has.

## Possible Responses *to Questions for Discussion and Writing*

1. The poet is showing that he's aware of the stale similes and excessive metaphors that other poets use to try to outdo reality. He is rejecting them in favor of a description that is more honest but just as complimentary.
2. He asserts that her beauty doesn't need to be exaggerated; she is just as attractive as any woman who has been falsely represented by conventional poetic descriptions.
3. See the discussion earlier.
4. The focus of this exercise is on language and its abuses. Commercials would be another good target for parody, especially those ads for medications that have a long list of dreadful side effects.

## Additional Questions for Discussion and Writing

1. How do the negative connotations of the words *false* and *belied* help you to figure out that the last two lines contain a true appraisal of the speaker's mistress?
2. How does the poem's argument divide up among the three quatrains and the couplet?

## Making Connections

→ What different attitudes toward the beloved are expressed in Shakespeare's sonnets "Shall I Compare Thee to a Summer's Day?" and "My Mistress' Eyes Are Nothing Like the Sun"?

## DEATH, BE NOT PROUD by John Donne [p. 584]

This sonnet is an intense and mocking (though not humorous) apostrophe (or address) to Death. Its central theme is based on the Christian belief in resurrection. The expression is paradoxical throughout. The speaker says Death should not be arrogant: Death is not final; neither is it "mighty" or "dreadful"; it's not even competent. Actually, Death is pitiful ("poor Death"); far from being terrifying, it really should be welcomed like "rest" and "sleep." And there are other reasons to deprecate Death: it's a slave to human will and depends on poison, war, and sickness. Sedatives are even more effective in producing sleep, so why is Death so swelled with pride? As the final couplet makes clear, we can transcend Death by robbing it of its dominion.

Donne wanted control of his own dying. He wrote a treatise in defense of suicide in which he claimed that Jesus committed suicide. To a friend he wrote: "I would not that death should take me asleep. I would not have him merely seize me, and only declare me to be dead, but win me, and overcome me."

## Possible Responses to *Questions for Discussion and Writing*

1. He dismisses Death as an overrated, ineffectual fraud.
2. The paradox is that Death will die (line 14). By personifying death, the speaker can assign human characteristics and fallibilities: Death becomes a "servant" and can be dismissed as "poor Death," weak and powerless.

3. The speaker advances three claims to argue against Death's power: that people don't really die (lines 1–4); that death is really just a pleasant sleep, a rest and delivery from life (lines 5–8); that Death must depend on murder, war, poison, sickness (lines 9–12).
4. One must share the speaker's unqualified belief in an afterlife for the arguments to be valid and meaningful.

## Making Connections

→ Compare Donne's attitude toward death with Dylan Thomas's in "Do Not Go Gentle into That Good Night."

## THE FLEA by John Donne [pp. 585–86]

If you want to give students an example of a startling metaphysical conceit, this *carpe diem* poem will serve nicely. The poem presents a playful plea to a lady to surrender her virtue because in the swollen flea that has bitten them both, their blood is already mingled (as the speaker hopes their bodily fluids will soon be mingled in sexual intercourse). Their union, argues the lover, would be no more shameful than the bite of the flea. In stanza 2, he pleads that she spare the flea since they are united in a blood marriage within it (even though her parents might not agree). If, from force of habit ("use" in l.16), she crushes the flea, she will be killing all mingled within it—self, lover, and flea, "three sins in killing three" (l.18). In the last stanza, "cruel and sudden" (l.19), the lady crunches with her fingernail the jet-hard shell of the innocent flea, who did nothing sinful beyond taking a drop of her blood. But, since she feels no weaker from this tiny loss of blood, he pleads that she need not fear a loss of virtue: it will diminish her honor no more than the trifling death of a flea. The lover's argument is clearly longer on wit than it is on logic, but the poem nonetheless is considered exemplary in its genre.

## Possible Responses to *Questions for Discussion and Writing*

1. She's denying him her virginity, which for a woman in the seventeenth century was not a "little" thing. Losing her virginity meant losing not only her honor and reputation but also whatever advantage she had in the negotiations of courtship and marriage.
2. She's about to crush the flea. It was believed that a commingling of blood during intercourse might result in conception. In the speaker's elaborate conceit, the lovers are united ("more than married") in the flea's body, which has become a kind of "marriage temple." Thus, in crushing the flea she murders the speaker, commits suicide, and (figuratively) destroys any possible offspring.
3. The argument is that the consummation of the love affair has already taken place—in the body of the flea (the "living walls of jet").
4. See the discussion earlier and the answer to question 2.
5. The lady's nail is bloody because she's killed the flea.

6. She killed the flea, which means she didn't take his farfetched appeal seriously. If she admired his wit and ingenuity, perhaps she also realized that he could conceive of some equally clever reason to dump her after he got what he wanted.

### Additional Questions for Discussion and Writing
1. In what ways is this a *carpe diem* poem?
2. Look up in the glossary the definition of a "metaphysical conceit." How would you describe the conceit in this poem? Is it effective?
3. How would you describe the tone of this poem? How serious is the speaker?

### Making Connections
➜ How is this poem different from or similar to other poems about sex and love, such as Whitman's "Song of Myself (Section 11)," Dickinson's "Wild Nights—Wild Nights!" or Olds's "Sex Without Love"?

### A VALEDICTION: FORBIDDING MOURNING by John Donne [pp. 586–87]
In his biography of Donne, Izak Walton claims that the poet wrote this poem for his wife in 1611, when he was about to depart on a diplomatic mission to France. In the course of the poem, the speaker uses five conceits or metaphors to define the calm and quiet that he thinks should characterize his departure: the death of virtuous men, movement of the celestial spheres, the assurance of spiritual love (as opposed to physical love), the expansion of gold beaten into foil, and the conjoined legs of a drawing compass.

The simile of the first two stanzas must be linked to the title. The point is that the parting lovers should be like virtuous people who accept death easily because they are assured of being in paradise. The contrast between earthquakes (which can be accounted for) and the "trepidation of the spheres" (which is more significant but less destructive) sets up the contrast between the love of earthbound ("sublunary") lovers and the spiritual love of the speaker and his beloved. Their love does not depend on physical contact; it is as refined as gold, which can be expanded into gold foil without any break or separation. The final three stanzas develop the famous conceit in which the souls of the lovers are compared to a drawing compass (some students may visualize a directional compass). The best way to illustrate this famous conceit is to bring in a draftsman's compass (even a dime store variety) to demonstrate the movements described in the poem.

The student paper "Images of Love," which is at the end of Chapter 14 in the text, analyzes these metaphors and their progression through the poem.

### Possible Responses to Questions for Discussion and Writing
1. "Valediction" is a Latinate term for saying goodbye. The speaker forbids mourning because it would be inappropriate, unseemly, and unnecessary to cry and carry on.
2. Virtuous men have nothing to fear or worry about when they leave this life, since they're sure they're going to paradise. The speaker says the lovers should face their separation with the same grace and confidence.
3. The "dull sublunary" (earthbound) lovers need physical presence to sustain their

relationship. The speaker and his beloved represent something more refined; their love transcends the sensual. They have attained the Platonic ideal.

4. His beloved, like the stationary foot of the compass, gives him strength and support and inexorably draws him back to where he started (with her). Because the compass is used to draw circles, it is a most apt simile to describe the unity and perfection that the speaker claims for his love.

## Additional Questions for Discussion and Writing

1. Explain the reference to astronomy in stanza 3. (In the medieval cosmos, the heavenly bodies were thought to be fixed, while everything under the moon was subject to change.)
2. What qualities of beaten gold make it an appropriate metaphor for the love that the speaker is describing? (Gold is refined, precious, durable, and capable of being expanded greatly without breaking apart.)

## Making Connections

→ Compare the vision of idealized love that Donne projects in this poem to the one presented in Shakespeare's "Let Me Not to the Marriage of True Minds."


## TO HIS COY MISTRESS by Andrew Marvell [pp. 587–89]

This is one of the most famous *carpe diem*, persuasion-to-love poems ever written. It incorporates a distinct syllogistic form (an if-but-therefore argument) that distinguishes it from other *carpe diem* poems. The title identifies the characters: the speaker is a would-be lover; he is addressing his "coy" (reluctant) lady. His argument is this: if there were time, I'd woo you properly, but life is short and we'll be dead soon; therefore we'd better become lovers now.

The first section sets up a hypothetical situation in which there is vast space and time. The Ganges and Humber rivers are approximately on opposite sides of the globe. The allusions to Noah's flood and the conversion of the Jews evoke a span from Genesis to the Last Judgment. The speaker's "vegetable" (as opposed to rational) love will grow "vaster than empires but more slow."

The next section, beginning with "but," refutes the hypothesis of the first section. There is a note of urgency in the image of time's chariot pursuing them like an enemy, and the vastness of time is changed to deserts of eternity. The lines are full of images of death, dust, dryness, and isolation. The speaker also bawdily sketches the consequences of too much coyness: no one makes love in the grave. In the last section, the speaker's logic (or pseudologic) requires that the lovers behave differently. The images change from slowness, distance, and great size to excitement and vitality: "fire," "sport," "devour," "roll," "tear," "rough strife," "run." Time becomes a slow-jawed, devouring beast that will itself be devoured by the vigorous lovers.

129

## Possible Responses to *Questions for Discussion and Writing*

1. The speaker acts the patient courtly lover in the opening stanza, content to wait and to love and appreciate from afar.
2. In the second stanza the lover reminds his lady of their mortality, the fleeting passing of time (life) and their approaching death (eternity).
3. The speaker changes from patient, to concerned, to seductive ("Now let us sport")— and aggressive ("like amorous birds of prey, / Rather at once our time to devour"). Other key words include "fires," "sport," "tear," and "rough strife."
4. The metaphor stands for the sexual consummation the lover envisions, a victory over his lover's "fortified" resistance.
5. The poem is a classic representation of the *carpe diem* theme of the period. Students will likely enter into lively debate about the various motivations of the two lovers.

## Additional Questions for Discussion and Writing

1. Why does the speaker use "amorous birds of prey" instead of more conventional love birds (like doves or larks)?
2. What words and phrases have sexual connotations?
3. Write an answer to the argument in Marvell's poem, either in poetry or in prose.

## Making Connections

→ Edmund Waller's "Go, Lovely Rose" is another *carpe diem* poem with a sexual proposition similar to Marvell's. Do the pleadings in these two poems differ? Which do you think would be more likely to overcome a young maiden's resistance?

## THE LAMB by William Blake [pp. 589–90]

The childlike purity and pastoral bliss of this song arise from the abundant, positive depictions of a beneficent lamb (Christ) who is nourishing, comforting, and joyful. The first stanza poses a question; the second supplies the answer with naïve enthusiasm and assurance. The speaker unites himself, the lamb, and the infant Jesus in a pastoral vision of innocence and bliss. This is a Romantic portrait of a benevolent world envisioned by the uncorrupted, natural child, although the potential sacrifice of the unwary innocent is implied in the identification of the lamb and child with Christ. The poem is best taught with "The Tyger," allowing a full contrast of Blake's two views of God.

## Possible Responses to *Questions for Discussion and Writing*

1. The lamb is both the symbol of humankind and of Christ and all that is associated with him, most notably innocence.
2. The poem explicates a New Testament God and the gentler side of human experience.
3. The two-stanza structure of the poem allows Blake first to ask the question ("Who made thee?") and then to provide the answer ("He is called by thy name"), thus yoking humankind to the Christ figure, who is both human and God.

**THE TYGER** by William Blake [p. 590]

Most interpreters of this poem see it as a treatment of the age-old question: how can we explain evil in a world created by an all-knowing, beneficent God? The fearful, ominous tiger burns brightly in the dark forests of primeval creation. The lamb is contrasted with the tiger in stanza 5, which apparently alludes to the expulsion of Lucifer from heaven (as described in Milton's *Paradise Lost*). The angels weep not only over Lucifer's rebellion but also over the introduction of evil into the world.

**Possible Responses to *Questions for Discussion and Writing***

1. The poem presents the primeval side of creation. "The Tyger" also implies the possibility of a second creator, unlike the benign figure in "The Lamb." From this second creator emanates darkness, power, violence, and evil.
2. The fifth stanza seems to allude to the expulsion of Lucifer from heaven; see the discussion earlier. Lines 7 and 8 refer to the myth of Prometheus, who stole fire from the gods. His rebellion parallels the Christian myth of Satan's rebellion. Notice the use of the word "dare" in the last line, replacing the word "could" in the first stanza.
3. In addition to the contrasting views of creation, the two poems contrast sharply in tone, rhythm, pace, and use of assonance and consonance. "The Lamb" asks only one question—repeated several times, as in a nursery rhyme for children. "The Tyger" asks a lot of questions, most of which go unanswered.
4. Answers will vary.

**Making Connections**

→ Why does Blake answer his question in "The Lamb" but not in "The Tyger"?

**THE SICK ROSE** by William Blake [p. 591]

Students usually enjoy figuring out what the rose and the worm signify—and then deciding what the sickness might be. Since the rose is an archetypal symbol of sexual love, the meaning should be easily identified. But the worm, "That flies in the night [and thus is hidden] / In the howling storm" (a hint of catastrophe to come), lends itself to speculation. Critics have suggested syphilis, which in Blake's time did destroy life literally, or adultery, which (if discovered) could destroy the love existing in marriage. Today, the threat of AIDS comes to mind.

Blake printed and illustrated the text of his own poetry; his design for this poem has a rose drooping around the lines, with a caterpillar eating one of its leaves and a spirit expelled from the flower's closed center. This suggests the theme of erotic love: the merely sensuous worm enters the rose and drives out the spirit of joy, of authentic love. One interpretation is that the caterpillar is the Church, with its sick preoccupation with sex as sin, eating away a life-giving leaf.

## Possible Responses to *Questions or Discussion and Writing*

1. See the discussion earlier.
2. The rose is a yonic symbol; the worm is a phallic symbol. See the discussion earlier.
3. See the discussion earlier.
4. Have students check out the term *allegory* in the glossary.

## Additional Questions for Discussion and Writing

1. How does personification expand the scope of this lament?
2. In what ways does Blake's design of the illustrated manuscript for this poem contribute to your understanding and appreciation of the text?

## Making Connections

➜ Why is Blake's use of the rose unconventional? Argue your claims by comparing "The Sick Rose" to other rose poems: Edmund Waller's "Go, Lovely Rose" and even Dorothy Parker's "One Perfect Rose."

## LONDON by William Blake [p. 592]

This poem reflects Blake's distress with the suppression of human spirit, which he blamed on custom and politics. His idea was that humanity could flower if institutions could be eliminated or at least redirected. London represents a fallen world: everyone is blighted or plagued, and the midnight streets are filled with danger and misery. By contrast, the reader is reminded of privilege, soldiers, and palaces, all of which are aspects of oppressive authority. But the churches are not uplifting and the soldiers are not courageous, as the descriptive adjectives make clear.

## Possible Responses to *Questions for Discussion and Writing*

1. The poet uses a number of auditory images to suggest pain and suffering. The speaker hears the "cry of every man," "every infant's cry," and "the chimney-sweeper's cry" along with the "sigh" of the "hapless soldier" and the "curse" of "the youthful harlot" that "blasts the new-born infant's tear." The "marks of woe," the "mind-forged manacles," the "black'ning church," and the blood running down the palace walls also add to the far from happy picture.
2. The venereal disease infects the children and the wife of the harlot's customers. Thus, the plague that starts with a young woman forced by poverty to sell her body infects the whole society.
3. See the discussion earlier.

### Additional Questions for Discussion and Writing

1. Why does the speaker use the word *chartered* twice? What are its different meanings? (The streets are mapped; the privileged can hire [charter] the river for their use—in contrast to the misery of the poor.)
2. Explain how this poem is different from "The Lamb" and "The Tyger" in terms of voice, language, and tone. (The voice is more sophisticated, the language more complex, and the tone harsher.)

### Making Connections

Carl Sandburg also wrote about a big city. How does his poem "Chicago" compare with "London" in terms of theme, tone, and form?

THE WORLD IS TOO MUCH WITH US by William Wordsworth [pp. 592–93]
This sonnet almost perfectly embodies the love of nature that lies at the heart of English romanticism. When the speaker announces that he would "rather be / A Pagan suckled in a creed outworn" (lines 9–10), he probably is thinking of the Greek culture, in which nature had its own gods and goddesses. Still, the statement would have bordered on blasphemy in Wordsworth's nineteenth-century Christian England, thus lending considerable power to the closing sestet. The message is one that remains relevant today—"Getting and spending, we lay waste our powers" (line 2), thus losing the spiritual connection with nature that could enrich our lives.

### Possible Responses to *Questions for Discussion and Writing*

1. The speaker laments his culture's focus on the material world and thus its alienation from nature.
2. The poet commences the sestet emphatically in the middle of line 9 with the exclamation, "Great God!"
3. The octet outlines the problem ("Getting and spending") and what is lost as a result (a failure to see and benefit from the glories of Nature); the sestet provides a rebuke to a Christian culture that has lost its way by offering a contrasting Pagan (classical mythological) example.

### Additional Question for Discussion and Writing

Who are Proteus and Triton, and why would the speaker be comforted by the sight of them?

### Making Connections

→ Contrast Wordsworth's view of the world with Matthew Arnold's in "Dover Beach" or with Richard Wilbur's in "Love Calls Us to the Things of This World."

**SHE WALKS IN BEAUTY** by George Gordon, Lord Byron [pp. 593–94]
This evocation of feminine beauty works from physical properties to an ethereal state, with the final emphasis on spirit and mind: the last stanza speaks of goodness, peace of mind, and innocent love. The opening simile may be accounted for by the fact that Byron was writing for his cousin, Lady Wilmot Horton, who was wearing a black dress with spangles when he first met her (because she was in mourning). Byron's description is rich in an abstract, allusive way, but it has no specificity to it.

## Possible Responses to *Questions for Discussion and Writing*
1. The light of the speaker's lover is the perfect melding of light and dark, the pitch black of night, the bright and sparkling light of stars—"all that's best of dark and bright."
2. The features of his lover's face bespeak her quiet, good, and peaceful life and nature.
3. In his lover's faultless beauty ("One shade the more, one ray the less, / Had half impaired the nameless grace"), the speaker locates his definition of the perfect woman, one who combines a pleasing appearance with virtuous and admirable character.

## *Making Connections*
→ Compare Byron's "She Walks in Beauty" with the depiction of a female lover in Thomas Wyatt's "They Flee from Me."


**OZYMANDIAS** by Percy Bysshe Shelley [pp. 594–95]
The name "Ozymandias" is the Greek rendering of Ramses II, who was pharaoh of Egypt in the thirteenth century BC. The sonnet's ironic comment on his pride suggests the futility of all pride based on great work. Line 8 may present a problem: the passions of Ozymandias were well read by the sculptor who mocked them (imitated them on the face of the statue and derided them as well). But the passions, explicit in the statue's ruined visage, survive both the sculptor who created the statue and the pharaoh's heart.

Shelley visited the British Museum in 1817 with fellow poet Horace Smith and suggested that they should both produce a sonnet on the subject of the recent Egyptian finds. Shelley's sonnet reflects his lifelong hatred of tyranny. In a book by the ancient Greek historian Diodorus, Shelley had read an inscription to an Egyptian monarch's monument similar to the one quoted in his poem.

## Possible Responses to *Questions for Discussion and Writing*
1. The inscription on the statue has been recast by Shelley, from the original challenge to future leaders who would dispute the king's greatness ("let him surpass me in some of my exploits") to the broader taunt of "Look on my works, ye Mighty, and despair," a twist that captures Shelley's romantic theme of the vanity of human wishes.

2.  The once great "king of kings" is now broken into pieces, partly buried, strewn about, and "shattered." And, most pointedly, "lifeless."
3.  The fallen remains of the statue and of the king's legacy are further isolated by the leveling sands of time.

### Additional Questions for Discussion and Writing
1.  Why did Shelley choose this decrepit statue of a great king as a subject for a poem?
2.  Do the words "that colossal wreck" refer to something more than the statue?

### Making Connections
→ Compare the form, tone, and content of "Ozymandias" with McKay's "America."


ODE ON A GRECIAN URN by John Keats [pp. 595–97]
This poem is structured as a reading of the urn. It also brings up the contrast between timeless art and human mortality. The speaker muses on the unchanging beauty of the urn and his own suffering mortality. Grecian urns were vessels for the ashes of the dead; their carved or painted figures depicted a joyous afterlife in the Elysian Fields. The design on the circular urn appears to continue forever (an image of eternity or the seamless perfection of art).

In the first stanza, the urn is addressed as a "bride," a "foster child," a "sylvan historian," and the poet sketches a montage of the pictures that cover it. In stanza 2, he moves closer and considers a piper and a lover, figures that animate the poem's central idea: some ideal, unheard music is more beautiful than that which can be heard. This idea is further illustrated in stanza 3 by a series of poetic observations. In stanza 4, the speaker imagines what is not represented on the urn and, in the final stanza, reflects on the conclusions to be drawn from the graceful ancient shape.

### Possible Responses to *Questions for Discussion and Writing*
1.  Like all of the sense experiences described in the poem, the sweetness of the painted melody is eternal, experienced by each viewer throughout time.
2.  The urn's figures will live, will be youthful and beautiful, eternally, never experiencing human frailty, frustration, loss, illness.
3.  The paradox of the "Cold Pastoral" imparts a mildly ironic reading to the poem, creating a tension between the cold surface of the urn and the romantic, warm pastoral images painted upon it. The promise of eternal beauty offers condolences to humans facing their own mortality, thus the urn acts as "friend to man."
4.  Keats's aesthetic theory, "Beauty is truth, truth beauty," should generate lively and useful debate among your students.

### Additional Questions for Discussion and Writing

1.  The urn is called "sylvan" probably because it displays woodland scenes, but in what sense is it an "historian"?
2.  What disadvantages do living lovers experience (lines 28–30)?

### Making Connections

→ Compare Keats's views about art—and a specific piece of art—to what W. D. Snodgrass says on the same subject in his poem "Matisse: 'The Red Studio.'"

**WHEN I HEARD THE LEARN'D ASTRONOMER** by Walt Whitman [p. 597]
Whitman clearly would rather gaze at the beauty of the stars than hear a scientific description of them. He was much interested in science and paid tribute to discoveries in the new science of geology (of fossils, strata, and earth's age) in "Song of Myself." But he was also a transcendentalist who found God in nature, so reducing the stars to figures, charts, and diagrams would surely strike him as misguided.

### Possible Responses to *Questions for Discussion and Writing*

1.  The speaker in the poem, like Whitman himself, would rather be enjoying the beauty of the starlit sky than listening to a lecture containing "proofs" and "figures," illustrated with "charts and diagrams."
2.  One important feature that makes this a poem is Whitman's use of *anaphora*, the deliberate repetition of "When I . . ." at the beginning of the first four lines. There is also *assonance* in "heard" and "learn'd" and in "rising and gliding" and *alliteration* in "mystical moist" and "silence at the stars." The fanciful choice in their contexts of the words "gliding" and "mystical" is somewhat poetic. The unusual syntax in lines 4 ("When I sitting heard") and 5 ("How soon unaccountable I become tired and sick") is poetic; and of course, Whitman's adjective "unaccountable" would in standard edited English be an adverb, "unaccountably." The iambic rhythm, although not strictly adhered to, moves the lines along, as does the use of series. Some student may volunteer, likely in jest, that this is a poem because it is divided into lines like a poem, but that is, in truth, the most obvious characteristic that declares it to be a poem.
3.  Writing topic.

### Making Connections

→ Compare this poem with the ideas expressed about nature and beauty in Keats's "Ode on a Grecian Urn" or with Emily Dickinson's comments on faith and microscopes in "Faith Is a Fine Invention."

**SONG OF MYSELF (SECTION 11)** by Walt Whitman [pp. 597–98]

Whitman's very long poem "Song of Myself" is a hymn to America, to democracy, and to human sexuality. Contemporary readers, including Ralph Waldo Emerson, were shocked by the eroticism of the work but praised it nonetheless for its power and probity. Lines like "The scent of armpits, finer than prayer" must have given Mr. Emerson quite a turn; yet he still welcomed Whitman as the outstanding new poet of his day.

"Section 11" presents a kind of parable of loneliness and desire. Some students today may still be taken aback by its boldness. Most of the imagery in "Song of Myself" is homoerotic, but these verses are couched, at the beginning, at least, in heterosexual terms as the lady in her imagination goes "dancing and laughing along the beach" for "she saw them and loved them." We envision her as a rich, lonely, and repressed woman, perhaps middle-aged, who is aroused at the sight of the presumably naked young men cavorting in the water near her "fine house." The images of the young men are pure Whitman—intensely erotic regardless of sexual orientation: "The beards of the young men glisten'd with wet, it ran from their long hair, / Little streams pass'd all over their bodies." And the lady's "unseen hand also pass'd over their bodies, / It descended tremblingly from their temple and ribs." She is overcome by desire, as she "puffs and declines with pendant and bending arch," in what is surely a delicate description of a sexual climax. One critic also notes homoerotic arousal among the young men who "float on their backs," as "their bellies bulge to the sun," with the final "souse with spray" suggesting male ejaculation. In his essay on Whitman, Havelock Ellis, a pioneering early twentieth-century sex researcher, paid tribute to the "Homeric simplicity and grandeur" of the poet's expression in this episode. There may be some significance in the number twenty-eight, which is the length of a lunar cycle.

## Possible Responses to *Questions for Discussion and Writing*

1. The woman is hiding behind the window blinds because she does not wish to be seen ogling a bunch of young men swimming in the nude. She is rich ("owns the fine house by the rise of the bank") and lonely ("Twenty-eight years of womanly life and all so lonesome") and apparently sexually attracted to the male nudity.

2. The woman can stay "stock still" in her room while splashing with the young men in her imagination.

3. The phrase "souse with spray" could describe male ejaculation, given the sexually charged language that permeates the poem: "she saw them and loved them," "glistening with wet," "little streams pass'd all over their bodies," "unseen hand also pass'd over their bodies," "descended tremblingly," "their white bellies bulge to the sun," "puffs and declines with pendant and declining arch."

4. Whitman seems way ahead of his times in presenting a woman with a lusty sexual interest. In his day, women were thought to be far less responsive to sexual urges than men. Consider the old joke about Queen Victoria, whose daughter complained that she didn't want to have sex. The queen supposedly responded, "My dear, it is your duty: just lie there and think of England!" But Whitman declared that he wanted his poetry to celebrate everything human: "sex, womanhood, maternity, lusty

137

animations, organs, acts." Your students today may find nothing unusual about the lonely twenty-eight-year-old woman lusting after the twenty-eight skinny-dipping young men.

The deliberate repetition of words and phrases at the beginning and end of the poem are characteristic of Whitman's freewheeling style and lends emphasis and cadence to the lines. The occasional unusually long lines of verse give an impression of breathless, unbroken speech, reflecting the excitement of the secret watcher. But consider, too, that since short lines give a choppy, abrupt feeling, the long lines give a fluent, flowing effect, as in lines 10 and 11 with water running down the hair and its little streams passing all over their bodies. Also in the long line 16, all the actions are run together—all three sentences—to keep the movement going.

## Making Connections

➔ How is this poem different from or similar to other poems about sex and love, such as Donne's "The Flea," Dickinson's "Wild Nights—Wild Nights!" or Olds's "Sex Without Love"?


**DOVER BEACH** by Matthew Arnold [pp. 598–99]
The persona in the poem is standing at a window with his beloved looking from the white cliffs of England across the moonlit channel toward France. (Since the poet is male, it seems reasonable to assume that the persona is also.) He calls his love to the window and muses on the beauty of the landscape and the "eternal note of sadness" in the sound of the sea. The tide is in, and he remarks that the "Sea of Faith" (religious belief) was once "at the full" but now has retreated (under the onslaught of scientific discoveries of Darwin and others that contradicted the biblical account of creation). The solution posed in the poem for the resulting uncertainty is to have faith in each other, because the poet envisions a world without religious faith as being a place of darkness and strife. ("Shingles" are gravel beaches.)

Most of Arnold's poetry was written by the age of forty-five and examined the theme of human alienation and disconnection from the changing world of the nineteenth century. He continued to write as a literary critic until the end of his life, believing it was the best vehicle for social reform.

## Possible Responses to *Questions for Discussion and Writing*

1.  The setting seems to be a drawing room at night ("the moon lies fair") with a couple standing at a long window, looking out over the English Channel toward the French coast. The persona is presumably male, speaking to a woman ("Ah, love, let us be true / To one another!"), who is perhaps the Marguerite to whom Arnold dedicated a poem in 1857.
2.  The "Sea of Faith" is retreating following the stir caused by Darwin's *Origin of Species* in 1859, his earthshaking book promulgating the idea of evolution.

3. The persona proposes the strength of human love with faith in each other as a solution to the loss of religious faith.
4. Images of sight and sound abound in the poem; the "lack of sight" image would be the "darkling plain . . . / Where ignorant armies clash by night." Your students could argue that these images contribute to the effectiveness of the poem by providing concrete evidence to illustrate Arnold's abstract ideas.

### *Additional Question for Discussion and Writing*
What is the cause of the "sadness" in line 14? What is the speaker's response to the ebbing "Sea of Faith"?

### *Making Connections*
→ Compare Arnold's ideas about the loss of faith around the world with Emily Dickinson's comments concerning faith and microscopes in "Faith Is a Fine Invention."

### FAITH IS A FINE INVENTION by Emily Dickinson [p. 600]
This poem humorously labels Faith as an invention rather than as a virtue or philosophy, and questions Faith's adequacy to perform well in an emergency. Microscopes, which are literally inventions, are preferable. The type of emergency microscopes usually address is medical—crises of life and death. Thus, Dickinson belittles Faith's power in these matters and advises turning to science instead. The microscope improves on vision, the limited power of "Gentlemen who *see*."

### Possible Responses to *Questions for Discussion and Writing*
1. Inventions are the products of human minds that usually improve human lives, like fountain pens, lead pencils, steam engines, or electric lights. By calling "Faith" an invention, Dickinson is slyly suggesting that religion is also a product of human minds—a product provided by the "Gentlemen" who see religious faith as a means of easing fears, doubts, and losses through the offering of comforting platitudes.
2. According to the poem, microscopes are better tools than Faith "in an Emergency," like in a crisis of life or death, because a microscope actually does improve vision by enlarging cells or whatever medical evidence needs to be examined, thus making treatment possible.
3. The poem has a light, humorous tone, which tends to mask the serious content, but cutting humor typically serves a major function in satire. Students need to get beyond the tone and see the poem as a brief satire of religious beliefs. Dickinson, who was not a Christian believer but was steeped in Christian lore, was perhaps thinking when writing this poem of a Bible verse, Hebrews 11:1: "Now faith is the substance of things hoped for, the evidence of things not seen"—a statement that must have seemed like flimsy evidence according to her transcendental belief in God as transfusing all of nature.

139

## Making Connections

→ Compare this poem to others that concern the nature and value of faith: Arnold's "Dover Beach" and Whitman's "I Heard the Learn'd Astronomer."

## I'M NOBODY! WHO ARE YOU? by Emily Dickinson [p. 600]

The speaker in this poem is one of Dickinson's favorite personas—that of a small, shy person or a tiny winged creature—a bee, a cherub, a bird. Since she was herself a small, shy person who refused to publish her work, this poem may explain why she preferred not to advertise either herself or her work. Incidentally, if you've ever heard a vast number of frogs croaking around a pond in mating season ("the livelong June"), you'll appreciate the perfection of her simile in the final lines.

## Possible Responses to *Questions for Discussion and Writing*

1. The "they" in the first stanza are the "Somebodys" in the second stanza. These self-important "Somebodys" would "banish" the "Nobodys" perhaps by looking down on them or else by ignoring them completely.
2. The speaker, the "Nobody" in the poem, thinks it would be "dreary" to be in the public eye—to proclaim himself or herself ("tell your name") loudly and often in public the way frogs (and famous people) do to attract attention to themselves. The simile is effective because frogs are basically unattractive, and the idea of a fat frog croaking endlessly to an adoring audience of other fat frogs presents a laughable, Disneyesque image—and frogs also make a *lot* of annoying noise.
3. The speaker is clearly a shy person who values privacy and would find it a torment to be famous. The writing prompt is suitable for a brief in-class impromptu writing.

## Additional Questions for Discussion and Writing

1. Who is Dickinson mocking, especially with her references to croaking frogs (those who seek fame) and an admiring bog (fans and groupies of celebrities)?
2. How is the message of this poem even more pointed than it was in Dickinson's time?

## Making Connections

→ Contrast the voice (or persona) in this poem with several others by Dickinson. Develop an argument about the poet's range and variety of speakers.

## HE PUT THE BELT AROUND MY LIFE by Emily Dickinson [p. 601]

The persona in this poem is addressing her new husband (or perhaps her father). The capital letter on "He" does not mean that the man is Christ since Dickinson was capricious in her capitalization. Notice the similarities to Browning's "My Last Duchess" in the general oppressiveness of the male, the reference to a duke, and the use of the word "stoop" in the second stanza. Since the ellipsis is easily filled in, the only difficulty in the first stanza occurs in the last line: the speaker envisions herself as hereafter "a member of the Cloud." This image could suggest the sort of "soft eclipse" (to use her phrase from a similar poem) that occurs when a woman surrenders her name and her individuality in marriage. Those "little toils that make a circuit of the rest" are all those small services that a genteel housewife would perform for her husband in order to make the household run smoothly. A circuit is one of Dickinson's favorite images for wholeness. At the end of the poem, the persona envisions herself, like Browning's duchess, not allowed to smile or associate with anyone other than her husband, since he demands her entire attention. Thus, the theme of the poem concerns the restrictive nature of marriage for a woman in the nineteenth century.

## Possible Responses to *Questions for Discussion and Writing*
1. The "He" in the poem is in all likelihood the speaker's new husband, whose new spousal role would in the nineteenth century allow him to take complete control over her life. The speaker seems cool and resentful but careful not to give offense by openly complaining.
2. See the discussion earlier.
3. The speaker exhibits all three of those attitudes: she is polite ("Yet not too far to come at call—"), modest ("To lives that stoop to notice mine—"), and submissive ("Whose invitation, know you not / For whom I must decline?"). Yet she is also resigned ("My lifetime folding up—") and considerably restive and resentful ("He put the Belt around my life— / I heard the Buckle snap—").

### *Making Connections*
→ Contrast this poem about male-female relationships with Lucille Clifton's "homage to my hips." Which attitude do you prefer?

## MUCH MADNESS IS DIVINEST SENSE by Emily Dickinson [p. 601]
Dickinson states quite succinctly in this little poem one of the important truths of human survival: it's dangerous to be a nonconformist—even, or especially, if you're right. She begins by pointing out that many things condemned as crazy by society actually make good sense. We think at once of Galileo and Darwin and others who discovered truths that society didn't want to hear about. She then says that much of what people accept as sensible is patent madness. Consider the nuclear arms race, for example. Her final line, asserting that dissenters will be "handled with a Chain," probably reflects the treatment in her day of chaining asylum inmates to the wall. Today, students are more likely to think of handcuffed protesters.

## Possible Responses to *Questions for Discussion and Writing*
1. As examples of something, perhaps historical, that was thought to be madness but turned out to be sensible, you might bring up the ideas of Darwin and Galileo to get your students started. They, then, may bring up the idea of travel in vehicles like cars, trains, airplanes, or even spaceships—all of which seemed wildly fanciful,

dangerous, deafeningly noisy, and (in the case of space travel) prohibitively expensive to many people when the concepts were first introduced.

2. Asking for something that is accepted by most people in society that you personally consider "madness" may bring responses ranging from nuclear proliferation, war, and the defense budget to personal peccadilloes like motorcycles, all-terrain vehicles, jumping out of airplanes for fun, the cost of the space program, and so on.

3. By "handled with a Chain," Dickinson could mean that dissenters will be treated the way mad people were handled in asylums in her day—by being chained to the wall.

### Additional Questions for Discussion and Writing
1. What does it mean that "the Majority / In this, as All, prevail"?
2. Discuss the conflict between the individual and society expressed in this poem.

### Making Connections
→ Compare this poem's message about conformity to the theme of "The Supremes" by Cornelius Eady. Do you think the speaker in Eady's poem would agree with Dickinson's views?

### BECAUSE I COULD NOT STOP FOR DEATH by Emily Dickinson [p. 602]
This poem reveals Dickinson's calm acceptance of death. She presents the experience as being no more frightening than receiving an unexpected gentleman caller. Stanza 3 presents stages that the persona reviews during this journey to the grave—childhood (the recess scene), maturity (the ripe hence "gazing" grain), and death (the setting sun)—as she passes to the other side, where she experiences a chill since she is not warmly dressed. In fact, her garments are more appropriate for a wedding—a new beginning— than for a funeral, which we tend to think of as an ending. Her description of the grave as her "House" indicates how naturally she depicts this new state. The eternity she spends there seems timeless to her. If the poem has a theme, it is a transcendental one—that death is not to be feared since it is a natural part of the endless cycle of nature.

### Possible Responses to Questions for Discussion and Writing
1. The action depicted in the poem is the traveling of a soul from death to whatever lies beyond ("the Horses' Heads / Were toward Eternity"). The action described in stanza 3 is a review of the journey to the grave: childhood (the recess scene), maturity (the ripe hence "gazing" grain), and death (the setting sun). The "House," of course, is the grave.
2. Death is personified as if he were a gentleman caller: he is kind, polite, unhurried, and civil.
3. The persona's attitude toward death is completely accepting. She has, apparently of her own volition, "Put away / My labor and my leisure too"; she says, "He kindly stopped for me"; she describes the grave in a comforting image as a "House" and reassuringly says that eternity for her is timeless.

4. The theme is transcendental: that death is not to be feared since it is a natural part of the endless cycle of nature. That attitude is very similar to Whitman's calm, welcoming acceptance of death at the conclusion of "Song of Myself": "I bequeath myself to the dirt to grow from the grass I love, / If you want me again look for me under your boot soles."

### Additional Questions for Discussion and Writing
1. Do the clothes the speaker is wearing suggest typical burial garments? If not, what do they suggest?
2. Why couldn't the speaker stop for death?

### Making Connections
➜ Contrast the personification of death in this poem with that of John Donne in "Death Be Not Proud." How do they differ? Which do you find more appealing?

SOME KEEP THE SABBATH GOING TO CHURCH by Emily Dickinson [p. 603]
Dickinson's poetry is filled with Christian imagery and terminology, but she was far from being a true believer. A great admirer of Emerson, she seems in this charming poem more transcendentalist than Christian. Transcendentalists believe that God is everywhere—in nature and all its creatures, as well as in human beings themselves, thus denying the Christian doctrine of original sin. The persona here is a small winged creature who celebrates the Sabbath not with a tolling bell but with birdsong in the midst of nature. Her concept of worship is one of joy here on earth, not the promise of heaven in the hereafter. The tone is light, playful, and a touch satirical.

### Possible Responses to Questions for Discussion and Writing
1. The persona in the poem presents herself or himself as a small creature with wings, a bird perhaps, or a bee or a dragonfly. Dickinson was a great lover of all of nature's creatures, although she admits to feeling "zero at the bone" when surprised by a smallish snake—that "narrow Fellow in the Grass."
2. The speaker celebrates the Sabbath by staying at home in the orchard, with the arching branches providing the "dome" of her church. Instead of donning an elaborate surplice, she says, "I just wear my Wings," meaning she goes as she is, and quite appropriately so in the midst of nature's unclothed creatures; instead of "tolling bells" as a call to worship, her "little sexton" offers bursts of birdsong; instead of a clergyman, God does the preaching (which, like the birdsong, is "never long"). In other words, in a transcendentalist manner, she communicates directly with God during her communion with nature's creatures.
3. The tone of the poem is playful, sprightly, and insouciant. The theme is clearly stated in the last two lines: instead of having to wait until after death to get to heaven, she experiences the joy of heaven all the time, filled with happiness by being in union with nature.

➜ How does this poem differ from Gerard Manley Hopkins's "Pied Beauty," which also praises the beauty of nature but with a different set of philosophical underpinnings?

**WILD NIGHTS—WILD NIGHTS!** by Emily Dickinson [p. 603]
Emily Dickinson was famously celibate, but she is known to have fallen in love with a married Boston minister. This poem may express her unrequited desire for the man she called her "master" in several poems. Notice that the poem is couched in the conditional ("should be," "might I"), so the passion expressed is a longing, not a fulfillment. The word "luxury" (line 4) formerly meant "excess," suggesting wild abandon—a surfeit of sensual delights. Stanza 2 (elliptical, with "are" understood in line 5) presents the image of a heart (source of love) as a vessel safely in port (no longer needing the compass or chart), united with the lover after weathering any storms that might have separated them. "Rowing in Eden" in the final stanza suggests the epitome of bliss, as the speaker longs to "moor" (to be held safely and securely) in the arms of the beloved. Probably the poem has no theme. It's a lyric poem expressing subjective emotion.

### Possible Responses to *Questions for Discussion and Writing*
1. The speaker is looking forward to being united with her lover for a night of ecstasy.
2. The word "luxury" in Dickinson's day meant "excess"—in this case the excess of wild sexual abandon that the speaker is hoping for.
3. A paraphrase of the second stanza might go this way:
   > Undamaging are the winds—
   > To a lover sheltered in port—
   > There is no longer need for a compass—
   > There is no longer need for a chart!
4. In stanza 2, Dickinson presents the image of a heart (the traditional source of love) as a ship safely in port, united with the lover after weathering any storms that might have separated them.
5. In the last two lines, the speaker longs to "moor" (to be held safely and securely, like a ship is in port) "in Thee" (in the arms of the beloved).

*Making Connections*
➜ How is this poem different from or similar to other poems about sex and love, such as Donne's "The Flea," Whitman's "Song of Myself (Section 11)" or Olds's "Sex Without Love"?

**PIED BEAUTY** by Gerard Manley Hopkins [p. 604]
Students will probably need to look up the meaning of "pied," or they may be able to guess that it means essentially the same as "dappled." The poem praises the variety and contrasts found in nature and in the work of human hands, since all is (in the poet's view) God given. The phrase "All things counter, original, spare, strange" suggests how

interesting as well as beautiful this variety makes our lives. The beauty of the poem lies in its imagery and word choice.

## Possible Responses to *Questions for Discussion and Writing*
1.  This poem illustrates Hopkins's use of numerous poetic innovations in style, structure, and word choice. The heavy emphasis on repetition, alliteration, consonance, and assonance, along with the difficult diction and the unconventional dependence on stress (called "sprung rhythm") can seem almost overwhelming. But the main point is fairly simple: to glorify God (the only entity "whose beauty is past change") by describing the great variety present in the earth and sky. The hyphenated words are the ones the poet coined. Ask students if they can figure out what the combined terms mean. Most of them are decipherable.
2.  If readers have ever looked at the countryside from an airplane, they'll have a good idea of a landscape that is "plotted and pieced"—i.e., divided into plots and fields and various parcels of land.
3.  Hopkins's religious creed would hold that human talents and artistry derive from God: "He fathers-forth" everything (the word "all" occurs three times in the poem). It's a mystery—"who knows how?" (line 7)—but the poet seems quite sure about the source of all beauty, as the opening and closing lines indicate. Darwinists would, of course, have another take on the matter, especially about the reasons for diversity and variation in the natural world.

## Making Connections
→ Compare Hopkins's attitude toward nature with the views expressed by Robert Frost in "Design" or by Maxine Kumin in "Woodchucks."

SPRING AND FALL by Gerard Manley Hopkins [pp. 604–5]
The poet here imagines Margaret grieving over the approaching death of nature in autumn (the grove "unleaving"—dropping its golden leaves). The syntax needs untangling in lines 3 and 4: can you with your fresh (innocent) thoughts care for human things as you do for these (falling) leaves? Lines 11 through 13 are also in need of paraphrase: "Sorrow's springs are the same" suggests that even spring leads eventually to fall (death), and no mouth or mind has expressed what the heart, the spirit, can understand. "Fall" in the poem also has the meaning of humanity's fall from grace—the fall that brought death into the Garden of Eden. Thus, the "blight man was born for" is both death and original sin. So Margaret, without knowing it, mourns her own death as well as that of the falling leaves.

## Possible Responses to *Questions for Discussion and Writing*
1.  The golden leaves in the grove are "leaving" the trees. Margaret is sad that the beauty of autumn is passing and winter is coming. And she's getting older (line 7).

145

2. The falling leaves could also allude to the fall of man, as hinted at in lines 4 ("like the things of man") and 15 ("the blight man was born for"). The biblical fall meant, among other things, that humans became mortal and would die.
3. This would be a good topic for students to work on in pairs or groups and come up with a short explication to compare and argue about.

### Making Connections
→ Compare this poem to others about growing older and facing the prospect of death, such as "My Son My Executioner" by Donald Hall, "The Force That Through the Green Fuse Drives the Flower" by Dylan Thomas, or "The Leap" by James Dickey.

### TO AN ATHLETE DYING YOUNG by A. E. Housman [pp. 605–6]
In this poem Housman appears to be congratulating a young athlete for having died in his prime, since his glory would have faded quickly as he aged. Presumably he is not serious in recommending early death as a remedy for loss of fame but is commenting on the way we tend to remember the best of those who die before their laurels (in the poem, wreaths of laurel bestowed on early gladiators to be worn as a crown of triumph) have faded. President Kennedy is one good example; Amelia Earhart is another; perhaps even Elvis Presley, although his laurels were beginning to go a trifle limp. You may need to explain the image in the first stanza of the athlete being carried in a chair through the town as a celebration of his prowess; he would, of course, be once more "carried shoulder-high" in his coffin. Note, too, the first stanza is in past tense, the rest of the poem in present.

See the student response to this poem, which misses the irony. It is presented for analysis and discussion at the end of Chapter 13.

### Possible Response to *Questions for Discussion and Writing*
1. The "road" down which "all runners come" is the road to the grave, that "stiller town," where the quiet dead are laid to rest. The laurel is an evergreen tree with leaves that, woven into a crown, bestowed honor on winners of ancient Greek athletic contests held at Delphi every four years (the early forerunners of our present-day Olympic Games). We learn in line 11 that the "laurel" (the honor won in the race) will fade all too quickly. The poetic voice continues his wry suggestion that the youth, "Smart lad," was fortunate to die before someone else broke his record, and his fame wore out, "And the name died before the man."
2. The final stanza suggests that actually the garland is not worth much at all since, even though "unwithered," it is "briefer than a girl's." (Garlands for girls, of flowers instead of laurel, encircle their heads, while those for males leave an opening above the brow—think of pictures of Julius Caesar.) But the greatest sadness is that the young athlete's garland, signifying his honor, will be acknowledged only by those silent "strengthless dead" in that silent "stiller town"—no cheering or waving flags. Most of us would not consider approbation by the dead worth dying for. But, on the other hand, we can all think of examples of famous people, gone to an early death, whose failings are now forgiven and forgotten as they live on in our collective

146

memories—President John Kennedy, Amelia Earhart, Janis Joplin, Elvis Presley, John Lennon, Michael Jackson, and so on.

3. Housman in this poem is undermining the widely accepted belief that athletic success is glorious.

### *Additional Questions for Discussion and Writing*
1. Why is it important that the young athlete be a runner (rather than a football player or a tennis champ)? What archetype does running a race suggest?
2. How does the poem undermine the belief that athletic success is glorious?
3. One reader has suggested that the speaker is almost envious of the young athlete because he (the speaker) has experienced the fate of watching his own glories fade and die. Can you find evidence in the poem to support this interpretation?

### *Making Connections*
➔ Compare this poem with Emily Dickinson's "Because I Could Not Stop for Death" or with John Updike's "Ex-Basketball Player."

### LOVELIEST OF TREES by A. E. Housman [p. 606]
If you ask your students to write on a slip of paper the age of the speaker in the poem, you'll probably be surprised by the variety of the responses. Perhaps they think it's a trick; perhaps they have no idea what "threescore" means; perhaps they don't know that seventy years is the expected human life span given in the Bible. In any event, you can use this opportunity to stress once more the need for close reading of poetry. You may also need to remind the class that cherry tree blossoms can be white, as well as pink. The poem is a lovely lyric using praise of nature's beauty to comment on the brevity of human life. Note also the suggestion of rebirth in the reference to "Eastertide" and also in the cyclical reference by which the white blooms of the first stanza become snow in the last.

### Possible Responses to *Questions for Discussion and Writing*
1. The speaker is twenty years old. In stanza 2 he says that of his biblically allotted seventy years on earth, "twenty will not come again": he's already lived them.
2. The images of white blossoms in spring and of white snow in winter reinforce the endless cycle of life in nature. The spring blossoms, coupled with the mention of "Eastertide," might be seen as promising the renewal of human life, which Easter celebrates in Christian dogma.
3. Since this is a lyric poem, a theme is not expected, but the wistful final stanza sounds a cautionary plea to make the most of time because life is fleeting and "Fifty springs are little room" to admire the endless beauty to be found in nature.

### Additional Questions for Discussion and Writing
1. What images connect the first and third stanzas?
2. What connotations does Eastertide (line 4) carry? How do these connotations fit into the development of the poem's theme?

### Making Connections
→ Compare this poem to "Spring and Fall" by Gerard Manley Hopkins.

### THE SECOND COMING by William Butler Yeats [p. 607]
Yeats developed a complex personal mythology, which sheds light on this poem, but it can be understood without special knowledge. He believed that civilizations moved in cycles of 2,000 years; the passing of one and the rising of the next would be accomplished in great upheaval. Although the poem makes use of Christian imagery (appropriate to the ending of the era following the birth of Christ), the "Second Coming" anticipated in the poem sounds anything but Christlike.

The first stanza depicts a world out of control, perfectly conveyed in the image of the falcon beyond hearing its handler. The "ceremony of innocence" (baptism) has been drowned in the "blood-dimmed tide." The lines "The best lack all conviction, while the worst / Are full of passionate intensity" are prescient in their apt description of what happened in Nazi Germany as Hitler rose to power. The huge beast that "slouches toward Bethlehem" can be seen as fascism, which drenched much of the world in blood during World War II. Yeats, of course, in 1921 simply saw it as the coming civilization—as violent and pitiless as the one that was passing. The phrase "twenty centuries of stony sleep" refers to the pre-Christian era, which was "vexed to nightmare by a rocking cradle"—by the birth of Christ, who did not, after all, prove to be the Prince of Peace.

### Possible Responses to Questions for Discussion and Writing
1. The world described by the speaker in the first stanza is in utter chaos, as if following some cataclysmic natural disaster or a bloody, destructive world war.
2. In the poem, the "ceremony of innocence" (perhaps baptism) is drowned in "the blood-dimmed tide." Yeats believed that ceremony was the civilizing principle that could save humanity from being engulfed in turbulence. In another poem he writes, "How but in custom and in ceremony / Are innocence and beauty born?"
3. Just as water, used in baptismal ceremonies, symbolizes sacredness and spirituality, a desert, devoid of life-giving water, symbolizes a total lack of spirituality. So it is entirely fitting that the "rough beast" appears from the "sands of the desert."
4. Yeats believed that history moved in 2,000-year cycles, with each cycle ending in upheaval and catastrophe. So the "twenty centuries of stony sleep" would be the pre-Christian era that was "vexed to nightmare by a rocking cradle," meaning by the birth of Jesus in that cradle in the manger.
5. Some early critics thought that the "rough beast" represents the 1917 Russian Revolution, but others later proposed that the image represents the rise of Adolph Hitler and fascism. Yeats accepted that interpretation as possibly being what his

148

unconscious mind had fashioned into the imagery in this poem. In *A Vision*, Yeats
wrote that he felt "we may be about to accept the most implacable authority the
world has known." He got that right.

### Additional Questions for Discussion and Writing

1. What image does the description of the beast—with the body of a lion and the head
   of a man—conjure up? (The Sphinx.) Why is this an appropriate form for the beast?
2. Write a paper discussing the bird imagery in the poem. Consider why the
   falcon/falconer image is particularly appropriate. Why is the beast accompanied by
   the reeling shadows of "indignant desert birds"?

### Making Connections

→ Compare this poem to "Fire and Ice" by Robert Frost.

SAILING TO BYZANTIUM by William Butler Yeats [p. 608]
Considered one of the finest poems in the English language, "Byzantium" presents an
aging man's response to his loss of sexual vitality. The "country" in the first line may be
Ireland, but it could also be the country in which we all must live—within our own
bodies. The speaker in the poem seeks to be freed from his body, that "tattered coat upon
a stick," and teach his soul to sing so that he can find satisfaction in "monuments of
unaging intellect," instead of the sensual pleasures enjoyed by the young. As a metaphor
to represent all artistic and intellectual accomplishment, he chooses "the holy city of
Byzantium," with its gorgeous mosaics in St. Sophia's depicting on the walls saints
"standing in God's holy fire." He wants to be freed from sexual passion ("Consume my
heart away; sick with desire / And fastened to a dying animal"—his body) so that he will
be able to concentrate on less earthly matters. In the final stanza he asks to be
reincarnated as a beautiful mechanical bird, such as an emperor might own, to entertain
the court with his song (poetry) about literally everything—past, present, or future.

   In 1913 Yeats wrote, "Now I am trying to write about the state of my soul, for it
is right for an old man to make his soul, and some of my thoughts on that subject I have
put into a poem called 'Sailing to Byzantium.' [In the eighth and ninth centuries]
Byzantium was the center of European civilization and the source of its spiritual
philosophy, so I symbolize the search for spiritual life by a journey to that city."

### Possible Responses to *Questions for Discussion and Writing*

1. The imagery in the first stanza depicts a land given to sexual activity: "The young /
   In one another's arms"; "The salmon falls" refers to the spectacular athletic feats
   performed by salmon, leaping up waterfalls in order to make it upstream to mate;
   "the mackerel-crowded seas" suggests the astonishing fecundity of fish in the sea;
   "the birds in the trees" (in line 2) may remind some readers of Cole Porter's "Birds
   do it, bees do it; even educated fleas do it." Yeats is saying the same thing, only a bit
   more poetically.

149

In the Renaissance, the verb "to die" had an additional meaning: to have an orgasm. So Yeats, in describing the young as "those dying generations," is saying that young people are dedicated to the same activity as the birds and the bees and the fish. (The phrase can also be read quite literally, though, as in Bob Dylan's line, "Everything not busy being born is busy dying.")

2. That "country," not for old men, is the country of youth, given to sensuous activities from which the speaker is now excluded by his age. (Remember, this poem was written pre-Viagra.)
3. The speaker wants to sail to Byzantium to be free from the siren call of sexuality ("sensual music") and find instead music for his soul in art and "unaging intellect." Byzantium, with its gorgeous glittering gold mosaics, is the perfect symbol for the solace he seeks because its beauty and intellectual appeal can be appreciated just as well, if not better, by an aged man than by a youth, distracted by "sensual music."
4. The "dying animal," of course, is the speaker's body, presented in the image of a scarecrow—"a paltry thing, / A tattered coat upon a stick."
5. The writing assignment is challenging, but adept students should be able to discover how the images interrelate. In the first stanza the sensual images (one critic has called these "the most spermy lines in all of English poetry") end with the introduction of a purely cerebral image, "Monuments of unaging intellect." In the second stanza the image of the weak "aged man" becomes reenergized through his soul's search for "Monuments of its own magnificence." In stanza 3 the speaker begs the "sages" to rid him of sexual longings ("Consume my heart away, sick with desire") and deliver him "Into the artifice of eternity"—meaning, probably, those same asexual monuments of intellect and soul searching that concluded stanzas 1 and 2. In the final stanza he seeks reincarnation as a gorgeous mechanical bird (completely freed now from his earthly body and from sexuality) to sing his poetic song ("Of what is past, or passing, or to come") as entertainment for "the lords and ladies of Byzantium." Thus each stanza ends with an image of intellectual or artistic achievement—the goal the speaker aims for—and the final image fulfills his intent.

### Making Connections
→ How does this poem about art compare to John Keats's "Ode on a Grecian Urn"?

## WE WEAR THE MASK by Paul Laurence Dunbar [p. 609]
Dunbar's poem, written half a century before the civil rights movement in this country, is an anguished cry of suffering and protest. The mask worn by blacks in the poem is the pretense of happiness, which contributed to the stereotype of those happy slaves down on the plantation—an illusion accepted by some southerners to justify their racist position during the Civil War and for a long time afterward. The debt paid "to human guile" would be the psychological cost of living a lie, of using guile in order to deceive whites into thinking black people are happy. The word "subtleties" in line 5 surely means subterfuges or deviousness, as Milton used the word to depict the "subtle serpent" in the garden.

**Possible Responses to *Questions for Discussion and Writing***

1. The speaker in the poem represents plural personae, most likely of black people, with whom Dunbar would identify, but he could be speaking for any and all persons of color in American society—black, brown, red, or yellow.

2. The smiling mask is necessary because a candid show of righteous anger would threaten the white people who control society, and the person of color would be seen as "straightway dangerous" and "handled with a Chain" (to quote Emily Dickinson).

3. The theme of this poem is a powerful protest against the indignity and injustice of racial discrimination, a protest that eventually became magnified, energized, and organized into the civil rights struggle of the 1960s.

4. This writing prompt may provide some students a chance to express their own righteous outrage. You may want to discuss with them the need to establish a rapport with their audience instead of just lashing out and losing their empathy.

*Additional Questions for Discussion and Writing*

1. Why does the speaker address Christ in line 10?

2. Why does the speaker say "the clay is vile / Beneath our feet, and long the mile" (lines 12–13)?

*Making Connections*

→ Compare Dunbar's feelings about living in a racist country to those expressed by Claude McKay in "America" and Langston Hughes in "Harlem (A Dream Deferred)."

MENDING WALL by Robert Frost [pp. 610-11]

This poem may or may not be about walls. Certainly the lines "Before I built a wall I'd ask to know / What I was walling in or walling out / And to whom I was like to give offense" call to mind several famous walls, like the Iron Curtain, the Bamboo Wall, the Great Wall of China, and the Berlin Wall, not to mention metaphorical walls that separate people who fail to communicate or who hold opposing positions. Frost portrays the neighbor (who finds walls necessary for no good reason) in such an unflattering light that most readers fail to notice that the speaker (who wryly questions the need for walls) is not exactly rational about them himself and also that he is the one who lets the neighbor know when it's time to repair the wall in the poem. One critic has suggested that the poem is about two kinds of people: conservatives and liberals; in which case, we can perhaps safely say that the poet favors a liberal bent.

**Possible Responses to *Questions for Discussion and Writing***

1. The speaker in the poem is a farmer, or at least the keeper of an orchard, who has a sense of humor (he wryly teases his neighbor about repairing this wall that they do not need in the first place) and seems a friendly, reasonable person who would prefer to get along without a wall. The neighbor, though, "moves in darkness" (meaning, in the speaker's opinion, in ignorance) and is deaf to the speaker's reasoned

arguments—he just keeps repeating an adage that he learned at his father's knee: "Good fences make good neighbors."

2.  The line "Something there is that doesn't love a wall" appears twice in the poem, but so too does the line "Good fences make good neighbors." Both express key concepts in the poem, which probably accounts for their appearing twice, but they also express opposing ideas. "Something there is that doesn't love a wall" suggests that perhaps walls cause animosity. And, indeed, that will serve as the theme of the poem, since the speaker supports it with good evidence, and the neighbor who wants the wall is described as looking "like an old-stone savage, armed." Quite a few people quote that line—"Good fences make good neighbors"—as if the advice makes good sense. So maybe ironically, in the real world, the "old-stone-savage" has the last word.

3.  The speaker is not in favor of walls. He keeps pressing his neighbor for reasons to think walls in general are good and reasons against them: "Before I built a wall I'd ask to know / What I was walling in or walling out, / And to whom I was like to give offense." But neither does he like hunters, who damage walls like his, just to "have the rabbit out of hiding, / To please the yelping dogs." Maybe he just gets tired of mending the troublesome wall.

4.  Ask your students to declare whether they are prowalls or antiwalls and put them into groups to brainstorm for a paper supporting their position. Then ask each group to write a claim in support of the opposite position. Finally, assign the class to write individual essays arguing for the position of his or her choice using personal experience as evidence.

### Additional Questions for Discussion and Writing

1.  Why is the wall in the poem made of stones? (It's located in Frost's native, rocky New England.)
2.  Is "mending" a gerund that denotes what the men are doing (mending the wall), or is it a participle that describes the wall? What kind of wall would a "mending wall" be?

### Making Connections

→ How do you think the neighbor in this poem might respond to the attitude toward nature expressed in Whitman's "When I Heard the Learn'd Astronomer" or in Thomas's "The Force That Through the Green Fuse Drives the Flower"?

### BIRCHES by Robert Frost [pp. 611–12]

Many students will have no idea what the activity of swinging birches is, and some will not even know what a birch tree looks like, so pictures may be useful in introducing the poem. The birch is a tall, straight, flexible tree, and it is possible to climb carefully to the thin top of the main trunk and then, flinging your body outward as a weight, make the whole tree bend down close to the ground and drop you off. In the poem, Frost uses this activity symbolically as a way of "getting away from it all" yet still feeling attached to the earth. The speaker does not wish for complete release from adult life but for a brief respite.

**Possible Responses to *Questions for Discussion and Writing***

1. The speaker prefers to think the birches have been bent by boys instead of by ice storms because, while a coating of ice makes them gorgeous in the sun, its weight drags them down, and "once bowed / For so long, they never right themselves." Luckily, though, a boy's "swinging doesn't bend them down to stay / As ice storms do." Instead, it merely takes "the stiffness out of them," as if somehow improving the trees.

2. In lines 41–49, the speaker is describing the tribulations of adulthood ("life is too much like a pathless wood") and longing to return briefly to his carefree childhood as "a swinger of birches" ("I'd like to get away from earth awhile / And then come back to it and begin over").

3. The speaker does not want fate to "snatch me away / Not to return." Make no mistake, he says, he does not want to die, because "Earth's the right place to love," meaning earth, not heaven, is the place one should love to be. The italics in "*toward* heaven" in line 56 emphasize that he is not ready to actually go there now. What he wants is a brief respite from life's cares and trials (those face burns, tickling cobwebs, and weepy eye of lines 45–47). He only wants to be free from earthly responsibilities once in a while and know once more the joy of being "a swinger of birches."

4. Perhaps this creative assignment will enable your students to recapture their moments of once having been swingers of birches.

*Additional Questions for Discussion and Writing*

1. What does the experience of swinging on birches mean to the speaker? (Limber freedom, a feeling of conquest, physical enjoyment.)

2. Why is blank verse an appropriate form for this poem? (The easy conversational feel fits the meditative recollection better than a rigid form would.)

### Making Connections
→ How does the attitude toward nature in this poem differ from the view in some other Frost poems, such as "Design" or "Mending Wall"?

### "OUT, OUT—" by Robert Frost [p. 613]
The title, which implies the theme of the poem, is an allusion to Macbeth's speech upon hearing of the death of his wife:

> Out, out, brief candle!
> Life's but a walking shadow, a poor player
> That struts and frets his hour upon the stage
> And then is heard no more. It is a tale
> Told by an idiot, full of sound and fury,
> Signifying nothing. (5.5.23–28)

The "brief candle" image conveys the senseless, almost capricious ending of the boy's life before he has a chance to live it. His short life can signify nothing, and his accidental death underscores the tenuous nature of all human existence. At the end, the attitude of those who are tending the boy ("since they / Were not the one dead, turned to their affairs") suggests the truism that life goes on. But not for the boy who has lost his chance at life. The personification of the saw (which "snarled and rattled" and "leaped out at the boy's hand") lends an air of fatalism to the accident, as if fate decreed that this boy should die, and for no reason. Like the passage from *Macbeth*, the poem seems to acknowledge, in a matter-of-fact way, the tenuous hold that we have on life.

### Possible Responses to *Questions for Discussion and Writing*
1. The speaker in the poem is an omniscient but impartial observer who sets the scene, describes the action, reports the tragedy, and summarizes the incident—all with minimum comment and little emotion. The characters are not named to convey universality to the brief account.
2. The personification of the saw creates a chilling response to the suddenness of the saw's attack, which is heartbreaking, just as the boy was done for the day.
3. The theme of the poem is conveyed by the allusion in the title: that life is a tenuous affair and can be dispatched in a moment without warning or reason.
4. This allusion is fully explained in the discussion of the poem earlier.

### Additional Questions for Discussion and Writing
1. What does the image of "Five mountain ranges one behind the other" suggest?
2. What do you think of the attitude of the survivors? Are they callous or just practical and realistic?

## Making Connections

→ Compare the attitude expressed in this poem toward the boy's death with the attitude toward the death of the young soldier in Tim O'Brien's "The Things They Carried" and/or the attitude toward the death of Jane MacNaughton in James Dickey's "The Leap."

### FIRE AND ICE by Robert Frost [p. 614]

Frost here considers the two popular concepts concerning the end of the world—the biblical apocalypse of fire and the scientific speculation during Frost's day of a gradually cooling earth ending in ice. The speaker associates the heat of passion with fire and the coldness of hate with ice. The key to the poem lies in the final coupling of "ice" with the ironic understatement of "suffice," to suggest that hate is ultimately stronger than desire.

## Possible Responses to *Questions for Discussion and Writing*

1. The metaphorical association of fire with sexual passion is archetypal (Johnny Cash's "Ring of Fire"); the association of ice with hatred is also universal ("an icy stare").
2. See the explanation earlier in the discussion of the poem.
3. The response to this question also appears earlier, but it should be noted that some readers conclude that the speaker's "I hold with those who favor fire" means that love is stronger than hate and hence the world will end in fire, not ice.

## Additional Questions for Discussion and Writing

1. What world-ending disasters can you think of? Which ones involve fire or heat (nuclear war, the greenhouse effect), and which ones involve ice or cold (nuclear winter, a return of the ice age)?
2. Why does the speaker say "I hold with those who favor fire"? How could the world "perish twice"?

## Making Connections

→ Compare this poem to "The Second Coming" by Yeats.

### DESIGN by Robert Frost [p. 614]

Frost's description of the spider in this sonnet presents the perfect image of innocence as plump and dimpled, like a baby, and white besides. As critic Randall Jarrell notes, the spider holds the moth up, like a priest presenting a "sacrificial victim" at a devil's mass, and the moth is "full of the stilling rigor of death." The line "Mixed ready to begin the morning right" makes this "witches' broth" sound like a nourishing breakfast cereal. And the flower that should have been blue has been turned to white—a white suggestive of Melville's whale. The speaker's questions in the sestet lead us to speculate on who or what controls the universe. The "design" of the death described seems so deliberate as to suggest some malevolent force "of darkness to appall" (the spider was "brought," the moth was "steered"). But perhaps even more chilling is the implication in the final line that nothing controls our fate, that there is no God, that all is pure chance.

## Possible Responses to *Questions for Discussion and Writing*

1.   The title relates directly to imagery throughout the poem, which conveys the theme, i.e., the "design" revealed in the death of the moth is not the divine providence promised by Christian doctrine, guiding and protecting the faithful, but rather a malevolent and treacherous luring of the innocent ("white") moth to its death; surely it is a "design of darkness to appall," a creation worthy of Satan, the Prince of Darkness.
2.   The spider is described in pleasant words usually bestowed on cute, plump babies— "dimpled" and "fat"; "white," of course, is the color of innocence. This "snow-drop spider" is a far cry from the usual image that the word *spider* calls up of a scary creature at Halloween, often black and potentially poisonous.
3.   The speaker's questions lead us to query the deceptively innocent appearance of the spider and how it came to be lurking on a white flower (providing perfect camouflage) when the flower should have been blue, and also the speaker wonders what "steered" the white moth to its hideous fate. The answer could be simply fate, but the poem points instead to a "design of darkness to appall." Although that answer is undercut by the final line, "If design govern in a thing so small," (meaning, "Oh well, maybe not to worry"), we are not much comforted by the suggestion that perhaps no one is in charge.
4.   Frost's use of white, the color of innocence and purity, to label all that is treacherous and deceptive in the poem invests the color with the horror of nothingness that chills to the bone.

## Additional Questions for Discussion and Writing

1.   What is the tone of "Mixed ready to begin the morning right"?
2.   This poem is a sonnet. What kind is it? How does the sonnet's limited rhyme scheme help to emphasize the interlocking of ideas and the impact of the last two lines?
3.   Analyze the use of white and whiteness in this poem. How does the word *appall* contribute to this motif?

## Making Connections

→ Compare the working out of theme in this poem with that of Matthew Arnold in "Dover Beach."

FOG by Carl Sandburg [p. 615]

This famous poem conveys a single image without making a point or establishing a theme. In this respect, it is similar to haiku. Your students will find it instructive to compare this poem (which they probably read in high school) with the fog-as-cat image in lines 15 through 23 of T. S. Eliot's "The Love Song of J. Alfred

156

Prufrock" [p. 603]. They should easily see that Eliot presents a far more effective picture of the behavior of both cats and fog.

## Possible Responses to *Questions for Discussion and Writing*

1. This poem has no theme, but its purpose is to convey what fog looks like by comparing it in a single image to a cat, stepping delicately ("on little cat feet"), then sitting quietly and looking "over harbor and city," and then moving on.
2. Since cats tend to move in a sinuous manner, as fog does, the image works fairly well for Sandburg in the first brief stanza, but the lines involving "looking" are strained since fog does not "look" at anything.

## *Making Connections*

→ Compare the use of imagery in this poem to the images in "Reapers" by Jean Toomer or "The Red Wheelbarrow" by William Carlos Williams.

## CHICAGO by Carl Sandburg [pp. 615–16]

Sandburg's debt to Walt Whitman is evident throughout this poem, beginning with his admiration for the subject (although it was New York, not Chicago, that Whitman loved). And Whitman loved city life for the same reasons Sandburg does: its vitality, its bustle, its excitement, its blatant maleness—"stormy, husky, brawling laughter of Youth, half-naked, sweating, proud. . . ." The construction and poetic elements of the poem are also Whitmanesque: the catalogs; the balanced elements; the bold, hard images; the powerful rhythms; the deliberate repetition of words at the beginnings of lines (8–9, 26–27, 28–31). The poem seems to sprawl like the city but is really quite nicely unified by the balanced structure and by the repetition of the catalog (with slight variations) at the end. The poem's enthusiastic embrace of the common man and admiration for masculine energy and accomplishments also capture the essence of Whitman's democratic spirit—and, one presumes, the essence of the city of Chicago not long after the turn of the century.

## Possible Responses to *Questions for Discussion and Writing*

1. The defining characteristics of Sandburg's Chicago are masculinity, vitality, excitement, coarseness, youthfulness, violence, and cunning.
2. He addresses the city's violence and brutality but seems to think it's acceptable because it's a part of the city's vital image. To those who would "sneer" at the painted prostitutes, the wanton shootings, and the hungry women and children, he would "give them back the sneer," saying, "Come and show me another city with lifted head singing so proud to be alive and coarse and strong and cunning," "fierce as a dog," "cunning as a savage." Students might enjoy discussing whether modern cities, including Chicago, would care to be characterized in these ways.
3. Sandburg employs the same poetic devices that Whitman used so effectively in "sounding his barbaric yap": catalogues; balanced elements; hard, clear, striking imagery; powerful rhythms; and deliberate repetition at the beginnings of lines.

157

4. Personification works well for Sandburg in presenting Chicago as a hard-fisted, hard-drinking, hard-fighting, hardworking masculine city.

## Making Connections
→ Compare this poem to Langston Hughes's "Saturday Night," set in Harlem, where people during the 1920s knew how to party hard. How do these poems differ in focus?

## DANSE RUSSE by William Carlos Williams [p. 617]
Presumably the poem is called "Russian Dance" because the Russians dance with a wonderful abandon, as does the speaker in the poem. The time is early morning, with the sun just rising through the mist, as he revels in his total freedom of expression achieved by being alone. His dance, both sensuous and self-centered, expresses his happiness in simply being himself as well as in being by himself while living in a household peopled by a wife and children. By declaring himself the "happy genius of my household," he envisions himself as the lucky icon, a sort of god figure, who in certain cultures is in charge of keeping everyone in the family contented. The dash before the last two lines gives emphasis to the speaker's final statement as well as separates the description of his activities from his observation concerning them.

## Possible Responses to *Questions for Discussion and Writing*
1. The title means "Russian Dance," and Williams must surely have chosen it because the persona in the poem is emulating the fervor of Russian dancers, who are famous for their wild, flailing exuberance.
2. The speaker is in his "north room," probably his private writing room where he can be sure he won't be interrupted or observed at that hour, just as the sun is rising through the early morning mists.
3. He dances naked because he exalts in being alone and free—for a brief time, at least—from the obligations of wife and family.

## Making Connections
→ Compare the theme of this poem to the theme of Kate Chopin's "The Story of an Hour."

## THE RED WHEELBARROW by William Carlos Williams [p. 617]
This piece, which has both baffled and delighted many readers, belongs to the school of imagism. The imagists wanted to be concrete and definite in their word pictures, to suggest rather than make complete statements, and to strive for concentration of expression, which to them was the essence of poetry. What makes Williams's poem more puzzling than most imagist poetry is the first two lines: "so much depends / upon," an assertion that seems to demand an interpretation. *What* depends upon this wheelbarrow and these chickens, students will want to know. One writer suggests that it could be "the sheer joy of the poet at bringing the outside world into the poem and thus into relation with himself." Another finds the poem sentimental: "At its worst this is togetherness in a

158

chickenyard." X. J. Kennedy reveals the circumstances under which the poem was written: Dr. Williams, he says, supposedly "was gazing from the window of the house, where one of his patients, a small girl, lay suspended between life and death." Knowing the occasion of the writing, observes Kennedy, allows us to read it as "a kind of prayer, a work of compassion." But since the poem itself provides no clue to the situation underlying its composition, you may want to consider whether it is successful or sentimental or simply incomprehensible.

## Possible Responses to *Questions for Discussion and Writing*
1. It seems reasonable to approach this poem as if it were like a haiku, presenting a brief poetic image that, as one critic puts it, "makes us aware of glories in common places." Of course, some may think that "glories" is too laudatory a word for white chickens and a wheelbarrow, even a red one, "glazed with rain water."
2. The images and, let's face it, the placement of the lines on the page, make this a poem; whether one considers it a good poem or not is an interesting topic that your students will likely relish discussing.

### Making Connections
→ Contrast the images in this poem with those in another poem where the images carry the meaning, like Blake's "London," Whitman's "A Noiseless, Patient Spider," Sandburg's "Fog," or Housman's "Loveliest of Trees."

PIANO by D. H. Lawrence [p. 618]
The persona recalls a childhood emotion from the vantage point of an adult's perspective. The poem hovers on the verge of sentimentality but is saved from it by the specific images that re-create for readers what he felt as a child—the joy and warmth and security associated with his loving mother. The soft singing of the woman in the first line triggers these memories of his mother. He manfully struggles to resist "the insidious mastery of song," but the sound "betrays [him] back." Eventually—despite the singer's change from a soft song to a loud lively one, played with feeling—the speaker can't keep from dissolving in tears. Even though he is aware that his recollections are nostalgic and heightened by memory ("the glamour of childish days is upon me"), he nonetheless cries "like a child for the past."

## Possible Responses to *Questions for Discussion and Writing*
1. In the first line of the poem the speaker is in the present with a woman who is singing to him; in the third line, he has gone back in memory to his childhood when he was sitting beneath a grand piano while his mother was playing.
2. We don't know who the woman is in the first line, but her singing stirs in him memories (in line 4) of his mother's singing.
3. Perhaps the speaker prefers not to dwell on the past because it was a much happier time for him and is now gone; perhaps also his mother is now gone.

### Additional Questions for Discussion and Writing
1. Why does the speaker say the music "betrays" him back to his childhood?
2. Is this poem sentimental? If not, why not?

### Making Connections
→ Compare the point of view of the young persona in "Piano" with the speaker's viewpoint in Audre Lorde's "Hanging Fire."

## THE LOVE SONG OF J. ALFRED PRUFROCK by T. S. Eliot [pp. 618–22]
The persona is walking through a rather rundown section of London to a highly fashionable late-afternoon tea at which he arrives just as the poem ends. Once students discover that the speaker is talking to himself, that he is both the "you" and the "I," the poem becomes manageable. They may also need help in seeing the "love song" of the title as ironic, since it is clearly not a love song at all but a wimpy debate about whether he dares to ask the lady an "overwhelming question"—probably whether he might sit beside her or take her to dine or some such inconsequential thing. Since the whole comic but somehow touching scene depends upon Prufrock's self-centeredness, coupled with his exaggerated fears of inadequacy, you might start with a thorough discussion of his character, beginning with his name (a "prude" in a frock coat, which happens to be what he is wearing). The poem doesn't reveal much about the lady he wishes to approach, but the response expected from her (in lines 96–99) suggests she has a demeanor of bored sophistication (which is reinforced by the refrain, ". . . the women come and go / Talking of Michelangelo"). So, poor Prufrock talks himself out of even asking her and resigns himself to walking alone on the beach, convinced that he will never hear the mermaid's sexy song. The "human voices" of the last line are the voices he hears upon arriving at the party, waking him from his reverie to "drown" in the sea of people among whom he feels so inadequate. Despite the comic tone, Eliot is seriously criticizing the triviality and sterility of the society presented here.

### Possible Responses to Questions for Discussion and Writing
1. The speaker of this interior monologue is the J. Alfred Prufrock of the title, who is speaking to himself.
2. He is walking through a rather rundown section of London to a highly fashionable late-afternoon tea at which he arrives just as the poem ends. He is both the *you* and the *I* in this ironic "love song."
3. J. Alfred Prufrock's name says a lot about the kind of person he is—pretentious, stiff, and wearing a frock coat. But he clearly lacks self-assurance in his wimpy debate about whether to ask the lady an "overwhelming question"—probably whether he might sit beside her or take her out to dine or some such inconsequential thing. The whole comic but somehow touching scene depends upon Prufrock's self-centeredness, coupled with his exaggerated fears of inadequacy, which make him wary about attending this party. He considers "parting his hair behind" in order to pull it forward to cover his bald spot. His life is no more than a series of these social

occasions where coffee and tea are served; so he measures "out his life in coffee spoons"—a perfect metaphor to capture the insignificance and sameness of it all. The women make him nervous because he expects them to be haughty and reject whatever he says: "That is not what I meant at all; / That is not it at all." He thinks he ought to be a crab, "scuttling across the floors of silent seas," where he would not be expected to converse and interact with others. His exaggeration is an attempt to cover his basic fear of being a social failure. He is like both Polonius and Hamlet since he shares Hamlet's hesitation to act, but he is far more like Polonius because he thinks of himself as a tragic figure, while he is actually somewhat pathetic. He wonders if he dares to eat a peach because he fears he would look foolish if the juice should drip down his chin, or perhaps he worries about his delicate digestion. He does not think the mermaids will sing to him because mermaids are all about sexual enticement, and he dares not even hope. By the end of the poem, Prufrock resigns himself to walking alone on the beach. The human voices of the last line are the voices he hears upon arriving at the party, waking him from his reverie to "drown" in the sea of people among whom he feels so inadequate. Despite the comic tone, Eliot is seriously criticizing the triviality and sterility of the society presented here.

## Additional Questions for Discussion and Writing
1. Why is this poem called a love song?
2. Consider what the sea might symbolize and how Prufrock is involved with it—especially in the last nine lines. Write an essay arguing that the sea (oyster shells, ragged claws, mermaids, walking on the beach) functions as a controlling image.

## Making Connections
→ What does J. Alfred Prufrock, the speaker in Eliot's "love song," have in common with the woman described in Walt Whitman's much shorter poem, Section 11 of "Song of Myself"?

AMERICA by Claude McKay [p. 622]
McKay is another black writer, like Paul Laurence Dunbar, who was expressing his resentment at the treatment of blacks in America long before the civil rights movement. In this sonnet the feelings of the persona are ambivalent: he loves the land that oppresses him and will not cry out against it. Instead, he delivers a warning: he sees the strength of America being undermined, worn down, by racial injustice (as a granite monument is eroded by the winds of time) and warns that the country cannot survive it. He predicts that her "granite wonders" (those splendid monuments, especially the Lincoln Memorial, which signify the ideals embraced by the country in theory but not in practice—liberty, equality, justice for all), those "priceless treasures," are crumbling and will end up "sinking in the sand." His tone is fervent but rational—and remarkably unresentful.

## Possible Responses to Questions for Discussion and Writing
1. The speaker in the poem is a person of color, probably black since McKay was black.

2.  In the first three lines, the speaker is being fed "bread of bitterness" (racial hatred) by a figure (representing white racism) whose attacks inflict pain like a "tiger's tooth," slashing his throat so cruelly that he is losing his "breath of life." Racial hatred, he is saying, can and does kill both the spirit and the body. [Both the figure and the country are presented as female since America is customarily personified that way (perhaps because of the Statue of Liberty?). Germans, on the other hand, think of their country as male, the Fatherland.]

3.  The speaker loves America for the same reason Carl Sandburg loves Chicago—"her vigor" and "her bigness." Implicit in the last four lines of the poem is the fear that America may lose her strength and greatness because of ingrained racial prejudice.

### Additional Questions for Discussion and Writing
1.  What are the "granite wonders" of line 10? What do they signify?
2.  Can you describe the tone of this work?
3.  Why is it surprising that this poem is a Shakespearean sonnet?

### Making Connections
➜ Compare McKay's feelings about living in a racist country to those expressed by Paul Dunbar in "We Wear the Mask" and Langston Hughes in "Harlem (A Dream Deferred)."

### OH, OH, YOU WILL BE SORRY FOR THAT WORD! by Edna St. Vincent Millay
        [pp. 623–24]
In this sonnet the speaker comes to the realization that her husband is perhaps more "enemy" than "friend" when he takes away her book and insults her intelligence (in line 5). Her strategy for dealing with him is to pretend for the present to be the pretty bubblehead that he apparently thinks he married. But she will also be "crafty, soft and sly," for she plans, on some otherwise ordinary day, to leave him flat. We may be quite sure that when he whistles, she will not come back. "Prink" (line 6) is an earlier form of "primp," a term applied only to females, meaning to fussily touch up makeup and hairdo.

### Possible Responses to Questions for Discussion and Writing
1.  The speaker is angry because her husband has taken away the book that she was reading, telling her, in effect, that she shouldn't trouble her pretty "little head" with intellectual pursuits.
2.  In response to the insult, she plans to conceal her intelligence from him ("never tell him what I think") and act like the brainless girl he apparently thinks he married and clearly wants. But she will be "sweet and crafty, soft and sly," as she quietly makes plans to leave him high and dry and wondering what happened.
3.  In 1923, when the poem was written, the qualities that would have been expected for a "wife to pattern by" would be the ones listed in the Marital Rating Chart on page 305 in the main text.

### Additional Questions for Discussion and Writing
1.  What is the speaker's tone in lines 5 and 6? Read the lines aloud in the appropriate tone.
2.  In the final line, what does the speaker imply that her role as wife is similar to?

### Making Connections
→ Compare and contrast the speaker in this poem to the wife/speaker in Linda Pastan's "Marks" or the one in "My Ex-Husband" by Gabriel Spera. Which wife would you prefer to be or have?

### FIRST FIG by Edna St. Vincent Millay [p. 624]
This delightful little verse praises hedonism. One might call it a *carpe diem* poem with Millay seizing the night instead of the day, which is appropriate since we associate romance and revelry with night rather than day. She borrows Shakespeare's metaphor of life as a candle and adapts it to suit her meaning of getting as much pleasure as possible out of living, even if it means enjoying a briefer span. The "lovely light" makes the trade-off worth it.

### Possible Responses to *Questions for Discussion and Writing*
1.  The central metaphor is the candle burning at both ends. See the discussion earlier.
2.  The author seems carefree and happy to be living her life in the fast lane. The reference to both friends and foes suggests she doesn't care what anyone thinks about her lifestyle choices.
3.  Millay first called the poem "My Candle" but gave it the title "First Fig" when it appeared in her 1920 collection *A Few Figs from Thistles*. What the new title means is not entirely clear. (There's another poem in the collection entitled "Second Fig.") Because of their shape and juiciness, figs are considered a symbol of female sexuality, and some people associate them with the forbidden fruit in the Garden of Eden myth. This association would be consistent with the hedonistic message of this flippant little verse.

### Making Connections
→ Compare this poem to other single-statement poems, like Dickinson's "Faith Is a Fine Invention" or Williams's "The Red Wheelbarrow."

### IN JUST- by E. E. Cummings [pp. 624–25]
On first reading, the lively and energetic sounds of this poem suggest the celebration of spring and the innocent fun for children that comes with this season. However, the strange little balloonman holds a mysterious power over the children with his whistle "far and wee," reminding some readers of the Pied Piper, who led all the children out of Hamlin. Be sure that your students understand that in this context, the word *queer* meant odd or strange, not homosexual, or they may come to some misguided conclusions about the poem's meaning. Sexuality, for sure, is what must be associated with the balloonman

due to his identification with Pan. The separate, gendered activities that the children come running from emphasize their separate realms of play, which they leave behind to heed the balloonman's whistle. Spring, of course, is also associated with sexual activity, so it seems clear that under the playful tone lies an end-of-innocence motif.

## Possible Responses to *Questions for Discussion and Writing*
1. The run-together names suggest the children are rushing headlong into spring and the rest of their lives. The boys, eddie and bill, were playing marbles and pirates; the girls, betty and isbel, were playing hopscotch and jumping rope. The children at the beginning of the poem are engaged in typical childhood pursuits, enjoying gender-associated activities.
2. Pan is closely associated with sexuality, so the balloonman serves as a sort of sexual Pied Piper, luring the children to follow him.
3. The compelling whistle that makes the kids come running from their play is the call of adult sexuality, with all its attendant delights and complications.

## Additional Questions for Discussion and Writing
1. Would you say that the poem suggests a positive or negative attitude toward growing up? Point out why you answer as you do.
2. What effect do the unusual line division and spacing have when you read the poem? For example, if you were reading the poem aloud, how would you intone and pace the last three words?

## Making Connections
→ Compare this poem to "Spring and Fall" by Gerard Manley Hopkins. How do the two poems view the coming of spring?

**PITY THIS BUSY MONSTER, MANUNKIND** by E. E. Cummings [pp. 625–26]
The enemy in this poem is "Progress," presented as a high-technology spiritual void, in which modern science performs miraculous feats that are ultimately meaningless. "Progress" is described as a "comfortable disease" but a fatal one. The poem suggests that humans have lost their place in the natural world by trying to control and analyze it. The clever wordplay emphasizes the negativity of science-mad humanity.

## Possible Responses to *Questions for Discussion and Writing*
1. The speaker defines "progress" as something dangerous, possibly fatal, a "comfortable disease," suggesting that we accept the danger because we enjoy the effects. The extended metaphor presents human beings as the victims of their own technological inventions, which could prove their undoing.
2. The lines "A world of made / is not a world of born" can be paraphrased as "A world of man-made technological gadgetry is not the same as a natural world of living creatures—human beings, animals, insects, all living creatures." The distinction is important because the speaker thinks that technology has achieved the capacity to

wipe out all life in creation (think atom and neutron bombs and all such weapons of mass destruction).

3. The poem suggests that technological advancement could be the death of us all; hence the suggestion in the last line that it's time to find another universe to inhabit.

## Additional Questions for Discussion and Writing
1. List quirky words in the poem. Explain how unusual words add to the meaning.
2. Can you see, in your own era, negative ideas about scientific progress? Write an essay in which you connect some of these to Cummings's theme.

## Making Connections
→ How do you think the sentiments of this poem match up with those expressed by William Wordsworth in "The World Is Too Much with Us"?

## NOT WAVING BUT DROWNING by Stevie Smith [pp. 626–27]
This poem concerns the difference between public image and inner reality. On a literal level, the drowned man (who, given poetic license, may speak for himself) was misinterpreted in his death throes; other people thought that he was cheerily waving. Even when these people find that he's dead, they misinterpret the cause of death. The dead man takes his insistence to a metaphorical level, saying that he was alienated and misunderstood all his life.

## Possible Responses to Questions for Discussion and Writing
1. The two speakers are the persona (presumably standing on the shore, addressing the dead man) and the dead man (presumably lying on shore, having just drowned). The persona misunderstood the man's gestures as he was drowning, thinking he was just giving a friendly wave, as a lark, to someone on shore, which was in keeping with the demeanor he had always exhibited and which led people to think he was carefree and happy.
2. The lines tell us that the dead man was, as he says, "much too far out all my life"— i.e., he was in over his head, drowning in troubles. His perpetual coldness stemmed from his alienation: nobody noticed or acknowledged that he was in trouble. Instead, everyone thought he was always "larking," horsing around and enjoying himself, when actually he was lonely and desperately in need of companionship and understanding.
3. Suggest that students use the poem as a starting point—as a way to get into the topic—for this essay.

## Making Connections
→ Compare this poem to another one that employs more than one speaker: "Not My Best Side" by U. A. Fanthorpe. What does each poet accomplish by using more than a single speaker (persona)? Do you think this multiple-speaker approach is equally effective in these poems?

**INCIDENT** by Countee Cullen [p. 627]

This simple lilting poem conveys a grim experience: a young boy's introduction to mindless racism. Although he is unfamiliar with the other boy's ugly reaction, somewhere deep within he understands how devastating and pervasive it is. It blots out nine months of experience in Baltimore. Of course, racist attitudes will shadow the speaker's life forever.

**Possible Responses to *Questions for Discussion and Writing***

1. The theme: this poem conveys the cruel, wounding unfairness of mindless racism.
2. The author chose the simple form and simple language to convey verisimilitude because the speaker is an eight-year-old boy.
3. Suggest that students begin their essays with a reference to this poem, using its theme as a jumping-off point for relating their own experience.

**Additional Questions for Discussion and Writing**

1. Look carefully at the stanza division in the poem. Can you explain why the stanzas are separated the way they are? (Each stanza is a sentence: the second and third stanzas are compound sentences. The third one acts as a summing up for the whole poem.)
2. How do the lilting meter and happy rhymes belie the ugliness of the incident? Why do you suppose the poet chose to present the brief story in this way? (The speaker seems to have made a kind of peace, or truce, with the incident, although he hasn't forgotten it completely.)

**Making Connections**

➔ Compare the attitude about racial hatred in this poem to those expressed by Amiri Baraka in "Biography."

**FUNERAL BLUES** by W. H. Auden [p. 628]

Auden's charming tribute to a dead (or perhaps only departed) lover gives modern voice to the traditional classical elegy in which a friend or admirer makes extravagant pleas that all of nature should mourn in respect for the departed—that stars no longer shine, rivers no longer flow, breezes no longer blow. Auden playfully requests signs of mourning both modern and distinctly urban: clocks, telephone, black-gloved traffic policemen, and (a witty touch) "crepe bows round the white necks of the public doves." Here instead of imploring the heavens to mourn, Auden would send airplanes to announce in skywriting his lover's death.

The tone is light, almost humorous, yet somehow the poem is still touching, especially the last two stanzas. Anyone who has lost a lover has felt the same. (And line 12 does suggest that the lover has left rather than died: "I thought that love would last forever: I was wrong.") To some readers, the images may seem exaggerated even in these final stanzas—but not to those recently bereft of love. The poem acquired some fame by its recitation in the popular film *Four Weddings and a Funeral* (1994). And your students may be interested to know that the lover Auden mourns was not a woman but a man (see line 6).

## Possible Responses to *Questions for Discussion and Writing*
1.  See the discussion earlier.
2.  Opinions will vary, making this a good question to use as an exercise in developing and supporting an interpretation. It's also an interesting example of how reader-response criticism applies. Ask these questions: What difference does the lover's status make to your response to the poem? How do your own personal experiences of lost love factor into your interpretation?
3.  The poem is light but also touching—see the discussion earlier. Ask if this mixed tone is effective.
4.  Again, opinions will vary. Remind students to give their evidence and their reasoning to support their answer to this question.
5.  Creative writing prompt.

### Making Connections
→ Compare this poem to "The Leap" by James Dickey or to "Do Not Go Gentle into That Good Night" by Dylan Thomas.

## I KNEW A WOMAN by Theodore Roethke [p. 629]
This poem draws its strength from its many evocative comparisons. The woman is compared to a goddess, a bird fancier, a dancing teacher, a sickle, a goose, and a musician, to name a few. The speaker is obviously obsessively in love with her but at least sees the humor in his own obsession. Notice that we almost always see the woman in motion; thus Roethke avoids the traditional objectification of the beloved woman.

## Possible Responses to *Questions for Discussion and Writing*
1.  The woman in the poem is compared to a goddess, a birdsong, a sickle, a goose, and a musician; however, the emphasis on her charming movements makes the dominant image one of dancing. The comparisons to a sickle and a goose are unusual but serve to convey the lovesick silliness of the narrator's point of view—everything the woman does is entrancing, even the most mundane.
2.  In stanza 2, "She was the sickle; I, poor I, the rake" requires a bit of farming knowledge. The sickle dramatically whacks down the crop with its razor-sharp edge; the rake comes behind it, methodically stacking what's left behind. Thus, the rake can never come before (or even alongside) the sickle but must slavishly follow it and pick up the leavings, as the smitten narrator is happy to do. Extra humor comes from contrast with the old definition of "rake" as a rather promiscuous ladies' man, which this devoted admirer certainly is not.

167

3. The joy of the poem is in the lover's conveyed understanding that he is foolishly in love—he is meek, a martyr, a gander, a compliant dancing student, so crazy about the woman that, glad to be a slave, he asks, "What's freedom for?"

### Making Connections
➜ How does the speaker in this poem differ from the persona in Byron's "She Walks in Beauty" in their idealizations of women?

### ONE ART by Elizabeth Bishop [p. 630]
This poem is a tightly crafted villanelle. Bishop manages to say something worthwhile while adhering to the tricky rules of this form, which require using only two rhymes and repeating two of the lines according to a set pattern. Line 1 is repeated as lines 6, 12, and 18; line 3 as lines 9, 15, and 19. The first and third lines return as a rhymed couplet at the end. The rhyme scheme is *aba* (*abaa* for the last stanza). Bishop varies line 3 as she repeats it; she also uses ingenious rhymes ("last, or" in l.10) and off rhymes ("fluster" and "gesture") to meet the demands of the very limited rhyme scheme.

The poem's meaning is also somewhat tricky. On the literal level, the speaker seems to say that it's easy to lose things (it's something you can "master"—or learn to deal with) and that loss is not "disaster." But as the poem progresses and the losses move from the trivial (keys) to more significant things (time, beloved places, a loved one), we realize the speaker is being ironic, that losing is difficult and not something one can "master" (except to ignore or accept the losses). The parenthetical imperative in the last line suggests that the speaker is forcing herself to admit that some losses are indeed disastrous.

The references to a lost "continent" and a lost love may be personal: Bishop lived for many years with a lover in Brazil and wrote this poem after she returned to America. Bishop's father died when she was eight months old, and she never saw her mother again once the latter was confined to a mental hospital. The draft of the poem was titled "How to Lose Things" and probably referred to her companion at the time.

### Possible Responses to *Questions for Discussion and Writing*
1. The poem is a villanelle. The repetition makes the theme seem light and emphasizes the dailiness of "losing," setting the reader up for the more serious closing twist and reversal.
2. The central experience of the poem is the narrator convincing herself that she can survive the loss of love as she has been able to deal with the many other changes in her life, from the insignificant ("lost door keys") to the life changing (moves from city to city, continent to continent).
3. The everyday losses include things that may or may not be able to be replaced (keys, a mother's watch); time ill spent; memory and the control of the details of our lives (names and places); homes and even countries. Most importantly, however, she explores the loss of a loved one.

4. Coming to terms with the idea of loss (and not the lost items themselves) is the art the narrator outlines. The emphatic and parenthetical *"Write it!"* reveals the truth of the difficulty of mastering the art.

### Making Connections
→ Compare this poem to Dylan Thomas's "Do Not Go Gentle into That Good Night," another villanelle.

## AIDS by May Sarton [pp. 631–32]
Sarton explores the ways in which AIDS affects everyone. (At the time Sarton wrote this poem, AIDS was almost always fatal.) The "we" of the poem clearly includes AIDS victims and their friends and lovers; your students may also point out that society in general has been challenged by the epidemic. The seeming oxymoron of "reckless design" is reflected in the subtle and irregular rhyme scheme of the poem. The speaker grapples with the strange mixture of "despair and hope" that the disease evokes and actually manages to end on a positive note, suggesting the renewal of love.

### Possible Responses to *Questions for Discussion and Writing*
1. The "we" of the poem is the collective of people who, unprepared, must find a way to respond to the AIDS crisis, especially as friends and lovers.
2. Used to turning for pleasure and "hope" to lovers and friends as part of an active present and an expected future, the friend must now act for these same lovers and friends in the face of death, loss, and "despair." His acceptance of this brings him the "discipline" and "grace" that lead to a new kind of expanded "love" that counters "fear."
3. They are "blest" in the sense of "grace" by being given the tragic but important opportunity to experience a deeper, more complex love.

### Additional Questions for Discussion and Writing
1. "AIDS" includes two unusual one-line stanzas. What is the effect of these stanzas? Why are they set off from the other lines?
2. This poem is more than twenty years old. Is its perspective on AIDS outdated?

### Making Connections
→ Compare the people in this poem who declare "We are blest" with the "people who take care" in the poem of that title by Nancy A. Henry.

## AUTO WRECK by Karl Shapiro [pp. 632–33]
This explicit and carefully structured narrative moves from the concrete description of the wreck's aftermath to abstract speculation about the meaning of life and death. The point of view is that of the unhurt witnesses of the accident, whose lives are unexpectedly touched with "richest horror." The suddenness and seeming arbitrariness of the auto wreck shakes up their ideas of life as a story or drama that makes sense.

## Possible Responses to *Questions for Discussion and Writing*

1. Until the nineteenth century, poems dealt mostly with what we consider "universal" themes—love, war, death, religion, heroic events (Tennyson's "The Charge of the Light Brigade"). Blake, Whitman, Dickinson, and others changed all that by writing about everyday events, some grim and ugly, in the lives of everyday people. Today we see nothing strange about a poem describing an auto wreck or a job in a sweatshop or getting beat up in high school. Shapiro's poem, though, is quite conventional in its form—line length, stanza divisions, deliberate repetition, hard and clear imagery, and vivid word choice.

2. The "we" in the poem is the bystanders or passersby who view the carnage and are struck with "richest horror," reminding them of their own mortality and of the split second in which they—or any one of us—may, in an instant, be killed.

3. Images that appeal to senses other than sight: "soft silver bell beating, beating," "the bell, breaking the hush, tolls once," "throats . . . tight as tourniquets," "speak through sickly smiles," "cancer, simple as a flower, blooms," "Cancels our physics with a sneer, / And spatters all we knew of denouement / Across the expedient and wicked stones."

### *Making Connections*

➜ Compare this poem to Sharon Olds's "The Death of Marilyn Monroe." How do the poets use reaction to a disaster as the basis for their poetic themes?

### THE STREET by Octavio Paz [pp. 633–34]

Four lines into this poem the reader has entered the sensory experience of the persona. The scene seems familiar, dreamlike, and cinematic. Stumbling blindly down a long, dark street is a bleak image of life's journey. Things don't improve, either. The persona is frightened by his own shadow (in Jungian terms) following him, and in the last four lines of the poem he becomes the shadow pursuing himself in the same nightmarish maze of streets, in which neither figure is quite real: both are "nobody." The poem can be read as a portrayal of anxiety or of identity dissolution.

### Possible Responses to *Questions for Discussion and Writing*

1. The first four lines of the poem are like a familiar nightmare, with its ominous and menacing tone. The poem drops the reader directly into the eerie scene with no explanation or orientation, much as a bad dream does. The first lines practically force the reader into an uncomfortable identification with the "I" of the poem.

2. The main sensory appeals are sound and silence; kinetic references such as stumbling, stepping, slowing, and running; and only a few visual images, usually of darkness and blindness. These combine to convey fright and confusion, with blindness not only literal but also in the sense of not understanding what is happening. Further dreamlike, the main character is himself pursued by his own shadow and then becomes the shadow pursuing himself, who then is named as

"nobody." The poem seems to be an extended metaphor for life's journey, or at least a particularly grim part of it. Some readers may have a psychological interpretation, in which the narrator is experiencing acute anxiety or losing his sense of self.

3. The image of the dry leaves suggests death and desiccation, while the doorless buildings that loom along the street suggest that there is no escape to a welcoming or rescuing household within. The doorlessness literally shuts the narrator out of ordinary social life.

## Additional Questions for Discussion and Writing
1. The persona is simultaneously being followed and following himself, never being caught or catching up, and always identifying himself as "nobody." This is obviously an extended metaphor, but a metaphor for what?
2. The street clearly stands for something. Is it a metaphor or a symbol or metonymy? What's the difference? Explain your choice.

## Making Connections
→ Consider the extended metaphors in this poem and in Hayden Carruth's "In the Long Hall." What do the poems suggest about the meaning of life?

## BALLAD OF BIRMINGHAM by Dudley Randall [pp. 634–35]
This poem derives from the civil rights movement in the United States. In 1963, during a series of demonstrations in Birmingham, white supremacists bombed a church where black people were worshipping; four school children were killed. "The Ballad of Birmingham" is about one of those children and her mother, who thought that although the streets were dangerous for black children, church was safe.

## Possible Responses to Questions for Discussion and Writing
1. The mother will not allow her child to go downtown and join a freedom march because she fears it will be dangerous; so she tells her "to go to church instead" and ironically sends the child to her death.
2. The poem has the rhyme scheme, the lilting rhythm, and the stanza length of a traditional ballad (it rhymes *abcb* and so on). It also uses the traditional question and response mode to advance the story, and the tragic outcome is revealed suddenly and unexpectedly. It differs from the traditional form by modifying the refrain at the end of each stanza (the third and fourth lines are different in each stanza) and in the shocking nature of the *envoy* (the final two lines of the poem), which here concludes with the cry of the anguished mother, "O, here is the shoe my baby wore, / but, baby, where are you?"
3. An account of the actual event appeared in the *New York Times* on September 15, 1963, reported by Claude Sitton and headlined, "Birmingham Bomb Kills 4 Negro Girls in Church; Riots Flare; 2 Boys Slain." Have students track down this article (or another newspaper account at the time) and then debate whether they think the poem

or the newspaper version does a better job of capturing the emotions of the situation—and explain why.

### Additional Questions for Discussion and Writing

1. Why do you think the poet chose to write about this incident in ballad form? What other ways might he have written about the event?
2. The second and fourth lines of each stanza rhyme: how do this pattern and the rhythm of the poem affect your response? Would your response be different if the poem has been written in couplets or with no rhyme?

### Making Connections

➜ Occasional poetry is written to mark or commemorate some particular occasion or event. In what ways is the "Ballad of Birmingham" an "occasional poem"? How does it compare with "The Death of Marilyn Monroe" by Sharon Olds or "Funeral Blues" by W. H. Auden?

## To the Mercy Killers by Dudley Randall [pp. 635–36]

This powerful rejection of euthanasia is a Shakespearean sonnet. The strong language, as well as the concise form, lends the poem its vigor. The speaker clearly feels that despite the outward appearance of suffering and the experience of pain, there is something still valuable in life, which should not be cut short.

### Possible Responses to Questions for Discussion and Writing

1. "Mercy" is not a word usually coupled with "murder," and "kindly killers" would—without the irony—be an oxymoron.
2. For people who believe euthanasia should be allowed to end the suffering of the terminally ill, the speaker's attitude is difficult to understand. Although some people object to mercy killing on religious grounds (that only God should decide when someone dies), the speaker in this poem doesn't seem to be taking that position. He (or she) seems determined to hang on to life as long as possible, even if it's painful—perhaps because the speaker feels that this life is all we have.
3. In the last line the speaker's life is compared to a light bulb: it could be "put out," but the speaker wants it left on, to "still glow."
4. A writer agreeing with the speaker's position might respond with the argument that only God can justifiably end a human life or that life is precious and should be clung to at all costs. Those choosing to argue against the speaker's position could point out the loaded language used in the poem: *murder, traitor, accomplice,* and especially *glow,* a word with pleasant, positive associations that are usually belied by the physical state of a dying person.

### Making Connections

➜ In what ways is the theme of this poem similar to the one expressed in "Do Not Go Gentle into That Good Night" by Dylan Thomas?

**THE FORCE THAT THROUGH THE GREEN FUSE DRIVES THE FLOWER** by
Dylan Thomas [pp. 636–37]
The first two stanzas of this poem set up the basic idea that all of nature, including
humanity, is driven by the same powerful life force. Throughout, the poem refers to the
speaker's inability to communicate with the other elements of nature, perhaps a
frustration for a speaker invented by a poet, to whom communication is paramount. The
third and fourth stanzas continue the life force idea but in images a bit more obscure and
with more of an orientation toward death. The death images are repeated in the final two
lines, which suggest a kinship that all mortals have with death.

**Possible Responses to *Questions for Discussion and Writing***
1.  That would be the life force that permeates and powers all living creatures.
2.  By our count, there are five images of growth and life and nine images of death and
    decay, so the emphasis is on the dark side, which makes sense in a poem whose
    message is that "he not busy being born / Is busy dying," as Bob Dylan puts it (out of
    admiration, Bob Dylan took the poet's first name as his stage name).
3.  The phrase "I am dumb" means literally "I am unable to speak," but by interpreting
    the speaker's imagery, we understand that he means, "I am unable to explain or to
    understand or to stop the process" of life proceeding relentlessly toward death.

*Making Connections*
➜ What similarities of theme can you find between this poem and "My Son My
Executioner" by Donald Hall?

**DO NOT GO GENTLE INTO THAT GOOD NIGHT** by Dylan Thomas [p. 637]
This poem was addressed to Thomas's agnostic father, who had cancer of the throat. One
interesting thing about it is its complex form; it's a villanelle, which you may want to
define for your class. The poem basically exhorts the father not to accept death passively.
Stanzas 2 through 5 give examples of people who admirably fight death: wise men
(writers, philosophers), good men (philanthropists, social reformers), wild men (poets,
artists), and grave men (scholars, perhaps religious philosophers).

**Possible Responses to *Questions for Discussion and Writing***
1.  The image of "that good night" represents death itself, while the "dying of the light"
    suggests the loss of health or gradual debilitation that often precedes death.
2.  The repeated pattern in those stanzas describes the different ways in which people
    ("men" in the poem) face death. The "wise" ones are not ready to die (and hence,
    "Rage, rage against the dying of the light") because they had not yet been able to
    inspire others with their ideas ("their words had forked no lightning"); the "good"
    ones are not ready to die because they have not yet been acknowledged for their
    modest ("frail") accomplishments; the "wild" ones, who partied hard and lived
    dangerously, are not ready to die because they mourn the coming loss of zestful

173

delight; the "grave" ones, "near death," who see metaphysically through "blind eyes," seem ready to die because they envision a scene of blazing light and joy; finally, the speaker addresses his father, near death ("there on that sad height") and begs him not to "go gentle into that good night," but "Rage, rage against the dying of the light."

3. In line 17, addressed to his father—"Curse, bless me now with your fierce tears, I pray"—the speaker begs to be cursed for his past misdeeds and then absolved with a blessing so that father and son could bid a final farewell on friendly terms.

### Additional Questions for Discussion and Writing
1. Do you think the speaker's reaction is normal? How would you react in a similar situation?
2. Examine the use of paradox in this poem ("blinding sight," "sad height," "fierce tears," "Curse, bless me now"). How does paradox fit the tone and message?

### Making Connections
→ Compare the attitude toward death in this poem to the ones expressed in Housman's "To an Athlete Dying Young" or Randall's "To the Mercy Killers."

### SADIE AND MAUD by Gwendolyn Brooks [p. 638]
This poem is dated in an interesting way. Clearly, the speaker thinks Sadie, who "stayed at home" and bore two out-of-wedlock children, had a better life than Maud, who "went to college." That "Ma and Papa / Nearly died of shame" seems quaint, even hard to believe today. But at the time Brooks wrote this poem, she felt the proprieties governing the lives of young women were too restrictive—as they were. Today, many people think we have moved too far in the other direction, since the cost of caring for literally thousands of out-of-wedlock children has become a heavy social burden.

Stanza 4 implies that Sadie's girls will follow their mother's lifestyle, not their aunt's, since Sadie "left as heritage / Her fine-tooth comb" (lines 15–16). That comb is the emblem of Sadie's irrepressible (irresponsible?) lifestyle, as "one of the livingest chits / In all the land" (lines 7–8). *Chit* means an immature young girl.

### Possible Responses to *Questions for Discussion and Writing*
1. The bare events of Sadie's life suggest a tragic arc: she stays at home and has two children—but never marries and dies young. Her short life is full, however, and her character is lively and strong. She passes this legacy along to two independent daughters. By contrast, Maud, who would seem to have had the greater advantage by going to college and living up to the cultural mores, lives an isolated, barren life.
2. Sadie is resourceful, ferreting out and taking advantage of every possibility.
3. By reversing narrative expectations, Brooks refocuses the reader's attention on character. It's not the events of life that matter but what one does with those events.

174

4. The discussion of this poem might focus on the contrasting choices the students' high school classmates made or perhaps the lives led by their parents and grandparents.

## Making Connections
→ Contrast points of view on what young black women should do: in this poem and in Toni Cade Bambara's story "The Lesson."

THE LEAP by James Dickey [pp. 639–40]
The speaker of the poem has vivid memories of seventh grade when he reads in the newspaper that an old classmate has killed herself. The visual imagery stands out in this poem—the racing children, the clumsy dancers, the dusty playground, and both leaps. The speaker wants to remember Jane as a lively, spontaneous seventh grader and is sad to hear that the "eternal process / Most obsessively wrong with the world" dragged her down. He feels his own age and mortality when he finds out Jane's fate.

## Possible Responses to *Questions for Discussion and Writing*
1. The "leap" refers to both Jane's buoyant reach for a paper decoration in seventh grade and also to her leap to suicide from the downtown hotel. Thus, the title names two contrasting events, one full of life and the other full of death.
2. Seventh grade is a time of puberty, when boys and girls become acutely aware of each other. The images that the narrator remembers are overwhelmingly physical. Yet, at the time Jane has an exuberance in her own physicality that we conclude is lost later in life. The lightness of Jane's spontaneous leap and the heaviness of age are emphasized in the poem.
3. The narrator looks at the newspaper and concludes that some man "caught and betrayed her." He thinks that the relationships between men and women are "wrong with the world" and provides the fact that Jane was a mother of four.

## Additional Questions for Discussion and Writing
1. What does the speaker mean when he says "My feet are nailed to the ground / By dust I swallowed thirty years ago"?
2. Why does he examine his own hands at the end of the poem? (Jane's hands are the focus of her reach toward the paper ring in seventh grade. Thirty years later, the narrator feels the physical weight of his own age, with his feet nailed to the ground and his aging hands a constant reminder.)

## Making Connections
→ Compare the reactions to death of the speaker in this poem to the ones expressed by the speakers in "To an Athlete Dying Young" or "Funeral Blues."

**WOODCHUCKS** by Maxine Kumin [pp. 640–41]

This poem has an easy conversational style and an unusual, inconspicuous rhyme scheme (*abcacb*). These fit with its offbeat subject—getting rid of the woodchucks that are eating the garden. The speaker first tries a cyanide bomb. When that doesn't work, she resorts to shooting the woodchucks one by one, which brings out a side of her that she didn't know about and is not very comfortable with. The effect of coming face to face with the prey instead of having them "die unseen" haunts her.

## Possible Responses to *Questions for Discussion and Writing*

1. The speaker says she is a "lapsed pacifist" because she "fell from grace" (lost her innocence) and started killing woodchucks. She is a kind-intentioned person who tried to get rid of the adorable little pests as humanely as possible by gassing them with a cyanide bomb, which was supposed to be "merciful and quick." If it had worked, it would have allowed her to kill them underground, without her having to watch them die. The tone of stanza 3 makes it clear that she does not want to have to kill the creatures but does so only because they are stealing "the food from our mouths." But she still acknowledges her role as a murderer, even though she finds the task displeasing.

2. Her admission of "righteously thrilling" to the feel of the gun lets us know that she is at some unconscious level enjoying her job, as she falls back on those "Darwinian pieties" (the strong survive, the weak die; nature is red in tooth and claw) to justify murdering the woodchucks. She kills first "the littlest," then picks off the mother, followed by four more babies, but even though "the murderer in me rose up hard," she cannot get the father, the "old wily fellow," who now haunts her sleep. She needs to kill him, too, now that the murderer in her has been loosed.

3. When the speaker asserts that it would have been better for her if the woodchucks had "all consented to die unseen," she is stating the theme of the poem: that killing is easy if you do not have to face the victim but can do it in "the quiet Nazi way," the way Hitler disposed of the Jews—unseen, in gas chambers.

## Additional Question for Discussion and Writing

Do some research about woodchucks (also called groundhogs). How destructive are they to gardens and such? Are there any ways to minimize their damage without killing them? Write a response (perhaps a letter) to the speaker in Kumin's poem about her methods and intentions.

## Making Connections

➔ Compare the attitude toward animals implied in this poem with the ones expressed in Stafford's "Traveling Through the Dark" and Oliver's "The Black Snake."

**YOU ALL KNOW THE STORY OF THE OTHER WOMAN** by Anne Sexton [pp. 641–42]

"She" in the poem is the other woman, the mistress of a married man. And the story, of course, is that she is a convenience, bound to ignominious secrecy and ultimate disappointment. "A little Walden" compares the love nest to Thoreau's idyllic retreat from civilization, but, as we find out in line 5, "it's a bad translation," not quite idyllic. All the comparisons emphasize the brevity and fleeting nature of the lovers' encounter, as well as the objectification of the woman, which is crystallized in the final simile.

## Possible Responses to *Questions for Writing and Discussion*

1. The story of the other woman may have changed since Sexton wrote this poem in 1967. The story in those days was that the unfaithful husband would tire of the other woman sooner or later, dump her, and continue in his marriage. The divorce statistics today suggest that perhaps in many cases the husband now dumps his wife and carries on with the other woman—or some brand-new other woman. (Also fairly common today is the dumping of husbands by wives who think they've found a more suitable mate, but the poem does not touch on this version of the marriage-go-round.)

2. Metaphors: "She is private in her breathbed"—Sexton coins a new term by combining the heavy breathing of sexual intercourse with the bed on which it occurs; "as his body takes off and flies"—not literally, but the rapid action and soaring feeling of the sex act is equated with flying; "God comes in like a landlord / and flashes on his brassy lamp"—the coming of daylight (God's "brassy lamp") ends the sexual idyll; "He puts his bones back on"—no longer the enfolding lover, the man, resuming his upright stature, puts his suit and tie back on; "when it is over he places her, / like a phone, back on the hook"—she's feeling at this point as if she's just been used and then discarded. The last metaphor is unmistakable because when a phone is placed back on the hook, the connection ends.

3. The man behaves as if he was only using the woman as a sex object. To paraphrase line 6 through 14: daylight is no friend to lovers; God, like a landlord, sends in the morning light to evict them; now she is no longer ecstatic; he is no longer cuddly and pliant, as he acts as if nothing has happened between them ("turns the clock back an hour"); lines 12–14 are difficult, but it helps to know that at the time the poem was written in 1967, many women still wore hats and girdles, which might explain the "boards" (perhaps the corset enclosing and binding her body) and the "roof, the removable roof" (perhaps the hat topping her head).

## *Additional Questions for Discussion and Writing*

1. Explain the house imagery in the poem. Is the speaker comparing herself to a house (rented and used by the landlord)? Look closely at lines 12–14.

2. What is the pun in the word "breathbed"? Why is daylight "nobody's friend"?

### Making Connections

→ How does the speaker in this poem compare to the speaker in Adrienne Rich's "Living in Sin"? What methods for coping with disappointment do they share? Which one seems to be doing better?

### AUNT JENNIFER'S TIGERS by Adrienne Rich [pp. 642–43]

The controlling image of the prancing tigers serves both to unify the poem and to amplify Aunt Jennifer's plight in her oppressive marriage. The gorgeous tigers, "proud and unafraid," provide a sharp contrast with the woman who created them with her "terrified hands." Unlike the tigers, who "pace in sleek chivalric certainty," Aunt Jennifer "flutters" under the domination of her husband. Although absent from the poem, the husband's domineering presence is felt in "the massive weight" of the wedding band that "sits heavily" on her hand. Unlike the tigers, which "do not fear the men beneath the tree," Aunt Jennifer was "terrified" into submission by unnamed "ordeals she was mastered by." In the last stanza we see that Aunt Jennifer will escape her confined, fearful existence only in death, but her spirited tigers "will go on prancing, proud and unafraid."

### Possible Responses to *Questions for Discussion and Writing*

1.  The tigers share the human traits of pride, bravery, stateliness, and self-assurance ("certainty"). They lead a life in which they are both feared and admired, and their "prancing" suggests that they very much enjoy that life.
2.  Aunt Jennifer's life, on the other hand, is fearful ("her terrified hands"), oppressed ("ringed with ordeals"), and restricted ("mastered by"). The tigers possess the freedom, strength, and bravery to live in freedom—a complete contrast with Aunt Jennifer's narrow existence. She probably chose the tigers for her tapestry because she admires them and longs to be like them.
3.  The "massive weight" of her wedding band symbolizes the weight of her oppressive marriage. Historically wedding rings were symbols of ownership of the wife by the husband, but today wedding rings are supposed to symbolize eternal love.
4.  Responses will vary, but certainly a strong case can be argued for reading the poem as sympathetic to Aunt Jennifer's plight and revealing as its theme that marriage can be bondage as easily as it can be bliss.

### Additional Questions for Discussion and Writing

1.  Although her husband never appears in the poem, what can you tell about him from the poem?
2.  Why does the poet use the word "mastered" instead of "defeated" or "beaten down"?
3.  Write a paper analyzing your response to the tigers in the last stanza, still "prancing, proud and unafraid." Are you comforted that Aunt Jennifer's artistic creation will live after her? Or are you sad that she was so unlike her tigers?

## Making Connections

→ How is the symbolic meaning of Aunt Jennifer's tigers related to "The Tyger" by William Blake?

## LIVING IN SIN by Adrienne Rich [p. 643]

This poem vividly defines the contrasts between the woman's expectations of "living in sin" and the rather grim reality. Her romantic vision is supplanted by a scruffy everydayness, with cockroaches, squeaky stairs, loud plumbing, and a lackadaisical lover. The piano isn't the only thing that's out of tune. The woman's disappointment subsides in the evening, when she is "back in love again," but the closing image of the impending morning foretells another day of disappointment.

## Possible Responses to *Questions for Discussion and Writing*

1.  The poem begins with the persona's illusion of living unmarried with her lover as being perfect bliss. Then this illusion is sharply contrasted with the reality revealed by the coming of the milkman and daylight: groaning pipes, squeaky stairs, grimy windows, dirty dishes, dusty furniture, unmade beds, and mice in the cabinets—not to mention a lover who plinks on the piano, shrugs at the mirror, and goes out for cigarettes, leaving her to do all the work. The reality of these drawbacks is emphasized because the idea of living blissfully "in sin" with a lover is a familiar one, promulgated in romance novels, trashy magazines, and B movies, so the poem brings up some of the drawbacks of the situation.
2.  The final image of "daylight coming / like a relentless milkman up the stairs" unifies the poem by reintroducing the earlier image of a milkman arriving with "that morning light" (line 9), shattering the persona's illusion of a perfect love nest. The poem was published in 1955 when gender roles still dictated that women do all of the housework, so the final image neatly reinforces the major claim in the poem that "living in sin" comes with some impediments for a female made perhaps a little dizzy with love.
3.  Writing prompt.

## Making Connections

→ How does the "she" in this poem compare with the "she" in Ann Sexton's "You All Know the Story of the Other Woman"? What methods for coping with disappointment do they share? Which one seems to be doing better?

## FLOWER FEET by Ruth Fainlight [pp. 644–45]

The 2000 *Oxford Companion to English Literature* describes Fainlight's work: "Her topics are both domestic and global; she combines, often in one poem, the personal and the austerely detached, and excels at the uncanny casual note of recognition." "Flower Feet" exemplifies this description well. The museumgoer, the narrator, appreciates the delicate beauty of the tiny slippers and then muses on the practice of foot binding that made them possible. The smiles and praise of women about the brutal practice, in the second stanza, clarify their complicity in this ritual. The last two lines provide the "uncanny casual note of recognition": modern women would also bind their daughters' feet if the practice were still popular. We naturally wonder what forms of cultural torture *are* still happily inflicted on girls. The photo on page 636 illustrates the ugliness alluded to in the second stanza.

## Possible Response to *Questions for Discussion and Writing*

1. The narrator is in the Whitworth Art Gallery at the University of Manchester, which holds a famous collection of fine art and design. The setting is important because the shoes she is pondering are considered historical objects of art, instead of instruments of torture.
2. The imagery changes from beauty to ugliness between the first and second stanza. The contrast between the lovely shoes and the process that made them possible is emphasized.
3. The last two lines suggest that "the times" dictate what the friends would do to their daughters. If the times had not changed, the friends would have felt the need to force their daughters to conform to the beauty norms of the culture.
4. The reports on Chinese foot binding will be repetitive, so you might choose to have them done by three or four small groups instead of by each individual student.

## *Additional Questions for Discussion and Writing*

1. What extreme measures and practices do some twenty-first-century females use to make themselves beautiful and attractive to males?
2. Why are no men mentioned in this poem?

## *Making Connections*

➔ How is the message of this poem similar to the point about female attractiveness that Marge Piercy makes in "Barbie Doll"?

## BIOGRAPHY by Imamu Amiri Baraka [pp. 645–46]

This chilling poem attempts to capture the lynching of the speaker's grandfather. The title implies that the victim's whole life is captured in the scene. The confused images reflect the nightmarish quality of the event, in the same way a filmmaker might use frantic splicing of shots. We can follow the focus from the hanging itself, to the Klansmen riding away laughing in the moonlight, back to the lonely figure as it "hangs / hangs." The shape of the poem on the page reproduces the image of something or someone hanging.

## Possible Responses to *Questions for Discussion and Writing*

1. The grandfather was lynched, probably by the Ku Klux Klan or some other racist vigilante group. We know that Baraka is black and involved in racial political movements, so even if the poem's images don't convey the context, the author's biography can fill in the blanks.

2. The images are broken apart and scattered (visual, tactile, audio images mixed together), reproducing one's perceptions when witnessing a highly disturbing scene—thoughts, feelings, senses jumbled without coherence. Students may bring up examples of when they have experienced such incoherence in the face of horror.
3. A *biography* is an account of a person's life. This may seem like an odd title for a poem that recounts only a person's death. The difference may be reconciled because the title suggests that the grandfather's whole life was a preface to this violent and hateful closing.
4. The poem is concrete because it is strung down the page in a narrow line, like a hangman's rope.

## Additional Questions for Discussion and Writing
1. Why are the words arranged on the page the way they are?
2. Write an account of how someone died or of some other intense experience, using a form and style like Baraka's in "Biography."

## Making Connections
→ Compare the stark images in Baraka's spare and scathing poem with the lilting meter and cheerful rhymes in "Incident" by Countee Cullen. Both poems strongly present the same theme. Which one do you think argues the point more effectively?

## HANGING FIRE by Audre Lorde [pp. 647–48]
This poem is an insightful reproduction of the train of thought of a fourteen-year-old female. The mixture of everyday worries ("I have nothing to wear tomorrow") and deep anxieties ("will I live long enough / to grow up") as they run through her mind is humorous but true to life for adults as well as teenagers. The refrain emphasizes that she feels a lack of attention from her mother. However, given the rest of the evidence, we are not sure whether her mother is knowingly neglecting her (in the bedroom with a lover, some readers believe) or whether the speaker is momentarily frustrated with her mother's absence and responding in an exaggerated way. The title has to do with firearms that fail to go off—"hanging fire." They are dangerous because they might explode at any time.

## Possible Responses to Questions for Discussion and Writing
1. The teen's insecurities and fears are typical: her body seems out of control, she feels misunderstood, and she's isolated from the security offered by a mother's love and simple answers.
2. See the discussion earlier. "Hanging fire" means to be in a state of suspension—in this case, between the securities of youth and the unknown and frightening realities of adulthood.
3. The refrain (in combination with the repeated references to death) suggests a darker reading of the teen's anxiety. Unable to turn to her mother for answers or support, the teen both fears death and finds it an escape from her other fears.

### Making Connections

→ How do you think Connie of the story "Where You Are Going, Where Have You Been?" (by Oates) would respond to this poem? Would she understand the feelings expressed by the poem's speaker? How about Sylvia in Bambara's "The Lesson"?

### BARBIE DOLL by Marge Piercy [pp. 648–49]

Though this condemnation of sex role expectations may seem heavy-handed to older students, younger ones usually appreciate it. The Barbie Doll is a perfect symbol of utterly unobtainable female appearance: if you have such a doll, you might measure the body parts and note the odd proportions of torso to leg, leg to neck and head, waist to bust, and so on. The girlchild in the poem is well socialized into her role, and the discovery that intelligence, strength, personality, and charm school self-improvement cannot redeem her "big nose and fat legs" drives her to suicide—or perhaps plastic surgery, a metaphoric death that "cuts off" the ugly parts and destroys her original looks (and her identity?). She looks perfect in her casket (her new self?), though, dressed in a nose and nightie like Barbie's.

### Possible Responses to *Questions for Discussion and Writing*

1. The young woman who finds herself unable to reconstruct her natural body to conform to social standards of beauty is, ironically, able to be made beautiful in death, in her casket.
2. Most often seen as an iconic figure of fashionable beauty, meant to teach young girls to aspire to standardized adult feminine beauty norms and behavior (set hair, appropriate makeup, high heels—as well as performing domestic tasks and projecting a feminine, passive affect), Barbie is the embodiment of what Piercy suggests is a plastic and dangerous kind of social enculturation.
3. While the poem perfectly captures Piercy's 1970s feminism, students are likely to enter into lively debate about its relevance to current beauty standards. A quick review of the covers of a few teen magazines would be an interesting addition to the conversation or useful evidence for student essays.

### Additional Questions for Discussion and Writing

1. Do you think the "girlchild" is literally dead at the end of this poem?
2. How might a male respond differently to this poem than a female would?

### Making Connections

→ Compare the issues about beauty and identity raised in this poem with those that Jane Martin explores in the play *Beauty*.

### DIGGING by Seamus Heaney [pp. 649–50]

The speaker in this poem admires the work done by his forefathers, who were potato farmers. Their strength and skill and their connection to the earth make him nostalgic.

Male virtues are venerated in the competition of cutting turf and in the way the grandfather tosses off his milk and returns to work without missing a beat. The speaker, a writer, has a pen instead of a spade to assert his manhood; the opening image of the pen as a gun supports this line of interpretation in an unsettling way.

## Possible Responses to *Questions for Discussion and Writing*
1. The speaker reveres strength, stamina, skill, and dedication in his forefathers.
2. Many students remember their grandparents as hardworking; maybe they even remember or hear tales of their great-grandparents' efforts. Second- or third-generation citizens whose forefathers immigrated to the United States may well remember the strengths of their parents and grandparents as they struggled to make their lives in a new country.
3. Writing poetry might be seen as nourishing the spirits of readers the way that potatoes nourish the body. Furthermore, the peat warms the household as poetry might warm the heart of a reader. The highly developed skill and exactness shown in the father's labor is also required of a good poet. *Digging* also has a double meaning—both digging into the ground but also digging into the consciousness and history of human beings. The last image contrasts with the very first image, when the pen is "snug as a gun," that is, an instrument of destruction. Instead, the poet turns to the craft as an instrument for life, not death.

## *Additional Questions for Discussion and Writing*
1. How can you fit in the disturbing image in the first two lines with the rest of the poem?
2. Do you think the speaker regrets that he's not doing the same kind of physical work as his father did?

## *Making Connections*
→ Compare this poem with these other poems about writing: "Sonnet" by Collins and "Theme for English B" by Hughes.
→ Compare "Digging" with other poems written by sons about their fathers: "Those Winder Sundays" by Robert Hayden, "My Papa's Waltz" by Theodore Roethke, "Like Riding a Bicycle" by George Bilgere.

## SEX WITHOUT LOVE by Sharon Olds [pp. 650–51]
The main difficulty in reading this poem is construing the tone or attitude of the speaker. Our own preconceptions about sex without love get in the way of clearly perceiving what the speaker's point is. Some of the images have a positive bent—the ice skaters, dancers, great runners, and true religious. There is also an attractive realism to those who have sex without love. Other images, though, are negative, like "fingers hooked / inside each other's bodies." Perhaps the speaker herself is struggling with mixed feelings on the issue. Some readers believe that the poem takes place during a sex act, citing lines 8–10 as the point of orgasm.

## Possible Responses to *Questions for Discussion and Writing*

1. The people are compared to dancers, ice skaters, unwanted babies, religious purists, and runners. These comparisons are mixed in connotation. However, they are all alone in an existential sense, as the closing of the poem confirms.
2. The speaker believes that people who have sex without love are realistic: "They do not / mistake the lover for their own pleasure." The theme of being ultimately alone is presented dispassionately.
3. Students may see a suggestion that people who believe that sex and love are intertwined are fooling themselves, escaping from the existential loneliness that is our true state. Love is presented as an illusion.

## *Additional Questions for Discussion and Writing*

1. Note how often the speaker uses the word *not*, ending with "not the truth." What is the truth? Why doesn't the speaker ever state her idea of truth directly?
2. Discuss the mix of religious and athletic metaphors. Do they work together or cancel one another out?

## *Making Connections*

→ Compare this poem with John Donne's "A Valediction: Forbidding Mourning." How does Donne's distinction between earthly and spiritual love parallel Olds's views?

## THE DEATH OF MARILYN MONROE by Sharon Olds [pp. 651–52]

Students need to understand what happened to Marilyn Monroe: she committed suicide by overdose at the age of thirty-six after many years of being a major sex symbol. Many commentators explain her suicide by the pressures of such fame and the relentlessness of the public gaze, which precluded a strong inner sense of selfhood. Some speculated that her death involved foul play by one of her powerful lovers who wished her silenced. Monroe was confined to being a fantasy woman rather than a real flesh-and-blood person, more public property than private human being.

## Possible Responses to *Questions for Discussion and Writing*

1. The first stanza emphasizes the depersonalized body of the corpse. The reader, knowing the title of the poem, is invited to think of the difference between the dead body and the living image of Marilyn Monroe.
2. The ambulance men act as carefully as they would carrying a living person. Marilyn Monroe had such a strong persona in life that the men still treat her as a live person when she is dead.
3. The men go out for a drink or two to soften their reactions to handling dead or dying bodies. The custom helps them cement their relationships to their workmates, perhaps the only people who could understand their experience.
4. All of the men have stress responses to their experience of carrying the dead body of a sexual icon. You might have your students look up PTSD (posttraumatic stress disorder) to help them understand various reactions. The description of the last man

is ambiguous—he may be grateful for his living, unglamorous wife, or he may be confused by the frailty of who lives and who dies, despite fame or fortune.

## Making Connections
→ Relate the themes or issues in this poem to those expressed by Marge Piercy in "Barbie Doll." Do you think Piercy would agree with the way Olds depicts Marilyn Monroe?

## MY MOTHER SEWS BLOUSES by Gina Valdés [pp. 652–53]
Students need to understand the garment industry in order to appreciate this poem. Along the U.S.-Mexican border, clothing factories are set up, and piecework is sent to the Mexican side to be done without union pay and U.S. safety controls (in other words, very cheaply). Final steps are taken on the U.S. side so that the garments can be considered U.S. made. In the poem, the speaker's mother risks her vision for one dollar a blouse while thinking about going to night school, no doubt to upgrade her job. The hope seems pitifully futile, given her circumstances.

## Possible Responses to *Questions for Discussion and Writing*
1. The mother is poorly paid because she works in a sweatshop—a place where undocumented immigrants to the United States or unprotected workers in other countries make goods, usually for U.S. markets. Much of the clothing we buy at least partly originates in such sweatshops (if it is finished in legally protected U.S. sites, it can be labeled "Made in the U.S.A."). You might ask your students to do some research on brand names and sweatshops.
2. The loss of sight is definitely a loss of power, which the mother experiences. Blindness is also symbolically associated with lack of knowledge, wisdom, or insight; perhaps the mother has little knowledge of her alternatives. The black lint symbolizes the evil effects of sweatshop work, using the conventional association of black with evil as well as its gradual incursion into the workers' lives.
3. The mother is "thinking about night school" because more education would qualify her for a better job. Students who work in sweatshop conditions often serve more than eight hours a day and often work nights, conditions that will interfere with going to night school and doing the necessary studying. Also, being near blinded every six months will impair her studying. Nonetheless, she is at least thinking about school, which could be interpreted optimistically.

## Making Connections
→ Compare this description of a parent's work with the one presented in "Digging" by Seamus Heaney.

## EXECUTION by Edward Hirsch [pp. 654–55]
The poem is a tribute to the speaker's former football coach, a man who loved football and loved winning even more but who is now dying of cancer, "wobbly and stunned by

illness" (line 28). His "favorite word, Execution" (line 9) is capitalized on the chalkboard by the coach and serves ironically as the title of the poem. The "awkward adolescent bodies" (line 16) of his high school players could never execute his clever plays well enough to achieve "the ideal game he imagined" (line 19). But the cancer is clearly going to perform its *execution* of the coach "with a vengeance" (line 32), like the team did from downstate, who "battered [them] all afternoon" (line 31) with "machine-like fury" and defeated them with its "perfect execution" (line 34).

## Possible Responses to *Questions for Discussion and Writing*

1. The coach is dedicated to football with "perfect unquestioning faith," as if to a new religion (line 11). The plays he outlines on the chalkboard are compared to a spiderweb, sprinkled with players like a "constellation" of stars (lines 7–8), "shining" under his motto "Execution" (line 9). The game is also compared to warfare and to the harmonious movement of the planets (lines 13, 15). In line 22, the young players are "challenged to hammer" the coach in practice sessions.

2. The downstate team played with the "perfect execution" that the coach tried but failed to achieve with his own team. The speaker remembers the long-ago game because he sees in the "wobbly and stunned" (line 28) demeanor of the coach a crushing loss in his battle with cancer like the defeat suffered by their team on the gridiron that day.

3. The coach's love of winning "more than his own body, maybe even / More than himself" (lines 25–26) accentuates his devotion as a religious experience, since the saints often mortified the flesh and gave their lives for the faith. The speaker is implying that the coach is an acolyte in the service of football.

4. Students could argue this one either way, possibly influenced by their own experiences with coaches. But the evidence in the poem presents the coach as a man who reveres the game and works hard (too hard?) to field a good team, including the "punishing drills" and doubled practice times (lines 20–21). His "elaborate, last-second plays" usually work, so he is good at what he does. He may be a sympathetic figure because he seems to be dying a long, agonizing death.

5. The irony of the title lies in the two meanings of "execution." As the coach's favorite word (lines 9–10), it means a skilled, near-perfect performance, but the term can also mean the taking of a life, as in the coach's slow "execution" by cancer. It is also ironic that the coach's players, who are diligently schooled but imperfect in executing plays, are defeated by a downstate team who have achieved "perfect execution" (line 34). Similarly ironic is the coach's "perfect unquestioning faith in . . . the idea of warfare" (lines 13–14), an idea that proves correct but unfortunately not for him. When tested in action against the team from downstate who attack with "Machine-like fury" and the "deadly, impersonal authority" of war (lines 34, 33), the coach's less warlike team goes down in defeat.

## Making Connections

→ Compare the situation of the coach in this poem with that of the dispirited young man in Updike's "Ex-Basketball Player."

## THERE ARE BLACK by Jimmy Santiago Baca [pp. 655–56]

The realities of prison life are expressed in this poem by an ex-convict. He focuses on the fact that both inmates and guards come from all races; the fact that the guards will keep their own people imprisoned and subject them to cruelty is especially brutal. The speaker understands the urge for power that makes a man a prison guard—the money and command that the same men could probably never find in other jobs open to them. He believes that they must harden their hearts, water down their blood, and turn off their minds in order to "seclud[e] themselves from their people."

## Possible Responses to *Questions for Discussion and Writing*

1. The horrifying element about the prison guards (and some of the prisoners) is their dehumanization. Eventually most fail to identify with their brethren.
2. The guards keep their jobs because probably these are much better jobs than they could get otherwise: their abilities to buy things and to become powerful are specifically mentioned. The poem also suggests that the power goes to their heads after some time in the job. You might discuss what other jobs dehumanize workers through money or power or both.
3. The two types of convicts are those that are nasty and brutal and those that are passive and daydreaming.
4. Most poetry lovers would say that all subject matter is appropriate for the genre. Material that is emotional, moving, and revealing about the human condition is traditional for poetry, and "There Are Black" certainly exemplifies this material. However, some readers may prefer poetry that emphasizes the beautiful, noble side of love, life, and nature, such as Carl Sandburg's "Fog" and John Donne's "Death, Be Not Proud." We notice the dearth of such poems in our anthology: this lack may be an interesting topic for class discussion.

## Additional Questions for Discussion and Writing

1. Why are the lines indented and arranged as they are? (The long lines build intensity and create a sense of the persistent noise and chaos of prison life.) What kind of verse would you call this? (Free verse.)
2. Can you explain the figure of the "ancient mummy"? (Possibly the dehumanized specters of the caring human beings the guards used to be.)

## Making Connections

→ Compare Baca's use of strong, vivid images to depict violence with the similar use of such imagery in "Biography" by Amiri Baraka and "Dulce et Decorum Est" by Wilfred Owen.

**LATIN WOMEN PRAY** by Judith Ortiz Cofer [pp. 656–57]

The Latin women (evidently, Latin American) are viewed by an outsider who sees them as unsophisticated dupes of the Catholic Church. The persona evidently sees the ridiculous aspects of these "brown daughters" praying to a white God derived from a tradition far away from their own ("with a Jewish heritage"). Appealing to this God is apparently useless, yet the women continue to so do with zeal. Their understanding of God is placed on a practical, worldly level—they hope he is bilingual, while more thoughtful believers would say that God understands all languages. The poem's God is not a sympathetic character. The women are driven by a pitifully misguided hope.

## Possible Responses to *Questions for Discussion and Writing*

1. The setting—with votive candles, kneeling, a white image of God—describes a Catholic church. Also, the idea that the women are Latina suggests that they are Catholic, Catholicism being the major religion of Latin America.
2. God is described as Anglo (with a Jewish heritage), a Great White Father, imperturbable, all seeing, unmoved. The women are described as brown, daughters, persistent, fervently hoping. The contrasts in these descriptions demonstrate the power relationship between the two, especially in terms of the detachment on God's side and the passion on the women's. They are complementary in the traditional father-daughter relationship. This view of the God-human relationship can be compared with other views; many believe in a loving, listening God who consists of a colorless force (not a white male); others define God as the energy found in the universe and in our souls, and so on.
3. The women probably pray for hope, health, money, love, happiness, a better life for their children, and an eventual home in heaven, but the society they live in almost ensures that they stay exactly where they are. They persist in their prayers because it is their only option, not seeing any realistic way their hopes will materialize. Being helpless, they hope that some father figure will intervene and save them.
4. The image of God as lustful adds an especially nasty and shocking note to the poet's description. Given the father-daughter relationship, incest is suggested, as well as the objectification of women. If any reader had a doubt about the poem's point of view toward the Catholic God, this image would make the hostility clear.

## *Additional Questions for Discussion and Writing*

1. What is the speaker's tone? What does the speaker think of the women she's describing? How can you tell?
2. What do you think of the last line? Is it a comic (perhaps sarcastic) line?

## Making Connections

→ Consider the women described in this poem, who need for God to be "if not omnipotent / At least . . . bilingual" in order for their supplications to be meaningful; compare them with the mother who wants to go to night school in order to escape her debilitating job in Gina Valdés's "My Mother Sews Blouses." Does the hope of the women in either poem seem rational or helpful? Or is it delusional?

## THE SUPREMES by Cornelius Eady [pp. 657–58]

The speaker in this poem explains his and his classmates' rebellious behavior as a response to the dull, life-numbing conditions of their lives in school and at home. The speaker justifies typical forms of adolescent acting out as doing "what we could / And all we could do was / Turn on each other" (lines 5–7). Students should recognize the various types and stereotypes that take the punishment. But the ending may elude them a little. The reaction of "some of us" to the stifling life mapped out for them was to "reach in self-defense for wigs, / Lipstick, / Sequins." Taken with the title, "The Supremes," these details suggest that this poem could be read as a coming-out statement, an explanation of why a young man would adopt flamboyant dress or even become a female impersonator. (Impersonating Diana Ross of the Supremes is a favorite choice of drag queens.) Instead of being born to be gray (line 1), the speaker might be saying some of us were born to be "gay." But these items could also be construed metaphorically—as colorful reactions of various kinds to the "gray" existence that the young people believed they were destined to lead.

## Possible Responses to *Questions for Discussion and Writing*

1.  The students in this school were "born to be gray"—that is, not colorful at all, the shade of dust and ashes. Eventually this first line contrasts with the final image.
2.  The students turn on each other by making fun of fat kids, freezing out shy girls, snapping butts in the shower, becoming brownnosers, and pinpointing each other's flaws. This behavior is typical of school children but only justified by their immaturity and the lack of an appropriate target for their anger or alienation.
3.  "This was to be the world": the students realized that even as grown-ups, their only rebellion was going to consist of hurting each other. Nothing exciting or engaging was likely to happen.
4.  The students' destined job opportunities were grim and boring. The tone of voice they heard was falsity, and those who detected it chose to become not-gray—instead, super colorful like the Supremes.

## Additional Questions for Discussion and Writing

1.  Why does the speaker say that being "desperately / Athletic or popular" was "training"? Training for what?
2.  Twice in the poem the speaker mentions "a long scream" in the back of "our small heads" or "our minds." What is he referring to?

## Making Connections

→ Compare this poem about growing up to others on the same theme: "Hanging Fire" by Audre Lorde and/or "Ex-Basketball Player" by John Updike.

**INDIAN BOARDING SCHOOL: THE RUNAWAYS** by Louise Erdrich [pp. 659–60]
From the 1870s to the 1960s, many Native American children were educated off the reservation at boarding schools run by the government or by religious groups. This poem tells the story condensed in the title. One night, the children hop a boxcar heading for their tribal home. They are not surprised to be found missing by the guard and caught by the sheriff before they reach their destination: the poem has a tone of calm resignation. The runaways have to scrub the sidewalks as punishment, but within the duty lie the marks they made when the cement was still wet, marks that confirm their identities. Throughout the poem, images of injury and violence provide the background, like the history of the children's people and lands.

### Possible Responses to *Questions for Discussion and Writing*
1. The story concerns some Native American children brought up in a boarding school instead of at home with their families and tribes. It appears that the boarding school is not voluntary, perhaps part of a government program displacing the children into something like an orphanage. Though they have lived there for a long time, the children still long for home and try to return by hopping a freight train. The sheriff catches them at midpoint as though he sat in his car expecting them, which implies that they have run away in this manner before and will do so again. The children's punishment is to wear ugly long green dresses and scrub the sidewalks back at the boarding school.
2. Images of injury and pain: *stumbling north, old lacerations, riding scars, it hurts to be here, cold in regulation clothes, a wing of long insults, worn-down welts of ancient punishments, the color you would think shame was, cut the stone, delicate old injuries.* The images are appropriate because of the emotional pain of the homeless children.
3. The children see the images of things they pressed into or wrote into the concrete when it was wet, long ago. In this way, the punishment actually connects them with a personal, collective history. This sense of unity will probably cause them to make a plan and rebel again.

## Making Connections

→ Compare the dreams of the children in this poem to those dreams expressed in other poems, such as Hughes's "Harlem (A Dream Deferred)" and Eady's "The Supremes."

**BULLY** by Martín Espada [pp. 660–61]
The irony of the poem is that the Boston school in 1987 is being taken over by the descendants of natives of the Caribbean, Cuba, Hispaniola, and Puerto Rico in much the

same ways as the United States defeated the Spanish in Cuba and the Philippines in the brief Spanish-American War in 1898. The Treaty of Paris, which ended this war, gave the United States Puerto Rico, Guam, and the Philippines, which the government proceeded to exploit ruthlessly and to suppress the native governments through wildly unequal power and resources. Several details in the poem are subtle parallels with events in the Spanish-American War, such as the "brown children devouring the stockpiles of the cafeteria," a reminder that starving, underprepared U.S. troops led by war hero Teddy Roosevelt devoured the food supplies of defeated Spanish troops in Cuba. Other parallels and historical references will come to light when your students research the topics in question 1 that follows.

## Possible Responses to *Questions for Discussion and Writing*

1. You might divide the four research topics (Teddy Roosevelt, the Spanish-American War, eugenics, and Taino Puerto Rican ancestors) among four groups of students, so that each group can collect information and then discuss together how their discoveries help them understand the poem.
2. The surprising images in the poem will also be illuminated by the understanding created by the exercise in question 1. It makes sense that Teddy Roosevelt's image is nostalgic for the Spanish-American War, where his bullying style made him a hero in the U.S. press; also, his fist would be lonely without a weapon or reins, because he was known for his masculine love for boxing, hunting, riding, and roping. Another telling image is in lines 23–24, "Once Marines tramped from the newsreel of his imagination," because scholars now believe that the purported justifications for the Spanish-American War were fictions developed by the U.S. news media.
3. The four stanzas relate to stages in the transition of the school. The first describes the conventional statue of Roosevelt in the school auditorium. The second depicts the invasion of the school by children (in the same way their ancestors were invaded by Roosevelt and his ilk). The third implies some symbolic revenge (being surrounded) on behalf of the peoples that Roosevelt belittled in the past. The fourth shows the conquest of the old statue, and what it stands for, by the new population.
4. The "bully" is Roosevelt and the expansionist and racist ideals he represents. The title is appropriate in terms of the massive superior force that the United States used to overwhelm a much less prepared Spain, and native movements, in the Spanish-American War. The city and date allow the reader to locate when and where the transition of the school's population was occurring. Students may find more reasons for the choice of Boston and 1987, specifically, through doing some research.

## *Making Connections*
→ Compare the attitudes toward wars and war memorials expressed in Komunyakaa's "Facing It" and in Espada's "Bully."

**COMMITMENTS** by Essex Hemphill [pp. 661–62]

Perceptive readers, especially after perusing the headnote, will discern that the poet is talking about the experience of being gay in a close family from whom he feels he must conceal his sexuality and be "the invisible son" (line 31). In the family photographs he is always "pictured smiling / among siblings, parents, / nieces and nephews" (lines 4–6), but his "arms are empty" (line 16) because he has never produced children of his own to hold in the family photos. Still he feels committed to his family: "I will always be there," "I am always there / for critical emergencies, graduations" and those calls in "the middle of the night" (lines 1, 28–29, 30). But his unspoken wish is for their acceptance—to no longer be invisible, always "in the background of the photographs" (line 7). Instead he wants to be fully himself, loved for himself despite his arms being "empty" (lines 16, 24), without children to hold. The second line is perhaps the only difficult one in the poem: "When the silence is exhumed." If you ask your students to look up the word *exhumed*, they may find that one meaning is "to bring to light; disclose, reveal"; so the "silence" could refer to his unmentioned homosexuality. If so, the line could be paraphrased as "When the secret of my sexuality is revealed"—something that might actually have happened to the poet while he was dying from an AIDS-related illness.

## Possible Responses to *Questions for Discussion and Writing*

1. The speaker's arms are "empty" because he has no offspring—nor a partner of his own—to hold in the family pictures. The aunts are "unsuspecting" because they have no idea that their nephew is gay (or don't want to acknowledge it).

2. He thinks of himself as "the invisible son" because the focus of the family is on the children, "his nieces and nephews" (line 6), and he has produced none.

3. The "commitments" of the title seem to be obligations the speaker feels toward his family—obligations to shield them from being distressed by the knowledge of his homosexuality. The aunts, who have no idea that he is gay, are "expecting to throw rice" (line 18) at his wedding when he marries a nice young woman. He is also committed to showing up at family gatherings—barbeques, Christmases, and Thanksgivings. And he's always on call for "critical emergencies, / graduations," and "middle of the night" counseling (lines 27–30). The family's commitments to him seem mainly to entail hosting picnics, Christmas celebrations, and Thanksgiving dinners. He may be fond of his family, but he feels marginalized because he cannot truly be himself around them without the risk of shocking or offending them (or being insulted by them) if he reveals that he is gay.

4. These writing suggestions will appeal to a number of students and should work well as an in-class writing assignment.

## Making Connections

→ What difficulties does the speaker in "Commitments" share with the speaker and his friends in Cornelius Eady's "The Supremes"? Do you see any differences in the attitudes of the two speakers toward their situations?

**PEOPLE WHO TAKE CARE** by Nancy A. Henry [pp. 663–64]
Nancy Henry's poetry seems deceptively simple, but as critic Gary Lawless observes, "These are not facile poems." The language is simple, yes, but gains power from its very simplicity. The impact of the plain words and short lines focuses the reader's attention on the unfairness of a health system that offers starvation wages for essential, grueling work quite deserving of high praise and good paychecks.

You might want to have your students suggest punctuation for the poem as they go through it in class, letting them see as they do so how punctuation aids clarity in writing. At the end of the poem, the "beautiful place" (line 31) where caregivers go could be described as nirvana and suggests that virtue is, in many cases, its own reward.

## Possible Responses to *Questions for Discussion and Writing*

1. It is considerably ironic that people who perform some of the most essential services in our society are paid the least for their hard, often unpleasant work.
2. If doing hard work with dedication deserves good pay, then caregivers should definitely be paid more. But it clearly does not pay well, possibly because it requires little formal education and no skills other than empathy—and a strong back.
3. The "secret" shared by caregivers is perhaps their feeling of satisfaction in doing good by performing services for people who need help.
4. That "beautiful place" is a place of spiritual satisfaction, like the concept of nirvana—a place where a person is content just by virtue of being a good person who helps others and is concerned about those less fortunate. The "clean important people / have never been" to the "beautiful place" because they are too self-involved, too busy telling others what to do (lines 13–14), and too involved in making money to take satisfaction in service.
5. This is another assignment suitable for in-class writing.

## *Making Connections*

→ Henry's poem and Jan Beatty's "A Waitress's Instructions on Tipping" both focus on stultifying occupations, but which type of work do you think would prove more tolerable in the long run and why?

→ How would the speaker in Dorianne Laux's "What I Wouldn't Do" respond to the sentiments expressed in Henry's poem?

## PAIRED POEMS FOR COMPARISON [pp. 665–82]

Some of these paired poems are parodies, making them ideal for teaching tone. Even the pairs that are not parodies provide useful insights into the nature of tone. Students who tend to dislike poetry often love parodies because they feel the original poem is being ridiculed—as sometimes it is. But none of the parodies we have included here make fun of the original. These are simply responses to other poems, often changing the content for humorous effect, as with the two poems about ex-spouses. There's nothing humorous about the two versions of "Richard Cory," which tell the same story but with a different tone and a very different theme. Most of the pairs don't involve conscious imitation or direct commentary on each other, but they approach similar themes and subject matter in different and enlightening ways, adding depth and understanding to our appreciation of both selections.

**THE PASSIONATE SHEPHERD TO HIS LOVE** by Christopher Marlowe [pp. 665–66]
Using the conventions of the pastoral (the speaker assumes the pose of a shepherd), the speaker-poet invites his loved one to join him in a carefree love. Students may not find the invitation convincing; it is too artificial and the enticements (which carefully avoid the mention of any sexual pleasures) are charming but modest. But what do contemporary swains promise their loved ones? Are the modern conventions any more persuasive? Certainly, the innocent tone will appeal to some students' romantic impulses. This poem should be studied in conjunction with Raleigh's reply.

### Possible Responses to *Questions for Discussion and Writing*
1. The speaker offers the joys of nature, clothes, jewelry, and entertainment. His repetition of the "If" clauses may suggest that he is uncertain whether the woman will accept his offers. Some readers may also think that making so many offers in a row sounds a note of desperation.
2. The speaker's promises seem lavish, though we note that most of the enticements are indeed available to a shepherd, being derived from nature. Only the gold buckles, coral clasps, and amber studs are extravagant items. However, it may seem doubtful to a modern reader that the shepherd can come through with all his promises.
3. Most modern readers would not be enticed by the appeal, unless they are attracted to rural pleasures. Also, there is no allusion, even a delicate one, to sexual or romantic attachment, which calls into question the speaker's passionate nature.

**THE NYMPH'S REPLY TO THE SHEPHERD** by Sir Walter Raleigh [pp. 666–67]
This is the famous critical response to Marlowe's poem. In it, the speaker (the "nymph") systematically points out the illusory nature of the world offered to her by Marlowe's shepherd: men lie, weather turns bad, flowers and young women fade and wither as do gowns, skirts, and posies. In short, the poem offers a wry comment on love and the passage of time. The speaker implies that the shepherd's carefree love could not survive the passing youthful joys and her loss of beauty. The allusion to Philomel (line 7) is heavily charged with the tragic consequences of untrammeled lust. Philomel was raped

by her brother-in-law, who tore out her tongue so she couldn't accuse him; the gods later turned her into a nightingale.

## Possible Responses to *Questions for Discussion and Writing*
1. The nymph points out the temporary quality of natural wonders—flowers fade, winter comes, love dwindles.
2. As noted earlier, the nymph's reply shows awareness of time's ravages on nature, people, and love.
3. Readers will disagree on whether they like the shepherd or the nymph's point of view better. It may depend on how many romantic ideals each reader harbors. Also, women readers may enjoy the nymph's reply because they too suspect a silver-tongued suitor. If you don't have time for each student to write an essay of comparison, you might list pros and cons on each side of the matter as a class.
4. The students' responses to either the shepherd or the nymph should be fun to exchange and read in class or electronically.

## MY LAST DUCHESS by Robert Browning [pp. 667–68]
This dramatic monologue seems to allude to the life of Alfonso II, Duke of Ferrara, in northern Italy, whose first wife died three years after she was married to him. She was rumored to be a victim of poisoning. Through the offices of an agent (to whom the Duke may be speaking in the poem), Alfonso married the sister of the Count of Tyrol four years later.

The Duke's cold arrogance emerges from the outset of the poem. Selfish pride controls all his relationships with people. The Duchess is not alive but the subject of a painting by a famous artist. (Wives and works of art seem identical to the Duke—both are collectibles.) In lines 21–31, the poet engages our sympathies for the Duchess, despite the Duke's contemptuous criticism of her failings. What were the commands that ended her smiles? Browning once explained: "That she should be put to death, or he might have had her shut up in a convent."

Lines 47–53 make it clear that the Duke has been addressing the emissary of the Count whose daughter he hopes to marry. Has the Duke unwittingly revealed too much of his cruel nature, or was he just making it clear what he will expect from his new duchess? Critics have taken both sides of this question: some seeing him as calculating and in control; others suggesting that his arrogance is almost pathological and leads him to say too much (note the abrupt shift in the subject in line 47—has the Duke realized he should shut up about his last duchess?).

## Possible Responses to *Questions for Discussion and Writing*
1. The Duke of Ferrara is showing a painting of his previous wife to a visiting emissary, whose visit evidently is aimed at arranging a marriage between Ferrara and a Count's daughter.
2. The last Duchess was easily pleased and amused. The Count believes that she was flirtatious in her friendliness to men from all ranks; however, we are led to think that

195

the Count was possessive and vain and may have misinterpreted his wife's high spirits. He thinks of her as property, like his acquisitions of highbrow art objects.

3. Readers may disagree on whether the Duke is accidentally or purposely showing his nature and his attitudes. Certainly lines 35–46 seem like clear messages about what happens to an uppity wife in his household. However, the Duke is so arrogant that he may not be sensitive to his own threatening tone.

4. Most readers would warn the Count about what kind of marriage he may be sending his daughter into. Especially if the Count's daughter is a lively gal, her future at the Duke's looks grim. The Duke might be described as jealous, possessive, arrogant, acquisitive, shallow, and sexist.

### Additional Questions for Discussion and Writing

1. How does Browning make us understand that the Duke's remarks are biased?
2. What evidence is there that hypocrisy is another aspect of the Duke's character? Why does he, three times, deprecate his ability to relate precisely what he wishes?
3. What is the effect of mentioning another work of art at the end of the monologue? What does this remark show us about the Duke? Is there any significance to the statue of Neptune taming a seahorse?
4. Although the Duke is unsympathetic, are you still fascinated by him? If so, explain why.
5. How would the Duke's refusal "to stoop" and his insistence upon the importance of his "nine-hundred-years-old name" (or comparable attitudes) be manifested today?

### MY EX-HUSBAND by Gabriel Spera [pp. 669–70]

You may want to reproduce both poems on overhead transparencies and project them side by side for purposes of comparison. Spera says, "A good parody (as opposed to satire) recognizes the merits of the original, highlights distinctive stylistic elements, accentuates the inevitable failure of imitation, and leads to a greater appreciation of the original work. I think that's what makes it fun."

### Possible Responses to Questions for Discussion and Writing

1. Students will have fun making the exact comparisons between the two poems—the fancy painting turns into a photograph, the ex-wife chooses "never to get stuck," and now "Claus" is a sharp divorce lawyer, for example. The ex-husband turns out to be a philandering cad, something that isn't suggested about the Duke in the Browning poem.
2. Both speakers make clear decisions to get rid of spouses they believe unfaithful and undiscriminating in their affections. The speaker of "My Ex-Husband" gets a divorce rather than having her husband killed.
3. Many readers, especially women, will identify more readily with the ex-wife in "My Ex-Husband" because she found herself in a situation that is familiar to most. She does show some defensive assertiveness—"No, / We'll take my car," for instance— but this is quite understandable after a humiliating marriage. On the other hand, the

Duke of Ferrara seems to have no redeeming qualities except for his wealth and power. Both speakers are preoccupied with their previous marriages and determined not to repeat their perceived mistakes. Both also have an element of snobbery—for example, the ex-wife hates to be in the same position as some "bimbo / In the steno pool." In both poems, the readers' sympathies lie with the wronged woman.


**OF THE TERRIBLE DOUBT OF APPEARANCES** by Walt Whitman [pp. 671–72]
These two paired poems, separated in time by 100 years or so, are close in sentiment. Both celebrate private moments between two people, when they are in perfect harmony. Each poem argues for the mysterious power of love, one in a serious manner and the other in a humorous way.

### Possible Responses to *Questions for Discussion and Writing*
1. The speaker of the poem has terrible doubts about whether what appears to be real is only an illusion. He wonders whether there is really a soul and an afterlife, whether reality is something completely different from what it seems to be, and whether there is meaning to life. These concerns are very common, especially among people with a philosophical bent.
2. The mood shifts in line 10: "To me these and the like of these are curiously answer'd by my lovers, my dear friends." The narrator finds comfort in being with his lover, because he feels that he possesses wisdom deeper than appearances when they are together.
3. The "they" may refer to the skies of day and night, colors, densities, and forms—that is, the visible appearances of things. These may "dart out of themselves" by suddenly seeming completely different than usual. Students may have had experiences in which ordinary things temporarily seem extraordinary and strange—for example, during times of mental alteration due to exhaustion, drugs, starvation, elation, trance, stress, meditation, or illness.

### *Audio*
→ Garrison Keillor reads "Of the Terrible Doubt of Appearances" on the radio show *The Writer's Almanac*: **http://writersalmanac.publicradio.org/index.php?date=2009/02/04**


**ROMANTIC MOMENT** by Tony Hoagland [pp. 672–73]
This is the humorous argument for the mysterious power of love.

### Possible Responses to *Questions for Discussion and Writing*
1. The first three stanzas of the poem set up the beginning of a story, like the beginning of a romantic film perhaps, and invite the reader to continue to find out what happens next. As soon as the narrator says, "And if I were a bull penguin right now I would lean over / and vomit softly into the mouth of my beloved . . ." we know that the

story doesn't continue as expected. Later, in stanza 11, the atmosphere shifts again and becomes more serious as the couple begin to talk.

2. The two characters are in a beautiful outdoor mall, maybe in California or Florida. They are thinking about animals because they just saw a nature documentary. The poem emphasizes the gross and blatant details of the sex lives of animals.

3. The human characters compliment each other by pointing out ways that males and females of other species have good qualities (not accidentally, qualities that humans would desire in their mates). This banter is leading up to a sexual encounter between the two humans. The idea that human sexual activity may be just as gross and ridiculous as animals', if seen from the outside, is possibly suggested.

4. Students will enjoy speculating on the changes in the poem over the years, especially the way the ending changes. This is a good opening to discuss the purposes of revision.

5. Both poems build to a conclusion in which human love is elevated above other worldly experiences. The unromantic twist in Hoagland's poem involves the mentions of the crude courtship behaviors of animals; and in Whitman's poem, the unromantic twist is the deep questioning of whether anything is real and enduring. In both poems, love does not erase or refute the unromantic side of life but manages to exist in peace with it.

### Video

→ Tony Hoagland reads a version of "Romantic Moments" in honor of Valentine's Day at **www.pbs.org/newshour/bb/entertainment/jan-june12/poem_02-14.html**. This video is illustrated with animal footage.

**RICHARD CORY** by Edwin Arlington Robinson [pp. 673–74]
Part of the success of this poem lies in the way it builds to an unexpected climax. But certainly the simplicity of the speaker's diction contributes to its effectiveness, as does the spare imagery ("he glittered when he walked") and the rhyme and rhythm. The theme addresses the problem of illusion versus reality. We are often deceived by the surface of things. Young people, for instance, often long for the life of a rock star—to be an Elvis Presley or a Janice Joplin—but when that idol dies of a drug overdose, the glittering life looks considerably tarnished. Students may state the theme as "It's better to be poor than to be rich and miserable," which is an acceptable response, but encourage them to learn to state themes in more sophisticated language. The theme may involve the idea that people who seem totally privileged can harbor inner tortures, unguessed by their fellow citizens. For instance, it could be that Richard Cory was horribly lonely in his singularity among the townspeople.

**Possible Responses to *Questions for Discussion and Writing***
1. The speaker is a working-class citizen of the town where Richard Cory lives.
2. Richard Cory is a rich, well-educated, gracious person. A gentleman is considered a person who is polite and careful of others' feelings, knowing how to behave properly in all situations.
3. Images of royalty include "from sole to crown," "imperially slim," and "richer than a king," among more subtle suggestions in lines like, "We people on the pavement looked at him." The onlookers of lower classes seem not to resent Richard Cory's status, only wishing that they had been born to a similar situation.

**RICHARD CORY** by Paul Simon [pp. 674–75]
The obvious thing to do with this song lyric is to compare it with E. A. Robinson's version, "Richard Cory." Listening to the Simon and Garfunkel recording will be useful in the comparison, for there the bitterness of this version is clear; it's available on the album *The Sounds of Silence* (a Columbia recording).
　　　　The Cory of Robinson was actually a gentleman, while the Cory of Simon is a playboy sleaze. Even his charity seems designed to elicit thankfulness and admiration rather than to relieve suffering. The persona in the Simon version hates Richard Cory, while the persona in the Robinson version adulates him. Both speakers are puzzled by Cory's suicide, but for different reasons.

**Possible Responses to *Questions for Discussion and Writing***
1. A difference that stands out is that Simon's speaker, voice of the everyday citizen, resents Richard Cory bitterly, while Robinson's speaker seems purely admiring. The character of Cory in the two versions may explain this—in Simon's song, Cory is a privileged playboy with yachts and orgies, while in Robinson's poem there is not a whiff of such a lifestyle for Cory. It could be that class warfare in the United States escalated between 1896 and 1966, changing the characterization of Cory.
2. Many students will enjoy changing an old poem into a modern rock song. These can be distributed among classmates and discussed, including looking at what qualities of the original had to be altered for the rock version.

**TRAVELING THROUGH THE DARK** by William Stafford [p. 676]
The moral ambiguity behind our everyday decisions is exemplified in the speaker's encounter with the dead deer on the road. He needs to do a violent act in order to save drivers behind him who might cause more death by swerving to avoid the deer on the narrow road. These drivers are humans like whoever has shot or run into the deer in the first place. Human needs and goals, signified by the loving description of the car, take precedence over wilderness ways, signified by the doe's pregnancy. These are probably some of the hard thoughts the speaker refers to in the last stanza.

**Possible Responses to *Questions for Discussion and Writing***

1.   The title can be taken on a literal level, because the driver is indeed traveling through the dark when the incident happens. Being "in the dark" also fits metaphorically, because the narrator is uncertain about the right course of action. Some readers will also think that he is "in the dark" because he does not see things clearly and does the wrong thing with the dead deer.

2.   The animal is dead, and it creates a danger for other drivers on the road. Whether they hit it or swerve to avoid it, they can cause further damage or even death to other animals or drivers. After the speaker thinks for a moment, he does not let the pregnancy make any difference in his decision.

3.   The car is described fondly and in animate terms—it purrs, breathes exhaust, and aims its lights on the scene. Because a car was likely the deer's killer, the description highlights an ambivalence about machines versus nature. The car also signifies human goals, carrying us to our destinations.

4.   The speaker "thought hard" about the nature of life and death. Some readers may think that he is considering heroic attempts to save the unborn fawn. It seems that "us all" means the speaker, the deer, the fawn, and even the car; in a broader sense, it could mean all human beings caught in morally ambiguous situations. The speaker's "only swerving" is his pause to think hard: this is his only deviation from his original goal, to get the deer off the road. Pushing the deer "into the river" (in contrast with "into the canyon") makes use of the association of rivers with the ever-ongoing processes of natural life. Thus, the effect of pushing the deer off the cliff is softened by its joining the river.

*Additional Questions for Discussion and Writing*

1.   Do you think the speaker is cold and emotionless? Or he is keeping his emotions in check in order to do what he thinks he has to do?

2.   What is the effect of the final stanza? Where does it place the focus?

3.   Do you think the speaker did the right thing? Explain.

**THE BLACK SNAKE** by Mary Oliver [p. 677]
The speaker's admiration of the snake in this poem contrasts markedly with the spare, unemotional description of the deer in Stafford's poem. The dead snake is "cool and gleaming," "beautiful and quiet / as a dead bother" and is given a ritual burial under the leaves. Oliver exhibits a heightened respect and fondness for this dumb creature. And her theme is quite different from Stafford's. In Oliver's poem, the accidental death of the snake leads the speaker to focus on the randomness of death—"its suddenness, / its terrible weight / its certain coming," this instantaneous obliteration of the life force, "the light at the center of every cell."

**Possible Responses to *Questions for Discussion and Writing***

1.   The speaker has a loving, admiring attitude toward the snake. She carries it off the road and puts it beneath the bushes, in its natural habitat. Many readers will see this

as a contrast with the speaker's action in the previous poem, pushing the dead animal off the cliff. However, the concept of returning the bodies to the river of life makes the two disposals more similar.

2. The usual connotations of a snake, especially a black snake, are fearsomeness, evil, and duplicity. However, this poem provides a different and unexpected point of view, describing the snake as beautiful.
3. The brighter fire is the life instinct, which allows us to live most of the time as though we are not destined to die. It resides in "the bones," which suggests that it is instinctive rather than emotional (in the heart).
4. The "light at the center of every cell" is the will to live and to enjoy life, reinforcing the poem's affirmation of the life instinct.

## THOSE WINTER SUNDAYS by Robert Hayden [p. 678]

This poem is about the expression of love, as is clear from the last line. The father's thankless and painful work to nurture his family is presented as a repeated ritual. The image is unusual, since it is conventionally mothers that do the unregarded labor that children grow up to recognize as valuable. On the other hand, the inability to communicate feelings verbally, which we see between men in this poem, is typically male. See the published critical article "The 'Banked Fire' of Robert Hayden's 'Those Winter Sundays'" by David Huddle at the end of Chapter 14.

### Possible Responses to *Questions for Discussion and Writing*

1. As an adult, the speaker realizes that his father repeatedly showed his love, while the child did not perceive the demonstration.
2. The home had "chronic angers," which suggests strife within the household or problems brought home from work. The father has a hard-labor job; thus, we can infer that the house is not luxurious. This idea is supported by the fact that it gets so cold during the night. The plural "angers" suggests that perhaps each member of the household harbors his or her own anger. It also suggests that more than one problem creates strife in the home.
3. Love can be expressed directly, through words, hugs, smiles, and caresses, or indirectly, through serving another person. The father's "austere and lonely" expressions of love are concrete services, such as polishing the boy's shoes and building up the fires in the cold, dark morning.
4. In religious observances, an "office" is a ceremony or ritual for a specific purpose, such as Office for the Dead. The father's repeated services to show his love for his family convey a ritualistic tone and do serve a specific purpose.

### Additional Questions for Discussion and Writing

1. This is a memory poem, looking back forty years. Which details are the ones the older speaker now realizes but which the boy wouldn't have noticed or cared about? How can a reader tell what the boy felt then and what the speaker feels now?

2. Describe the father based on the speaker's sparse description. What does the word "too," in the first line, imply about the father?
3. Can you describe the speaker? How does he contrast with his father?

## LIKE RIDING A BICYCLE by George Bilgere [pp. 679–80]

This poem, like "Those Winter Sundays," describes a father as loving but troubled. The father attempts to help the child learn to ride a bike, but he is too impaired himself to perform the job he knows belongs to him. The speaker contrasts an ideal, fairy tale situation with the reality of his father's failure. Nonetheless, this failure is linked to the child's and then the adult speaker's prized self-reliance. The forgiving and even thankful attitude toward an inadequate parent makes the poem's message unusual.

The beautiful, nostalgic opening narrative (stanza) about a boy learning to ride a bike from his supportive, effective father is tinged with sadness when the adult speaker refers to a "perilous adult launch," which appears to be his own recent divorce. Yet the emotional guidance of the father remains in this scene, helping the adult son move "forward / Into the future's blue / Equilibrium." However, the whole scene is undercut by the next stanza, a narrative that describes the real story: a fat, drunken, stinking, stumbling father who was too much of a mess to support the boy's clumsy efforts and who finally "swore and stomped off / Into the house to continue / Working with my mother / On their own divorce." The boy went on to learn to ride the bike alone, finding some bittersweet pleasure in being a "lonely western hero." The closing stanza suggests that the adult speaker nonetheless managed to get launched and can now enjoy the pleasures of life with a "soft urgency all over." Unlike other poems implying that inadequate or cruel parents ruin their children's lives, Bilgere's presents a refreshing alternative point of view: that a person can overcome abuse and disappointment and make a virtue of loneliness.

### Possible Responses to *Questions for Discussion and Writing*

1. A gantry is the huge metal frame that holds a missile up at a launch site and then releases the missile, remaining attached to the ground as the missile flies upward. This image is the romantic ideal of father and son presented in the first stanza.
2. The boy's relationship with his father, as expressed in the second stanza, first seems dominated by disgust at his drunkenness, smoking, and physical clumsiness. After the father gives up, the boy appears to have some sympathy for him, suffering his own divorce, and uses the image of both parents about ready to hit the hard ground. Some students might say that the boy's disappointment with the real-life situation was probably influenced by the idealized vision he wishes for, expressed in the first stanza.
3. The first stanza describes the ideal scene of a loving father teaching his boy to ride a bike with just the right amount of support and release, while the second stanza presents the reality. The third stanza, somewhat unexpectedly, pulls the reader into the mind of the grown-up boy, who has learned not only to survive disappointment and loneliness but also to enjoy life.

4. Most students will focus on the contrast between the men who narrate the poems. Hayden's speaker, as an adult, regrets that he had so little appreciation for a devoted father, while Bilgere's speaker is able to appreciate what he learned from an incompetent and careless one. Bilgere's attitude is definitely more complex, in our view.

## THE BEAN EATERS by Gwendolyn Brooks [pp. 680–81]
Perhaps inspired by Picasso's "The Frugal Repast," this poem also paints a picture of a poverty-stricken couple who continue to live after life has lost its zest. Reminders of their past surround them in their "rented back room." Although the overall tone remains grim, the word choice makes the description tender, respectful, and deeply human.

### Possible Responses to *Questions for Discussion and Writing*
1. The aging couple eats beans because they lack money—and choices. Their frayed surroundings reinforce this image.
2. The beads and other objects are the remains of their past lives, suggesting beauty (the beads, cloth) and perhaps children (dolls) but also a frugally lived life (receipts).
3. "Mostly good" makes the couple human, subject to our common weaknesses and thus more easily identified with by the reader. Further, with this modification, Brooks resists romanticizing the poverty she examines through the poem.
4. The daily life of the elderly, especially of the poor, is reduced to a smaller stage, with fewer events and choices. Eating, dressing, and cleaning become the major events of the day.

### *Additional Questions for Discussion and Writing*
1. What is the effect of describing the couple as "yellow"?
2. What does the line "Dinner is a casual affair" suggest?
3. Why is the word "remembering" repeated, and why is the couple remembering "with twinklings and twinges"?
4. Write an essay on the use of concrete details in this poem, focusing on how they contribute to tone.

## THE OLD NEIGHBORS by Katha Pollitt [pp. 681–82]
Both "The Bean Eaters" and this poem place the old couples in what seem to be urban settings, apart from the families they have raised. This offers an opportunity to discuss not just aging but also family issues more generally—for example, the impact of urban versus rural and nuclear versus extended family experiences. Pollitt's poem models new ways to define family in order to solve many of the problems found in traditional families.

**Possible Responses to *Questions for Discussion and Writing***

1.  The speaker of the poem is a neighbor of Mr. and Mrs. Tozzi, Stanley, and Mrs. Sansanowitz, a part of the community the speaker wants us to envision and appreciate.

2.  The aloe is a succulent best known as a healing plant that is used in nontraditional medicine for burns and skin treatments. It is most often an indoor plant in northern climates and thus its survival in the Tozzi yard mirrors their own tenacious lives.

3.  In a very few lines Pollitt captures the gap between immigrant dreams and the realities of American life, especially the contrast between the hopes of the parents and the American-centered values of their children. The sadness of these lines, however, is offset by phrases such as "beautiful babies" and "sweethearts." Further she quickly shifts from the losses in their lives to the fullness of their everyday routine, a shift signaled by the word "still" in line 14.

4.  The speaker believes that as with the "gnarled" wisteria, the value of life is to be found in even "the feeble shower of purple blossoms." The tension in the phrase "stragglers basking" embodies this same complex reality.

5.  Both couples in these poems are old and alone in urban settings. Though there seems to be more optimism in Pollitt's poem and a more immediate sense of community, both couples take comfort in one another and find meaning in their routines. The phrase "twinklings and twinges" in "The Bean Eaters" might be a good place to begin the comparison.

6.  See question 5.

# A PORTFOLIO OF POEMS ABOUT WORK

**REAPERS** by Jean Toomer [p. 683]
"Reapers," with its steady rhythm and onomatopoetic *s* and *c* sounds, drives home the inexorable process of the world's work. Students may need to look up *reapers*, *scythes*, and *hones* to visualize the poem's images. The slaughter of the field rat makes the work seem heartless, as do the silence and the color black. The fact that death is called the "Grim Reaper" must come into play here. The poem is an excellent example of crystallized imagery.

## Possible Reponses to *Questions for Discussion and Writing*
1. The steady rhythm of the poem perfectly fits the activity described—the sharpening of the scythes and the rhythmic swishing of the cutting swings. The mowing in the second stanza with the horses slowly and steadily stepping follows a similar steady rhythm of the working animal.
2. Far from being a "joyful romp," the plodding rhythm, combined with the description of the repetitive action of mowing, suggests a dreary boredom. The silence of the workers (line 4) also suggests their draining tiredness.
3. The bloody slicing of the innocent field rat introduces the Grim Reaper. There is an undercurrent of seething anger in the poem, and the whetting of steel on whetstone suggests that the farm implement could easily become an instrument of death to others, not just field rats. If the black reapers are slaves, they might be envisioning in the scene the possibility of insurrection followed by freedom.

## *Making Connections*
→ Compare the use of imagery in this poem to the images in "Fog" by Sandburg or "The Red Wheelbarrow" by Williams.
→ Compare the difference in tone concerning the work being done in "Reapers" with that being done in Heaney's "Digging." Can you account for the difference? Or compare to the tone of "My Mother Sews Blouses" by Valdés?

**EX-BASKETBALL PLAYER** by John Updike [pp. 684–85]
Though aging ex-cheerleaders are a common target of sympathy, ex-basketball players rarely get much. This poem chronicles in rich detail the dead-end life of a man whose only golden moments were as a sports star—and that, only in a small-town high school. Your students may know such a person. The details, which give the poem its authentic flavor, also date the poem, and your students may want to look at the picture of the old-fashioned gas pump on page 639 to appreciate the personification in stanza 2. You may also need to explain what Necco Wafers, Nibs, and Juju Beads are.

## Possible Responses to *Questions for Discussion and Writing*
1. Flick Webb had all his moments of glory as a high school basketball player and drifted into the life of a mundane worker as an adult. His name reflects his past—in

205

that he could *flick* the ball and handle it as though he had *webbed* hands—as well as his present—in that his heyday was over in a *flicker*, and he's now caught in a *web* of ordinariness and boredom. We have no clue that he has a rich inner life to supplement his tiresome existence.

2. The "I" of the poem is a citizen of the same town as Berth's Garage. He knows the streets, people, stores, and sports lore of the town well. The speaker seems to be the same age or a bit older than Flick—at least, he was of an age to go to games Flick played in high school.

3. Each line has five stressed syllables (pentameter), more or less. The stanzas are like paragraphs in a prose essay. Each one takes up a new topic developing the overall theme: the town, Berth's garage, Flick's basketball feats, his current work, his current leisure. The thesis is implied.

4. Flick's job is described as routine and nonchallenging, and his attitude is resigned, even though once in a while he dribbles an inner tube. His life off work is similarly dreary, and the last three lines suggest that his inner life is stuck back on the high school basketball court. Some students may know people who have lived and worked like this, or they may have been such people themselves, motivating them to return to college.

### Additional Questions for Discussion and Writing

1. Note that Pearl Avenue runs past the high school, stops, and is "cut off / Before it has a chance to go two blocks." How does this relate to Flick Webb?

2. Explain the extended personification in the second stanza. What does "Five on a side" refer to? What do "rubber elbows hanging loose and low" suggest? What is the personification in lines 29–30, and how does it relate to the second stanza?

3. Try writing a description of some familiar part of your hometown with as much detail as Updike gives in this poem. You might add a town character if you want.

### Making Connections

➜ Compare this poem to A. E. Housman's "To an Athlete Dying Young" or Edward Hirsch's "Execution."

➜ Compare "Ex-Basketball Player" with "The Supremes" by Cornelius Eady, another poem about growing up.

### TO BE OF USE by Marge Piercy [pp. 685–86]

In contrast with "Beside the Point" and some other selections in this portfolio, this poem argues that the desire for work is indeed natural and beautiful. The argument concurs with humanist psychological theory, which says that people have a natural urge to do things they are able to do well.

**Possible Responses to *Questions for Discussion and Writing***
1.  Stanza 1 compares good workers to swimmers, Stanza 2 to farm animals, Stanza 3 to laborers. Notice the strong nature imagery, which emphasizes the good workers' harmony with nature instead of their struggle against it.
2.  Stanza 4 argues that work *is* art. The metaphor is that the lowly medium of mud is used to make the clay of a beautiful amphora (pitcher), which in turn does the work of carrying water. Students, we hope, will provide examples of ways in which ordinary materials, experiences, or actions can become beautiful or meaningful. Most of us have felt happiness and pride in a job well done, even when it is unpretentious. Examples from work abound, and the poem in this portfolio "What I Wouldn't Do" by Dorianne Laux is full of images showing how the narrator found beauty in humble jobs.


DAYSTAR by Rita Dove [pp. 686–87]
A question about who in the class identified with the woman in the poem may start an interesting discussion. Many of us wish for a solitary time in which we do not have to fulfill any of our roles, even freely chosen ones. Notice that the things the woman watches are utterly undemanding. The last stanza suggests that she does not welcome sex with her husband. Perhaps she feels that she is not real to him at the time ("nothing"), or perhaps she is avoiding the thought of conceiving another child. Though the night is usually associated with solitude, in this case the noon hour is associated with it. This irony may be the source of the title (the "daystar" is the sun).

**Possible Responses to *Questions for Discussion and Writing***
1.  The sun is the daystar. Instead of doing her daydreaming under the romantic night stars, the woman in the poem dreams under the daystar, behind the garage, in a decidedly contrasting setting.
2.  The speaker needs "a little room for thinking" because her day is full of childcare duties. She is never alone to think, nor does she really have partners for conversation.
3.  Perhaps older students will identify with the woman in the poem because they have experienced times when they feel that the demands of their roles overburden them and obliterate their individual identities. Students of any age may also relate to the stress of daily activates that are contradictory to their ideas of self and to the lack of time to relax and daydream. In your class discussion, these may be times when students mention needing solitude. The persona wants "a little time for thinking," implying that the rest of the day is taken up with unthinking activities.
4.  Liza is the toddler daughter, and Thomas is the husband. They are important characters because their demands run the woman's life. The writer refrains from identifying them because the point of view is interior to the woman. It would break the point of view to inwardly ponder, "Lisa, her toddler," or "Thomas, her husband." Students may think of several reasons why the woman herself has no name. The lack of a name may emphasize that she represents a whole class of women and not just an

individual; she may have no identity other than her role as wife and mother and thus no name; and again, in interior monologue, one rarely thinks of oneself by name.

## Making Connections
→ Compare the coping mechanisms used by the persona of Rita Dove's "Daystar" and the persona of Emily Dickinson's "He Put the Belt Around My Life."

### IN SECOND GRADE MISS LEE I PROMISED NEVER TO FORGET YOU AND I NEVER DID by Alberto Ríos [pp. 686–88]
Most of us can remember a teacher or other adult who did not conform to our childhood expectations of what grown-ups were like. The second graders' opinion of Miss Lee was markedly different from that of their parents, who most likely disapproved of her unkempt blonde hair and sexiness. Even the lack of punctuation in the poem's title emphasizes that we hear a child's voice as the narrator.

### Possible Responses to *Questions for Discussion and Writing*
1.  Miss Lee broke the mold of a stereotypical grade school teacher: she was too sexy and exotic, too cosmopolitan. Even the first line of the poem describes a "letting-go moment," something a second-grade teacher is not supposed to have in front of her class (or in some communities, even outside of class). She was probably fired when students carried stories from her classroom home to their parents, and the parents complained to the principal.
2.  Second-grade students are around seven years old. The apple story no doubt impressed the narrator and other students because they were totally unused to being told about French lovers and kissing. Generally, children remember incidents having to do with sex and bodily elimination, as well as surprising things that adults and other children did. They also remember people who were very different from their parents, who so far constituted their world of adults. Students may bring up anecdotes on these themes in your class discussion of childhood memories.
3.  The child obviously has a crush on Miss Lee and sees nothing inappropriate about her appearance or behavior. In fact, he finds her "Like a real movie star," an image of the ideal woman that reinforces his naïve point of view. He even believes that Miss Lee returns his feelings (lines 16–17). In contrast, from the parents' point of view, she is threateningly single and sexy and unfit for grade school teaching. The fact that the narrator has no insight into how parents might feel about Miss Lee sustains the childish point of view. He also seems to have no insight into the severe demotion from teaching to selling encyclopedias door to door!

### Additional Questions for Discussion and Writing
1.  What is a "letting-go moment"?
2.  If you were a parent, what would you think of a teacher telling second graders about the habits of French lovers?

### Making Connections

→ Toni Cade Bambara's story "The Lesson" also considers a teacher from a child's point of view. In both "The Lesson" and "Miss Lee," explain how an adult point of view would change the narrative.

### WHAT I WOULDN'T DO by Dorianne Laux [pp. 688–90]

This poem is structured by a bracket topic, the job the narrator quit: selling *TV Guide* over the telephone. This topic begins the poem intriguingly, because the reader must wonder what the other jobs were. The question is quickly answered by a sequence of descriptive passages about menial jobs that many people would not like. Each job is described in highly sensory terms, and each is presented with both good and bad elements. When the narrator returns to say finally what she hated about telemarketing, we have a good idea of her character. We are prepared for her keen sensitivity to the disappointment in the strangers' voices.

### Possible Responses to *Questions for Discussion and Writing*

1.  The narrator has worked in a fast-food place, at a Laundromat, cleaning houses, cooking at a sanatorium, and at a gas station and donut shop. All of the jobs were lowly and probably not well paid, and all included serving others, though in an impersonal, structured way. She describes each job with lots of sensory details and without resentment.
2.  You can tell that the narrator is sensitive to colors and sensory appeals and that she was efficient at all of the jobs and enjoyed her own efficiency. Also, she is good-natured about them, even though many people would abhor the work.
3.  In contrast with other jobs, in the *TV Guide* job the narrator was a supplicant and was supposed to use persuasion. This may be a position she was poorly suited for. She also had to deal with the disappointment of others when they found out she was a salesperson rather than a loved one calling. The nature of *TV Guide* may be that it is a text for the lonely or that it is a fairly useless item, furthering her dislike of trying to sell it.
4.  Students may share their writings about the jobs they hated or loved with classmates. Consider holding a discussion about which writings are more effective, negative or positive ones, or what other features make certain writings stand out.

### ACCEPTANCE SPEECH by Lynn Powell [pp. 690–91]

Though this poem conveys a playful tone, it also hints at some of the speaker's resentment about her undervalued role in the family.

## Possible Responses to *Questions for Discussion and Writing*

1. The main character is listening to a recap of the Oscars, Emmy Awards, or some program like that. When the poem begins, the winners are making their fulsome thank-you speeches.
2. In the fantasy, the speaker is one of the award winners for her work in the kitchen. She is actually a wife and mother, as far as we know. She includes the ingredients in her soup in her thank-you speech, because they support her performance.
3. When the narrator addresses the celery and parsnip, "only there to swell the scene," and says that "sometimes I know exactly how you feel," we are aware that she feels like a bit player in her own family and not a star at all.
4. Lines such as "without all of them," "I could not have made it without . . .," "Special thanks, as always," sound like they came straight out of the standard acceptance speech.
5. The poem appeals especially to taste and touch, helping to put the reader right in the kitchen with the narrator.


## BESIDE THE POINT by Stephen Cushman [pp. 691–92]

To be fair, we included a poem that provides a completely different point of view on work. Be sure that students know the phrase "Buck up" and the word "superfluity."

## Possible Responses to *Questions for Discussion and Writing*

1. Natural phenomena don't have motivations like achievement, admiration, and power. The words used to describe what is *not* in nature are *prize, careers, my work, productive, pragmatic,* and *useful.*
2. In the third stanza, the speaker addresses someone else as "my fellow superfluity." He also describes himself and the addressee using the words *self-indulgent, self-absorbed, inconsequential, good-for-nothings,* and *irrelevance.*
3. The speaker wants the other person to join him—most students will agree that a sexual encounter is suggested. Like this piece and "The Passionate Shepherd to His Love," poems have often used the beauty and the evanescence of nature as arguments for seeking immediate gratification in sexual union.

# A PORTFOLIO OF WAR POETRY

**TO LUCASTA, ON GOING TO THE WARS** by Richard Lovelace [p. 693]
This poem may be related to an actual parting: Lovelace fought in the service of Charles I during the Puritan Revolution (1642–1645). The theme, which seems to be a serious one, is that honor (duty to country and king) takes priority over duty to Lucasta. She is "chaste" and "quiet"; war is personified as a "new mistress" with greater vitality, and the speaker calls his departure an instance of "inconstancy." This comparison is in keeping with the light and witty tone (which may confuse some readers because of the seriousness of the message). The closing line makes a serious affirmation: the speaker's love for Lucasta is based on a greater love of honor, which is a driving force in the speaker's life.

## Possible Responses to *Questions for Discussion and Writing*
1. The speaker appears to be a young, idealistic man who has a romantic view of fighting for his country.
2. The speaker's "new mistress" is "the first foe in the field," meaning that he will aggressively chase the first enemy he encounters.
3. The virtues of loyalty to a beloved woman versus loyalty to duty to country, or "honor," are contrasted. The speaker argues that he could not love the woman properly if he did not put honor first, implying that he would lack character strength and therefore not be capable of the love she deserves.

## *Additional Questions for Discussion and Writing*
1. What is the tone of the poem?
2. What is the meaning of "nunnery" to the speaker?
3. Look up the term *synecdoche* in the glossary. Find several examples of the poet's use of this figure of speech. (Lucasta's "chaste breast and quiet mind" stand for her physical and mental attributes; "A sword, a horse, a shield" stand for war.)


**WAR IS KIND** by Stephen Crane [p. 694]
By far Crane's finest and most widely reprinted poem, "War Is Kind" presents the same strongly antiwar theme as *The Red Badge of Courage*. Stanzas 1, 3, and 5 directly address those who survive war but lose those they love, whereas stanzas 2 and 4 seem to be spoken to the military (especially in lines 20–21). Notice that the meter changes in the indented stanzas, suggesting the cadence of marching men—until the final melodious line, "A field where a thousand corpses lie." The incongruity between the sound and the meaning reinforces the already acute irony of the line. Lines 25 and 26 are admired for the moving simplicity of the image (the "bright splendid shroud" being the son's dress uniform) and the wonderfully effective use of alliteration. The short three-word lines, which serve as a refrain, are most emphatic.

## Possible Responses to *Questions for Discussion and Writing*

1. Stanzas 2 and 4 act as refrains: notice the similarity between them. These stanzas take a general point of view on patriotism and war, while stanzas 1, 3, and 5 deal with specific situations (the bereaved maiden, babe, and mother).
2. The flag is called "the unexplained glory," suggesting that most citizens don't understand the policies and philosophy of their country. They are taught to respond emotionally to patriotic symbols and exhortations.
3. The tone is ironic—there is a discrepancy between the words on the page and the intended meaning. The poem's message is that war is *not* kind but cruel and stupid.

### Additional Question for Discussion and Writing

In stanzas 1, 3, and 5, who is being addressed? Why did the poet write three long lines and two short ones in those stanzas instead of four long lines?


### DULCE ET DECORUM EST by Wilfred Owen [pp. 695–96]

Owen died in the trenches near the end of World War I not long after writing this powerful poem, which was published posthumously. The persona describes weary troops slogging through the mire (which often literally sucked the boots off their feet) away from the front, so exhausted that they fail to hear the "hoots" of the gas canisters dropping just behind them. These canisters have spent their fuel; thus they, like the men, are exhausted ("tired") after their journey through the air. One soldier fails to struggle into his gas mask in time, and his death throes—described in telling detail—haunt the persona. The last lines condemn the ancient practice of glorifying war (in epic poems, in popular songs, in heroic monuments, in John Wayne movies, in patriotic speeches) that for ages has served to fire the ignorant enthusiasm of young men to seek the "desperate glory" mendaciously associated with war. (Students may remember Crane's "unexplained glory" in "War Is Kind" [p. 705] and Henry Fleming in *The Red Badge of Courage*, who, at the beginning of that novella, was desperate for glory.)

The following account of the effects of mustard gas was written by a nurse in World War I:

> With mustard gas the effects did not become apparent for up to twelve hours. But then it began to rot the body, within and without. The skin blistered, the eyes became extremely painful and nausea and vomiting began. Worse, the gas attacked the bronchial tubes, stripping off the mucous membrane. The pain was almost beyond endurance, and most cases had to be strapped to their beds. Death took up to four or five weeks.

## Possible Responses to *Questions for Discussion and Writing*

1. Five-Nines are 5.9-caliber explosive shells, in this case apparently filled with poison gas. They are "tired" because the shells are falling behind the men as they stumble away from the battle toward a place to rest. Poison gas fills the lungs with fluid, giving the effects of drowning.

2. The "you" in the third stanza is someone in civilian life who evidently has passionately defended war. Most readers will hear "My friend" as having an ironic tone—the person who defends war is not really a friend. However, it could also be that the person is a real, noncombatant friend whose ideas are uninformed.
3. The "desperate glory" would involve battlefield heroics of some kind, desperate because there are other, less suicidal ways of being a hero. Norman Mailer's *Naked and the Dead* is a famous example of desperate glory.
4. The "old Lie" is "It is sweet and fitting to die for one's country." This philosophy lies behind suicide bombers in our current age. It is also used to comfort citizens whose loved ones die in contemporary wars.

### *Additional Questions for Discussion and Writing*
1. Why is the man in stanza 2 described as "drowning"? What is the "green sea" actually?
2. What is the source of the title of the poem? Why is it in Latin?

**NEXT TO OF COURSE GOD AMERICA I** by E. E. Cummings [pp. 696–97]
By the end of the poem, we realize that it is a political speech, given perhaps at a campaign rally. The high-sounding illogic of it is simply an exaggeration of the empty and frequently contradictory rhetoric found in patriotic diatribes. The lack of punctuation and meaningless line breaks emphasize the smooth flow of nonsense pouring from the speaker's lips. The last line points up the speaker's blustery style and also his comfortable position (in contrast to the young men who died in the war).

### **Possible Responses to *Questions for Discussion and Writing***
1. The poem begins with quotation marks to immediately indicate that it's a direct quotation from someone's speech.
2. Within the first three or four lines, the reader is aware that the patriotic phrases are jumbled together and often incomplete. This mixed-up rhetoric suggests that it is a parody of political speech.
3. Some clichés include "land of the pilgrims," "oh say can you see by the dawn's early," "my country 'tis of." The clichés don't go together sensibly. An example of a contradiction is that in one spot is the statement "thy sons acclaim your glorious name," while at the end, the speaker asks "then shall the voice of liberty be mute?"
4. The closing of the quotation marks before the last line of the speech shows that this line is not part of the speech. Now the position of the political speaker is clarified— he is comfortably out of the real line of fire.

### *Additional Question for Discussion and Writing*
Why is this poem included in a portfolio of war poems? What is the connection to war?

**SIX NATIONAL GUARDSMEN BLOWN UP TOGETHER** by Peg Lauber [pp. 697–98]
Peg Lauber's poem is a requiem for six national guardsmen whose remains are being returned by the military after they were killed in the Iraq war. She tells us in the opening stanza that they "grew up together on the bayous" (probably in Louisiana), where they "hunted, fished, trapped together." But on the other side of the globe they themselves became the prey, as the enemy hunted them down for the slaughter. Setting is important in conveying the contrast between the world of nature, where the young men once held sway, and the world of war, where now their shattered bodies are delivered home. Nature is impotent in the face of war machines: the "lumbering" cargo plane carrying "what is left of the men" frightens away the "Cajun Air Force" of seventeen white pelicans. Only the screeching gulls are left to cry an "appropriate requiem." The final image shows families, "bent / weeping into their small children's hair," as those crying children realize that their fathers, in those "flag-draped" boxes, are never coming home again.

**Possible Responses to *Questions for Discussion and Writing***
1. The title sounds like a newspaper headline. It provides the factual background necessary to understand the poem from the first lines.
2. The setting for the poem is the naval base airfield where the families wait for the plane to bring the remains of the six soldiers home. The natural setting of this home is emphasized, at odds with the war experience. Seven local animals are mentioned. The ones that the boys hunted are contrasted with the idea that in war, the boys themselves are the prey. The pelicans and gulls represent two natural responses to the effects of war—to flee and to mourn. In the second stanza the pelicans are frightened and scattered by a huge war machine, the "cargo plane carrying / what is left of the men" (lines 15–16). In the final stanza only the gulls have not been frightened away by the fearful plane or the flag-draped coffins. They swoop and glide, crying a mournful dirge over the weeping survivors.
3. The jack-in-the-box simile in the final lines reflects the bereft children's point of view—they might think in terms of a familiar toy. The realization that war is not play but a deadly pursuit changes their thinking and feeling forever.

**FACING IT** by Yusef Komunyakaa [pp. 698–700]
Students must understand the visual situation in order to appreciate this poem; the photo on page 694 should help. You may want to show other pictures of the Vietnam Veterans Memorial. Get people who have visited there to talk about the experience. The highly reflective surface of the wall, on which the names of Vietnam dead are engraved, mirrors the people who are visiting the memorial as well as the scene behind them. The speaker in "Facing It" captures the odd sensory experience thus created when he says, "I'm stone. I'm flesh." He moves in and out of the wall, becoming part of the names and also merging with the other visitors (who are reflected). Metaphorically, he is part of the Vietnam tragedy (the wall) but also he is still alive. Students might also want to explore

214

the various meanings of the word *facing* in the title. The speaker is facing (in front of) the monument, but he's also facing (confronting with awareness) the wall's significance and, thus, the meaning of his war experience (and perhaps the war's meaning to the country).

## Possible Responses to *Questions for Discussion and Writing*

1.  The "It" in the title, literally, is the Vietnam Veterans Memorial, which is made of polished stone with the names of the dead engraved into it. On another level, the speaker of the poem, a war veteran, is facing the war experience and its aftermath, as well as his own responses. The speaker's intention not to cry helps readers understand the point of view in the poem.

2.  The speaker is a Vietnam veteran himself and so identifies strongly with the names on the wall, so he half expects to see his own name there. Readers might also interpret these lines to mean that he feels half dead himself or that he feels survivor's guilt when confronted with the names of the dead.

3.  A woman visiting the memorial is able to walk away (unlike the war dead), but first she is imprinted with the experience (the names reflected on her blouse). The red bird may represent the power of nature over human artifice. The plane in the sky is a peacetime plane, perhaps chosen in contrast to the planes over Vietnam. The white vet's image is close to the black vet's (the speaker's), and their eyes' meeting might further an interpretation that the war brought the two races together. The white vet probably has not really lost his arm, but it looks that way in the mirror of the monument. This image reminds the reader of all the vets who didn't die but lost limbs in the war. The final image is explained in the next question's response.

4.  The speaker thinks for a moment that the woman is trying to erase the names of the dead—to obliterate the experience, or to bring them back, a reader may think. However, she is really brushing her son's hair. The error in perception reveals the vet's point of view, which is distorted in such a way that he instantly sees everything as pertaining to the war experience, even when it does not. The woman's act is really one of nurturance, not destruction. Many readers will also see a symbolic meaning in that the woman is literally grooming the boy and figuratively grooming him to become a soldier like the ones in Vietnam.

IN RESPONSE TO EXECUTIVE ORDER 9066 by Dwight Okita [pp. 700–02]
Some students may need a little background beyond the headnote in order to fully understand this selection. In 1942, at the beginning of WWII, President Franklin D. Roosevelt signed Executive Order 9066, forcing over 100,000 Japanese Americans then living in this country, whether citizens or not, to be sent to relocation camps in the West and the arid Southwest. Their property was confiscated, and most Americans went along with the injustice, considering it necessary for national security. Paranoia was rampant as the nation geared up for war. The young Japanese American narrator's classmate Denise has moved away to the other side of the room because her former best friend now

represents "the Enemy" to Denise, who fears she'll be "giving secrets away" to the Japanese military, thus endangering the American populace.

## Possible Responses to *Questions for Discussion and Writing*

1. The internment camps were located mostly in dry, arid (desert) places.

2. Okita's poem gains impact and empathy by being conveyed through the innocent voice of the young girl. We are touched by the unfairness to the child who in no way understands why she is being taken from her home or why her best friend rejects her in such a hateful manner. "I didn't know what to say" (line 21) is her helpless response. The tomato seeds, which would have produced abundantly in her home near Fresno, California, simply "won't grow" (line 6) where the family is being sent. Since water symbolically represents life and spiritual fulfillment, the arid desert of the relocation camp suggests the loss of those vital elements. We fear that the young girl may, like the tomato seeds, find it difficult to flourish there.

3. The narrator feels that her aversion to chopsticks and her love of hot dogs will make her seem truly American, not Japanese, and thus dispel her friend's suspicion that she might be "The Enemy."

4. Denise has been caught up in the anti-Japanese fervor that swept this country following the attack on Pearl Harbor. While she is not justified in rejecting her totally innocent friend, her behavior is quite understandable. Since tomatoes were sometimes called "love apples" (line 4), the seeds can be seen as a gift of love, a long-lasting token of their friendship; but Denise, caught up in her patriotic hostility to the Japanese, would not be likely to nourish the seeds.

# A PORTFOLIO OF HUMOROUS AND SATIRICAL POETRY

**THE LESSON OF THE MOTH** by Don Marquis [pp. 703–4]
Archy the cockroach has a rough time understanding the philosophy of the moth, who would rather "be burned up with beauty" than to live sensibly for a long time. While Archy sticks to his belief that a longer life with less ecstasy is preferable, the lesson of the moth is not lost. The last stanza shows that Archy understands the deficiencies of his own attitude. The moth's description of human beings as "too civilized to enjoy themselves" indicates the lesson for readers of the poem.

## Possible Responses to *Questions for Discussion and Writing*
1. The moth's philosophy is that "it is better to be happy / for a moment / and to be burned up with beauty / than to live a long time / and be bored all the while." The cockroach goes for long life, even with half the happiness.
2. Even though Archy rejects the moth's point of view, he understands the pull of intense desire.
3. Though some students of various ages may have trouble understanding the moth's point of view, all of us understand at some level the wild and dangerous impulses versus the pleasures of safety in life.

## *Making Connections*
→ Compare the moth's philosophy (about death and time) with the lover's persuasive strategy in Andrew Marvell's "To His Coy Mistress."


**MARKS** by Linda Pastan [p. 705]
The speaker in this poem is clearly a woman, a housewife and mother, who has grown tired of being underappreciated by her family. Her husband does give her "an A for last night's supper," but the "incomplete" in ironing tells us that particular chore is unending, and she apparently can't keep up. Her husband's "B plus" for her performance in bed indicates that he finds room for improvement. Her son judges her "average" as a mother but thinks she could do better if she "put her mind to it." Her daughter's "pass," on a pass/fail basis, says essentially the same thing—that as a mother she's just getting by. Continuing the academic grading system (the "marks" of the title), she predicts they'll all be surprised when they learn she's "dropping out." The poem is in the vein of humorous light verse, but readers may be brought up short by the serious note in the last line.

## Possible Responses to *Questions for Discussion and Writing*
1. The speaker of the poem is like a student trying to do well in a class instead of in regular family life. The other members of the family look at her this way, too. They act as though she is a subordinate and gradable being, not a human being of her own estimation.

217

2. The title, "Marks," may be a bit outdated; now, "Grades" might be a better title. Other meanings—like "a spot or dirty area that spoils the appearance" or "a cut, hole, or other small sign of damage"—might also come into play.
3. The attitudes toward the speaker are reflected in her family's grading attitude toward her. She is not a full member of the family; in fact, she could flunk out! The last line takes care of that possibility, though.
4. Many students have been evaluated on an inappropriate grading system, such as the 0-to-10 grading system for women's attractiveness. Many students will want to discuss their evaluation on ineffable qualities.


## HOMAGE TO MY HIPS by Lucille Clifton [p. 706]

Clifton's piece depends on its unusual topic for praise, poetry, and power. Notice that throughout the description, the hips are depicted in images that connote freedom and self-determination. Considering that the poet is an African American woman, the images are no doubt purposeful, suggesting that her spirit has "never been enslaved" (line 8).

### Possible Responses to *Questions for Discussion and Writing*

1. The unexpected element is the object of the homage. Have your students look up *homage* in the dictionary. What are some typical targets of homage? The hips are an unusual choice, being an ordinary body part and often unwanted at a certain size. Thus, Clifton is celebrating something that is usually mundane or even ridiculed in our society.
2. There are a number of racist remarks and jokes about black women with large hips; however, within the black community, differing beauty aesthetics make large, strong bodies both positive for the woman and attractive to others. Clifton mirrors her community's rejection of normative beauty standards and turns the racist attitudes upside down in writing an homage instead.
3. In the last three lines Clifton also turns the power relationship between the sexes upside down, as she glories in the mysterious effects her hips can have over men.
4. Answers will vary, but you may need to start a discussion to capture students' imaginations. For example, being an intellectual or a nerd can be negative at certain ages, yet turn out to be a major advantage. Furthermore, some physical problems can work for, as well as against, people: for example, controlling diabetes or allergies can be important practice in self-regulation, a true strength.


## CINDERELLA'S DIARY by Ron Koertge [p. 707]

Like "homage to my hips," Koertge's poem also depends on a reversal from the expected. Fairy tales end happily ever after, we hear, but in "Cinderella's Diary" the enraptured Prince Charming fails to deliver. Cinderella is bored and, it appears, horny, in her new perfect life, which she describes as insufferably routine. She even misses the passion of having a vicious stepmother to escape from.

**Possible Responses to *Questions for Discussion and Writing***
1. Usually, people write in diaries about thoughts and feelings that they would not share in conversation with other people. Therefore, the title of the poem suggests that we are hearing Cinderella's private thoughts about her outwardly perfect life.
2. In the poem, Cinderella clearly wishes for a more earthy life; in particular, some hot, dirty sex! She is frustrated with Prince Charming's kisses on the forehead, and she fantasizes about the cute page who holds the door and the rough huntsmen outside her window. Notice that she is trapped indoors, like a beautiful bird in a cage. Even the harshness of her stepmother appeals to her in retrospect, while her mother-in-law's home is relentlessly artistic and genteel.
3. The writer seems sympathetic to Cinderella, locked into a sterile and superficial life. The writer emphasizes the passivity of Cinderella's fate and the boring aspects of waiting for her prince to take four hours to dress to meet the cheering throng, and so forth. The last lines, in which she admits she wishes she'd never seen the glass slipper, show the author's point of view on the situation.
4. This writing assignment may necessitate some classroom brainstorming to get students started. Students can name stories and films that have ridiculously happy endings and think about what might happen if the story went on into future years. You can be prepared with some titles of recent popular movies to start the discussion.

### Making Connections
→ Pairing this poem with Margaret Atwood's "Happy Endings" might produce interesting discussions about the contrasts in the authors' views of fairy tales.


### INTRODUCTION TO POETRY by Billy Collins [p. 708]
Why is "Introduction to Poetry" humorous? Perhaps it reverberates with many students' experience in a required literature course, where the secret meaning of a work seems to be something extricated by barbaric means and then inflicted upon bewildered students. The first five metaphors for approaching a poem are what a professor would wish from his or her students, but the sixth one, torture, is the one they perceive as potentially effective. Asking your students what their experience with Intro to Lit classes was like will help most of them understand the point of view.

### Possible Responses to *Questions for Discussion and Writing*
1. It's crucial to understand that "I" is the instructor of poetry, and "they" are the students in class. The title is a common name for a college course, and it also describes the experience of students who are forcibly introduced to poetry as a genre.
2. The five metaphors provided by the speaker evoke exploratory methods that are experimental and active: looking at it as a picture, listening to its sound, watching an animal navigate the piece as though it were water, illuminating the poem by turning

on a light switch, and even skimming over the surface. These methods are quite different from most people's classroom experiences with learning to appreciate poetry. Thus, the metaphor that describes the students' approach is one of torture, suggesting that the poem will only give up its real meaning through violent methods. Students will vary in describing their processes of understanding an unfamiliar poem; perhaps they can choose from one of the six metaphors in the poem and expand upon it.

3. The torture approach is humorous because it appears at odds with the goals of poetry, such as expressing emotions and providing enjoyment to the reader. It also is a bad approach because it suggests that each poem has one secret interpretation that it purposely attempts to hide from the reader, like a spy with a clandestine plot.

## EMILY DICKINSON'S TO-DO LIST by Andrea Carlisle [p. 709]

This poem is humorous mainly in the form it takes: a modern to-do list apparently written by a very old-fashioned narrator. You will definitely want your students to review the poems by Dickinson in this book in preparation for understanding Carlisle's poem. As a prereading exercise, discuss students' impressions of what types of people make to-do lists. What can you tell about a person from their to-do list?

### Possible Responses to *Questions for Discussion and Writing*

1. The connotations of a to-do list usually describe the person who makes one: organized, busy, efficient, widely committed, diversified, and so on. From Emily Dickinson's biography, it appears that she would not need a to-do list at all, since she lived such an apparently restricted and routine life.

2. All of the tasks on the to-do list are stereotypically feminine. Perhaps the serious point has to do with the recurrent theme of hiding—that is, hiding her true thoughts (expressed in poems) from the world. Women traditionally have been encouraged to keep their thoughts to themselves.

3. White dresses, narrow fellows in the grass, T. W. H., Lavinia, gardening, and hair in a bun are all references that students will identify with parts of E. D.'s life and poetry. Students may find several more allusions and references.

4. It should be fun to write a to-do poem that reveals something basic about one's life. For example, some students' lists could show that their lives revolve around school, while others' show that their focus is family life, social life, or sports.

### Video

→You can hear readings of fifteen Emily Dickinson poems at **www.youtube.com/course?list=EC7950B98DB6F76E24&feature=plcp**. Each poem is accompanied by a written commentary.

**A MARTIAN SENDS A POSTCARD HOME** by Craig Raine [pp. 710–11]

The joy of "A Martian Sends a Postcard Home" derives from slowly coming to understand what the Martian is describing from his own alien point of view. At first, most students will only grasp one or two of the images—it took three of us to figure them all out completely! The idea that culture and its artifacts are not natural but created by tacitly agreed-upon meanings within the culture is a difficult one, resembling a fish trying to describe water or a teenager explaining what all that texting is about.

## Possible Responses to *Questions for Discussion and Writing*

1. Things look different to Martians because they are totally unaware of the culture and context surrounding the thing they are observing. The poem shows that the Martians infer meanings and purposes to common items and actions: the inferences are interesting in both their inaccuracies and their occasional odd correctness. Students who have visited foreign countries may have had something like the Martian experience in trying to grasp the significance of alien customs and arrangements (for example, the way grocery stores are organized varies from country to country, and the etiquette of visiting other people's homes is quite different from culture to culture). Even when we change from one subculture to another within our own, like moving from our family home to college, or from a city neighborhood to a small town, we can feel like Martians for a while.

2. The images in the postcard can be translated in these ways:
   Caxtons are books: their wings are the pages, the markings are the printed words and pictures; they perch on the hand when the reader holds them open to read.
   The sky is personified as a human tired of holding up the mist machine.
   The rain is compared to a visual effect on television.
   A Model T is a car, with the scenery whizzing by compared to a film.
   Time is conflated with its measurement devices, wristwatches and clocks.
   The "haunted apparatus" is a telephone.
   Customary manners of dealing with human excretion are the topic of lines 25 to 30.
   Going to bed in the dark and dreaming are described last.

3. You can bring other riddles in to help your class with this assignment or ask students to bring them in. The key words "medieval riddle" will lead you to examples from the Internet. It may be easiest to start with a list of possible answers to riddles and then work out the riddles backward from there.

## A WAITRESS'S INSTRUCTIONS ON TIPPING by Jan Beatty [p. 712]

Point of view is the key to this poem's charm and effectiveness. Many times, the speaker of a traditional poem is invisible: the character of the writer is not right on the surface. If identifiable, the speaker is often an intellectual, a lover, an artist, or a crazed person. We rarely see an everyday person like a waitress narrating a poem about the everyday hassles of an ordinary workplace. It can only be beneficial for students to consider the thoughts going on within workers who too often seem invisible nonpersons.

## Possible Responses to *Questions for Discussion and Writing*

1.  The speaker is an experienced waitress. She is tired and disgusted with most customers, as evidenced by such phrases as "don't wait around for gratitude" and "Better yet, do it yourself," as well as many more examples your students can point out. The language is informal but not slangy or ungrammatical, with extremely short sentences (imitating lists of official rules).

2.  The poem teaches the customer several things about the waitress and customer relationship. These will differ according to the students' degrees of experience in either role. For example, we didn't know that we should leave a $5 bill if just having coffee or pull out a $10 bill if the wine costs $50. We believe that Beatty must have been a waitress at one time because of the rich detail in the poem: for instance, the exact quotations from jerky tippers in lines 26–29 come from the voice of experience.

3.  The last two lines, "Don't say, *I'll make it worth your while.* / If you're miserable, there's not enough money in the world," tell us that the waitress hates her job. Even the biggest tip will not make the work worth her while. These lines are important because they stress the fact that we are hearing from an extremely dissatisfied worker. Other waitresses might have similar experiences but find them balanced out by the good points of the job or the positive aspects of customer contact.

4.  Most students have held crummy jobs and will be more than happy to make a list of rules for their customers, clients, or bosses. You might start with a brainstorming session about the worst jobs everyone has ever had. Some students may have never had paid jobs, and so they will have to write from a student's point of view to other students or to teachers. You can also discuss the different ways that Beatty develops her rules—for example, giving "nevers" and "don'ts," providing exact amounts of money, describing specific situations ("If I call a taxi for you"), and giving direct quotations. Students can imitate these methods of development.


### AFRAID SO by Jeanne Marie Beaumont [pp. 713–14]

Part of what we find funny about this poem, even outside of the familiar situations it evokes, is that rarely does anyone really answer the questions with the true answer, "Afraid so," especially in the more dire situations. Just think of what a doctor or nurse says in response to your question, "Is this going to hurt?" You'd be surprised to hear "Afraid so," instead of "You'll feel a little pinch," or "There will be some temporary discomfort." A straightforward answer to a distressing question is unusual in our culture. You might ask your students to give some real-life examples of answers to Beaumont's questions, such as "Your luggage will now go through Caracas instead of Detroit but should arrive in Houston within just a few days."

**Possible Responses to *Questions for Discussion and Writing***

1.  The answer to all of the questions is the title, "Afraid so." Most readers get the joke by question 5 or so. However, we believe that the humor stands up through the whole poem, because the questions keep bringing up familiar (but maybe forgotten) situations of life.
2.  If we look only at the first and last lines, we might decide that the questions build up from the least to the most serious in consequences. However, this organization doesn't seem to hold up because number 5 is the very serious, "Could you lose your job?" while the next-to-last question is "Are we lost?" which could be of varying levels of seriousness, depending on the situation. It could be that Beaumont listed the questions in order to go back and forth between obviously severe consequences and not-so-severe ones, the way real life works. It would be interesting to have each student rearrange the questions from the least to most serious and then compare their orders to see how much agreement there is.
3.  The poem requested in this assignment will probably be a series of questions, like Beaumont's. However, if you give your students latitude to make the questions any length they want, you could get more interesting variety. You might want to list a few other title answers, other than "Probably Not" and "You Bet," in a class exercise. Current slang (like "whatever") might provide some humorous possibilities.

**RECONSIDERING THE SEVEN** by Peter Pereira [pp. 714–15]
Like the poems "homage to my hips" and "Cinderella's Diary," this piece depends on a reversal of expectations. Rethinking the advantages of the seven deadly sins, and considering the peskiness of their opposites (such as people who can't sit quietly through a sunset), Pereira makes us smile in recognition that maybe perfection is not so ideal after all.

**Possible Responses to *Questions for Discussion and Writing***

1.  The seven deadly sins are pride, lust, envy, greed, gluttony, sloth, and wrath. These are faults that supposedly seriously impede spiritual development. Our current list comes from the thirteenth-century Catholic priest St. Thomas Aquinas, though lists of fatal sins originated as early as with the fourth-century Greek theologians. Efforts to make ideas of the worst possible behavior succinct and clear to everyone have probably always been around.
2.  The speaker reconsiders the seven deadly sins in terms of their usefulness and in terms of their opposites, which are not always desirable either (like false modesty and restlessness). The reconsideration is funny because it takes a lighthearted approach to such a serious subject. Students will vary in whether they found the poem persuasive or funny or both, and you might explore the reasons for individual differences in people's responses.
3.  The assignment is to take a different negative and present its positive side in a poem

or prose poem (paragraph). You may want to start with a class discussion of some appropriate negatives, such as having a messy desk, skipping class, dressing or acting too sexy, being overweight, or other forms of violating society's rules and expectations. What could be the positive sides of these violations?

### Making Connections [p. 715]

1. This exercise on tone helps students understand the concept by assigning emotion words to all of the ten poems in the portfolio. Each student does so individually; subsequently, comparing their choices with a group of three or four others helps them see where readers hear the same tone and where individual readers hear something idiosyncratic.

2. All ten of the poems in this portfolio can be seen as some kind of puzzle—even the relationship of the title to the questions in "Afraid So" and the nature of the narrator in "A Waitress's Instructions on Tipping" must be unraveled like a puzzle. So your students can't really go wrong here. For the two poems they choose from the Anthology of Poetry, the possibilities are myriad: you might ask them to look for poems that gave them an "aha!" moment, when they grasped something basic to the meaning.

# Selected Audio and Video Resources for Teaching Poetry

The following list of audio-visual resources is not meant to be exhaustive. There are numerous videos and recordings that can be used to supplement and stimulate the study of poetry. Most of the distributors listed here will send catalogs that give details of their holdings. (For addresses and telephone numbers, see the Directory of Audio and Video Distributors found at the back of this manual.)

**W. H. Auden**
Recording: 1 cassette
Read by the poet
Available from Spoken Arts

**W. H. Auden Reading**
Recording: 1 cassette
Available from Caedmon/HarperAudio

**The Poetry of William Blake**
Recording: 1 cassette
Available from Caedmon/HarperAudio

**William Blake: Something About Poetry**
Recording: 1 cassette, 22 min., 1969
Available from Audio-Forum

**Gwendolyn Brooks**
Video: 30 min., 1966
Brooks talks about her life and poetry.
Available from Indiana University Center for
    Media and Teaching Resources

**Gwendolyn Brooks**
Recording: 1 cassette, 29 min., 1989
Available from New Letters on Air

**Robert Browning: My Last Duchess and Other Poems**
Recording: 1 cassette
Available from Caedmon/HarperAudio

**Treasury of George Gordon, Lord Byron**
Recording: 1 cassette
Available from Spoken Arts

**The Poetry of Countee Cullen**
Recording: 1 cassette
Available from Caedmon/HarperAudio

**E. E. Cummings: The Making of a Poet**
Video: 24 min., 1978
Available from Films for the Humanities & Sciences

**Poems of E. E. Cummings**
Recording: 1 cassette, 60 min., 1981
Available from Summer Stream

**Emily Dickinson: The Belle of Amherst**
Video: 90 min., color, 1976
With Julie Harris.
Available from The Video Catalog

**Emily Dickinson**
Recording: 1 cassette
Available from Recorded Books

**An Evening with Emily Dickinson**
Video: 60 min., 2 videos: Claire Bloom in
"The World of Emily Dickinson" and Julie Harris in
"A Certain Slant of Light."
Available from PBS Home Video

**Poems by Emily Dickinson**
Recording: 2 cassettes, 236 min., 1986
Available from Audio Book Contractors

**Dickinson and Whitman: Ebb and Flow**
Recording: 2 cassettes
Available from Audio Editions

**Treasury of John Donne**
Recording: 1 cassette
Available from Spoken Arts

**Rita Dove**
Recording: 1 cassette, 29 min.
Available from New Letters on Air

**Poet Laureate Rita Dove**
Video: 60 min., color
Available from Films for the Humanities & Sciences

**Paul Laurence Dunbar**
Video: 22 min., color, 1973
Available from Pyramid Film and Video

**T. S. Eliot: Selected Poems**
Recording: Read by the poet. 49 min., 1971
Available from Caedmon/HarperAudio

**Robert Frost: A First Acquaintance**
Video: 16 min., color, 1974
Examines Frost's life through his poems.
Available from Films for the Humanities & Sciences

**Robert Frost Reads**
Recording: 1 cassette, 55 min., 1965
Available from Audio-Forum

**Nikki Giovanni**
Recording: 1 cassette, 1988
Available from New Letters on Air

**The Poetry of Donald Hall**
Recording: 1 cassette, 26 min., 1964
Available from Audio-Forum

**Poetic Voices of Thomas Hardy**
Video: 20 min., color
Available from Films for the Humanities & Sciences

**The Poetry of Gerard Manley Hopkins**
Recording: 1 cassette
Available from Caedmon/HarperAudio

**A. E. Housman: A Shropshire Lad and Other Poetry**
Recording: 1 cassette
Available from Caedmon/HarperAudio

**The Poetry of Randall Jarrell**
Recording: 1 cassette, 67 min., 1963
Available from Audio-Forum

**John Keats: Odes**
Recording: 1 cassette
Available from Audio-Forum

**Treasury of John Keats**
Recording: 1 cassette
Available from Spoken Arts

**Yusef Komunyakaa**
Video: 60 min., 1997
Pulitzer Prize winner talks with author Tori Derricotte
and reads from his works.
Available from Facets Multi-Media: www.facets.org

**Maxine Kumin: Progress Report**
Recording: 1 cassette, 42 min., 1976
Available from Watershed Tapes

**Audre Lord: Shorelines**
Recording: 1 cassette, 53 min., 1985
Available from Watershed Tapes

**Christopher Marlowe: Elizabethan Love Poems**
Recording: 1 cassette, 50 min.
Available from Spoken Arts

**Ralph Richardson Reads Andrew Marvell**
Recording: 1 cassette
Available from Audio-Forum

**Edna St. Vincent Millay: Renascence**
Video: 60 min., color
Directed by Vanessa Barth.
Available from Films for the Humanities & Sciences

**Poems of Edna St. Vincent Millay**
Recording: 1 cassette, 60 min., 1981
Available from Summer Stream

**I Am Pablo Neruda**
Video: 28 min., b&w
Available from Films for the Humanities & Sciences

**Sharon Olds: Coming Back to Life**
Recording: 1 cassette, 60 min.
Available from Audio-Forum

**Wilfred Owen: The Pity of War**
Video: 58 min., color, 1987
Available from Films for the Humanities & Sciences

**Linda Pastan: Mosaic**
Recording: 1 cassette, 51 min., 1988
Available from Watershed Tapes

**Marge Piercy: At the Core**
Recording: 1 cassette, 58 min., 1976
Available from Watershed Tapes

**Sylvia Plath**
Video: 4 programs (30 min. each), color, 1974
Examination of the poet and her work.
Available from New York State Education
    Department

**Sylvia Plath Reads**
Recording: 1 cassette, 60 min., 1987
Available from Caedmon/HarperAudio

**The Poetry of Adrienne Rich**
Recording: 1 cassette, 36 min., 1968
Available from Audio-Forum

**Theodore Roethke**
Recording: 48 min., 1972
Available from Caedmon/HarperAudio

**Anne Sexton Reads Her Poetry**
Recording: 1 cassette
Available from Caedmon/HarperAudio

**Shakespeare's Sonnets**
Video: 150 min., color, 1984
In-depth look at 15 sonnets, with readings.
Available from Films for the Humanities & Sciences

**The Sonnets of Shakespeare**
Recording: 2 cassettes
Read by John Gielgud.
Available from Audio Editions

**Treasury of Percy Bysshe Shelley**
Recording: 1 cassette
Available from Spoken Arts

**William Stafford: Troubleshooting**
Recording: 1 cassette, 50 min., 1984
Available from Watershed Tapes

**Wallace Stevens Reads**
Recording: 1 cassette, 60 min., 1987
Available from Caedmon/HarperAudio

**Dylan Thomas: A Portrait**
Video: 26 min., color
Available from Films for the Humanities & Sciences

**Dylan Thomas Reading His Poetry**
Recording: 2 cassettes
Available from Caedmon/HarperAudio

**The Poetry of John Updike**
Recording: 1 cassette, 47 min., 1967
Available from Audio-Forum

**Walt Whitman: The Living Tradition**
Video: 20 min., color, 1983
Allen Ginsberg reads Whitman.
Available from Centre Productions

**Walt Whitman**
Recording: 1 cassette
Read by Alexander Scourby.
Available from Filmic Archives

**William Carlos Williams Reads His Poetry**
Recording: 1 cassette
Available from Caedmon/HarperAudio

**Treasury of William Wordsworth**
Recording: 1 cassette
Available from Spoken Arts

**The Poetry of William Butler Yeats**
Recording: 1 cassette
Available from Caedmon/HarperAudio

## GENERAL COLLECTIONS

**Caedmon Treasury of Modern Poets Reading Their Own Poetry**
Recording: 2 cassettes, 95 min.
Available from Caedmon/HarperAudio

**English Romantic Poetry: Coleridge, Shelley, Byron, Wordsworth**
Recording: 3 cassettes
Available from Recorded Books

**The Harlem Renaissance and Beyond**
Video: 31 min., 1989
Available from Insight Media

**Medieval and Elizabethan Poetry**
Video: 28 min., color, 1989
Available from Films for the Humanities & Sciences

**Moyers: The Power of the Word**
Video: 6 programs (60 min. each), color, 1989
Bill Moyers talks with modern poets.
Available from PBS

**Victorian Poetry**
Recording: 3 cassettes
Available from Caedmon/HarperAudio

**Voices and Vision**
Video: 13 programs (60 min. each), color, 1988
Available from Annenberg Media

**With a Feminine Touch**
Video: 45 min., color, 1990
Readings by Valerie Harper and Claire Bloom of poetry by women.
Available from Monterey Home Video

# PART IV  WRITING ABOUT DRAMA

## Chapter 16  How Do I Read a Play? [pp. 718–22]

Our advice in this chapter focuses on reading drama. A useful activity might be to have your students read a scene to themselves, using the suggestions in this chapter, and then play a recording or video of professional actors doing the same scene. Discuss these questions:

> Was the actor's performance similar to your interpretation?
> Were there any readings that surprised you?
> Did the performance change any of your ideas about the scene?

If you show a video, you might also ask students to consider what effect the sets, lighting, costumes, gestures, and movements had on their understanding and response to the scene, reminding them to imagine these elements as they read the plays that are assigned.

### *Activities for Creative and Critical Thinking*

The following projects and writing assignments will help to engage your students in their study of drama.

- How would you stage a television or film production of any play in this book? Items to think about are set design, location, lighting, music, costumes, camera shots, special effects, changes in the script, casting choices.
- Write the detailed stage directions for a particular scene in a play of your choice. Describe the characters' moves and decide what the characters will do with any props or set features. Explain your decisions.
- Put a character "on trial" for actions that he or she took in the play. Some obvious choices would be Antigone, Othello, Tom Wingfield, Walter Younger, or the women in *Trifles*.
- Write a letter to a character from a play, offering advice or asking questions about the person's motives and behavior.
- Write a prose account of a minor character's thoughts about the play. For example, what might the Gentleman Caller think about the Wingfield family and his dinner with them?
- Take a poem or short story and transform it into a dramatic script.
- Write a scene that continues, updates, or provides an alternative to the action from a play. For instance, you might write about what happens when Mrs. Hale and Mrs. Peters visit Minnie Wright in jail (in *Trifles*) or what happens to Laura and Amanda after Tom leaves.
- Create the "background story" for one of the characters in a play. What crucial events have occurred in this character's life before the play opens?

# Chapter 17   Writing About Dramatic Structure [pp. 723–64]

Although dramatic structure is in general quite similar to the structure of traditional short stories and novels, the terminology for describing it is somewhat more technical. Many instructors use these same terms in discussing structure in any literary work. Certainly by now your students will be familiar with most of these concepts.

ANTIGONE by Sophocles [pp. 725–53]

As indicated in the introduction to the play in the text, *Antigone* is the third and last play in the Oedipus cycle. Sophocles could have counted on his audience to know something of the legend of Oedipus; this knowledge allows readers and viewers to recognize and appreciate the series of dramatic ironies and foreshadowings contained in the play. You may want to supplement the brief summary of the Oedipus legend on p. 725 in the text with this longer version:

In Greek mythology, Oedipus was the son of Laius and Jocasta, king and queen of Thebes. Laius was warned by an oracle that he would be killed by his own son. Determined to avert his fate, he bound together the feet of his newborn child and left him to die on a lonely mountain. The infant was rescued by a shepherd, however, and given to Polybus, king of Corinth, who named the child Oedipus ("Swollen-foot") and raised him as his own son. The boy did not know that he was adopted, and when an oracle proclaimed that he would kill his father, he left Corinth. In the course of his wanderings he met and killed Laius, believing that the king and his followers were a band of robbers; and thus he unwittingly fulfilled the prophecy.

Lonely and homeless, Oedipus arrived at Thebes, which was beset by a dreadful monster called the Sphinx. The frightful creature frequented the roads to the city, killing and devouring all travelers who could not answer the riddle that she put to them. When Oedipus successfully solved her riddle, the Sphinx killed herself. Believing that King Laius had been slain by unknown robbers, and grateful to Oedipus for ridding them of the Sphinx, the Thebans rewarded Oedipus by making him their king and giving him Queen Jocasta as his wife. For many years the couple lived in happiness, not knowing that they were really mother and son.

Then a terrible plague descended on the land, and the oracle proclaimed that Laius's murderer must be punished. Oedipus soon discovered that he had unknowingly killed his father. In grief and despair at her incestuous life, Jocasta killed herself, and when Oedipus realized that she was dead and that their children were accursed, he put out his eyes and resigned the throne. He lived in Thebes for several years, but was finally banished. Accompanied by his daughter Antigone, he wandered for many years. He finally arrived at Colonus, a shrine near Athens sacred to the powerful goddesses called the Eumenides. At this shrine for supplicants Oedipus died, after the god Apollo had promised him that the place of his death would remain sacred and would bring great benefit to the city of Athens, which had given shelter to the wanderer.

Students need to see that the main conflict in the play is not just a political battle; it's also part of the ongoing struggle between members of the cursed family of Oedipus. At the end of *Oedipus the King*, Oedipus blinds himself and goes into exile, being guided in his wanderings by his faithful daughter Antigone. After their father dies in exile, Antigone and Ismene are returned to Thebes, where they are taken in by their uncle Creon. Oedipus's sons, Polyneices and Eteocles, share the throne of Thebes for a short time, under the guidance of Creon, their mother's brother. But the two brothers soon tire of sharing, and Creon supports Eteocles for king. Polyneices angrily retaliates by joining six other leaders (including Megareus, one of Creon's sons) in an attack on Thebes. This attempt to overthrow the Theban government fails, but it results in the deaths of both Eteocles and Polyneices. Once we understand that Polyneices is a traitor to Thebes, we can see the merit in Creon's decree to deny him glory by leaving his body unburied. But Polyneices is also a Theban, was once a ruler, and is the son of the former king. He is also survived by two sisters, Antigone and Ismene, who are torn between loyalty to Thebes and loyalty to their brother, despite his treason.

It's important to note that Creon was the one who exiled Oedipus from Thebes; he also backed Eteocles for king, providing the spark that ignited Polyneices's rebellion. Moreover, Creon has become king himself, now that the sons of Oedipus are dead. In other words, Creon has a lot of personal investment in preventing any further rebellion that might arise from honoring Polyneices. It's also important to know that the family obligation to bury the dead and to cry out in mourning was one of the few public roles allowed to women. The conflict in the play, then, can also be seen as a conflict between men and women—between the government's laws (an exclusively male domain) and the tradition of honoring the death of a loved family member (an activity important to women). Antigone takes on male prerogatives when she takes public action, speaks boldly to the king, and argues openly for political change. That is why Creon accuses her of *hubris* and sees her defiance as a challenge to his right to rule. In the end, however, it is Antigone's love that distinguishes her from Creon. He loses the family he rejected, the state he ruled over briefly, and the favor of the gods. Antigone, on the other hand, loses her life, but her stand turns out best for her family, for the gods (whom she honors), and for the state that she had opposed.

## Additional Questions for Discussion and Writing

1. What ideas does the play *Antigone* express about duty and obedience? In what ways do these ideas conform or fail to conform to your own concepts of duty and obedience?
2. The Chorus expresses the values of the community. Is Antigone a danger to this community? How far do you believe a community should go to protect its values?
3. Both Creon and Antigone defend rights that they believe are sacred. What rights are in conflict? Is there any room for compromise?
4. Do you sympathize with Antigone or with Creon? What characteristics of each do you find admirable? Do you ever lose patience with either of them? Explain.

5. Is there any justification for Antigone's cold refusal to allow Ismene to share her martyrdom? Explain. Is Ismene entirely without courage?
6. Creon says at the end, "The guilt is mine." Do you agree?
7. What is your judgment of Antigone as the tragic heroine? One critic has questioned her "total indifference to the rights of the city" and claims that no one in the play really praises her, except her fiancé. She herself says that if the gods allowed her to suffer death for her stand then she would know she was wrong. Was she wrong?
8. Can *Antigone* be read as a justification for civil disobedience? Explain.

### Analyzing Dramatic Structure [p. 758]
1. Individual responses to this question will vary.
2. The Prologue introduces the major conflict of the play and reveals this background information:
   - The sisters are living under a curse (placed on their family because of their father's involuntary incest, we later learn).
   - Antigone and Ismene have lost two brothers who killed each other in a recent battle during which the invaders, led by Polyneices, were repelled.
   - One of these brothers was buried with military honors, but the other (who led the invaders) was left to lie in the field where he died.
   - Creon, uncle to these two sisters and their dead brothers, is now the king.
   - Creon has decreed that Polyneices must not be buried, under penalty of death to anyone who tries.
   - The girls' father, Oedipus, put out his eyes when he learned that he had unknowingly married his own mother.
   - The girls' mother, Jocasta, hanged herself when she learned that she had unwittingly married her own son.
3. From the Chorus and the Choragos we learn the following:
   - Thebes won the battle, repulsing at dawn the invaders who were roused to fight by Polynices.
   - God favored the Theban warriors by sending a thunderclap when the first invading soldier scaled the wall.
   - Again we are told that the brothers both died in combat.
4. The sentry serves to let the audience know that someone has attempted to bury Polyneices, in defiance of Creon's law. This character also serves to emphasize the absolute power of the king by showing the fear he inspires in his followers. Clearly the sentry and his fellow soldiers do not expect Creon to be just or fair. They know that he has a terrible temper and mistrusts everyone.
5. The major conflict involves the clash between duty to one's beliefs or conscience (Antigone's determination to bury her brother) and one's duty to authority and to the state (Creon's decree that Polyneices be denied burial).
6. Antigone (whose name is the title of the play) is the protagonist. Our sympathies are always with her. Creon is the antagonist, causing the conflict by his unjust ruling. Although Antigone can accurately be called a heroine (she gives her life for what she

believes to be right and holy), Creon is not precisely a villain because his intentions are not evil. Clearly misguided by pride and ambition to be a strong ruler, he does relent and try to save Antigone once he sees his wrongdoing.

7. Identifying the climax in this play is somewhat difficult because the plot takes several turns *after* the climax. But press your students to decide at what point the remainder of the action is predetermined (i.e., when clearly the die is cast). This turning point occurs when Creon declares that Antigone must die for not obeying his law. This act signals the turning point because the remaining actions result from this injustice.

   Some might reasonably argue that the climax occurs when Creon rejects the plea of Teiresias to spare Antigone and Tiresias then pronounces his curse. But since we do not know exactly when Antigone kills herself, Creon might have been too late even at this point to forestall the fateful chain of events leading to Antigone's death and his own downfall.

8. The climax does come unusually early in this play, but Sophocles maintains suspense by having Teiresias reason with Creon. The audience keeps hoping that Creon will relent in time to avoid the tragedy. Then the series of reported deaths surprises the audience—as well as Creon, who is shattered by losing his son and his wife in rapid succession.

9. The catastrophe in the extended denouement of this play begins with the report of Antigone's suicide, followed by Haimon's suicide, followed by Eurydice's suicide, the news of which prompts Creon's utter collapse. The outcome becomes inevitable once Creon has caused Antigone's death, thus depriving his son of his bride. Haimon's death causes Eurydice's suicide since she is thus deprived by her husband's willfulness of her last living son.

10. Your students might state the play's theme as "Pride goeth before a fall." Certainly, the major theme of this and many other Greek dramas warns against *hubris*, overweening pride, a character flaw which makes human beings think they know better than the gods. Also important in *Antigone* is the implication that one must stand up for one's beliefs and resist unjust laws. Antigone's refusal to allow Ismene to share her punishment underscores this idea, suggesting that because Ismene lacked the courage to stand up for her convictions, she should not be allowed to share Antigone's martyrdom.

11. Ismene's willing conformity provides a sharp contrast with Antigone's brave defense of what she considers right and just. Ismene simply accepts that the law was "made for the public good."

    Haimon serves as a foil for his father, Creon. The young man boldly stands up to his father and voices reason in contrast to Creon's inflexible, authoritarian stance. His suicide upon finding his beloved Antigone dead suggests fidelity, tenderness, sensitivity—traits entirely lacking in his father until Haimon's death.

12. Eurydice seems to be in the play primarily to show that, as Tiresias prophesied, everyone blames Creon for the deaths of the young people. Her suicide leaves Creon alone, and her dying curse places the guilt squarely on his head as the murderer of her sons.

### Avoiding Unclear Language [pp. 757–59]

Have students look through several essays they've written recently—for any of their classes—and ask them to identify any examples of Engfish, jargon, and abstractions they used. How would they revise these usages? Bring in further examples of pretentious language and jargon from a variety of sources (textbooks, journal articles, committee reports, and the like) and discuss ways to improve the clarity and fluency of the language. Also make sure that unclear language is one of the elements that students look for in peer reviewing. The three points discussed in this section—Engfish, jargon, and abstract words—should give peer reviewers something definite and productive to focus on.

### Sample Student Paper [pp. 759–63]

Since this student paper employs an approach to *Antigone* that your students might not have considered, you may want to let them respond to the "Questions for Discussion" (p. 764) after you have gone over with them in class the standard questions concerning the rhetorical components of the essay: Is the introduction effective? Is the thesis clearly stated? Are the paragraphs adequately developed? Are the sentences clear? Is the conclusion emphatic? Is the entire paper unified? Is the argument convincing? This last question should spark disagreement, which the discussion questions will allow you to explore.

### Questions for Discussion [p. 764]

1. Since the writer focuses on the gender issue as her thesis, one could not say that she overemphasizes it. She acknowledges in her second sentence that she is not going to deal with "the more obvious conflict between the state and the individual." She deliberately chooses to discuss an aspect of the play that many readers might overlook.

2. Because the student was working within a 700-word limit for her essay, she was not able to include all of the evidence that might be used to support her thesis. During the argument between Creon and Haimon, Creon denigrates females: "So you are right / Not to lose your head over this woman. / Your pleasure with her would soon grow cold, Haimon, / And then you'd have a hellcat in bed and elsewhere" (III.21-24). The implication of his speech is that Haimon is interested only sexually in Antigone, and that once his ardor cools, she will make him miserable with her aggressiveness. Creon's contempt for women as mere sexual objects is first voiced crudely: when Ismene expresses dismay that the king would condemn to death his own son's bride and Creon retorts, "there are other fields for him to plow" (642). Creon also tries to disparage Haimon's arguments by saying to the Chorus, "This boy, it seems, has sold out to a woman" (III.113), and calling him a "girlstruck fool."

234

If the student had been given a less restrictive word limit, she might have discussed Eurydice as providing yet another example of the conflict between male and female. Although we know little about the marital relationship between Creon and Eurydice, we can be certain that she blames her husband for the deaths of her sons and curses him as their murderer. (Women, traditionally, have been opposed to war. Men make war, in which women's sons are killed.)

3.  Antigone's purpose is more noble than mere sexual rivalry, but then, so is Creon's, supposedly. Although Antigone resents Creon, she clearly resents his power as a male. And in her final speech she places the blame for her death on men: "You will remember / What things I suffer, and at what men's hands" (IV.82-83).

4.  The student who wrote the essay naturally found the best evidence for her thesis ("The antagonist, Creon, is fighting to retain control over Antigone, not only as king over subject but also as man over woman") by analyzing the character of Creon. His misogynistic attitude forms the basis for her argument, since no other characters in the play appear openly antifemale. Her conclusion—that his fear of being beaten by a woman causes his rash action—is tied only by implication to his pride: "Creon's pride has made him blind to his mistake" (last sentence, next-to-last paragraph of the essay). She might well have stated this connection outright, thus emphasizing that her reading of the play supports and illuminates the usual interpretation. She argues that pride causes Creon's fall: her paper attempts to explain why he was so touchy, stubborn, and insecure in his pridefulness.

As a matter of background information, you might want your students to know that during the period in Greek history before this play was written, the state was governed by a matriarchy. Once women were ousted from control, it became expedient to keep them from regaining power. Scholars believe that the political threat that women perhaps posed underlies Sophocles' presentation of Creon as a tyrant unjustly persecuting an assertive woman of noble blood who shows qualities of leadership. Antigone's insistence that the citizens are on her side suggests that she already has followers.

## Making Connections

→ Compare Antigone to Mama Younger in *Raisin in the Sun* and the women in *Trifles*. How do these women deal with the laws and conventions of the male-dominated societies in which they live?

## Videos

→ *Antigone*. 88 minutes, b&w, 1962. With Irene Papas. In Greek with subtitles. Available from Insight Media and Filmic Archives.

→ *Antigone*. 95 minutes, color, 1991. With Carrie O'Brien and Chris Bearne; directed by Arlena Nys. Available from Insight Media.

→ *Antigone*. 120 minutes, color, 1988. Third part of the BBC production of the Theban Plays. With Juliet Stevenson, John Shrapnel, and John Gielgud. Adapted and translated by Don Taylor. Available from Films for the Humanities & Sciences.

# Chapter 18   Writing About Character [pp. 765–812]

Analyzing characters provides a convenient and rewarding way of getting at the intent of a play. Students enjoy talking about the characters and speculating on their motives. For further exploration of character, you will find at the end of this chapter a casebook including selections from professional critics offering diverse interpretations of Amanda's character.

## What Is the Modern Hero? [pp. 765–66]

Discussion of both *hero* and *tragedy* (or *tragic*) will reveal rather loose and broad-ranging definitions of these terms. It might help to ask students to distinguish between *heroic* and *courageous* or *bold* (Are heroes ever *foolhardy*?) and between *tragic* and *sad* (or even *pathetic*). Some discussion of the limits and problems with abstract value words may also be necessary. Asking students to write out definitions of abstract terms—with examples or illustrations—and then to compare answers can be an enlightening, if sometimes perplexing, activity. Another useful prereading activity for this chapter is to ask students to name a modern-day hero and defend or explain their choice.

Miller's definition of tragedy—"being torn away from our chosen image of what and who we are"—seems overly broad, one that can be applied to almost anybody. If Miller's concept is applied to the characters in *The Glass Menagerie*, it's possible to see most of them as displaced and at odds with the cosmos (or society). How useful, then, is this definition? Some readers may pity Laura but will not say that she is tragic. Even Amanda's single-minded determination, which is akin to Antigone's in some ways, seems, to some, more foolish and misguided than heroic or tragic. Perhaps there are no modern heroes.

## Analyzing the Characters [p. 808]

1. Some deceptions include Laura's dropping out of business school and pretending to continue; Amanda's pretense or hope that Laura is attractive and will have lots of gentleman callers; Tom's failure to pay the light bill and his keeping his plans to himself; Amanda's insincere sympathy for the "Christian martyrs" she solicits for magazine subscriptions; Jim's failure to tell anyone about his engagement until after he's built up some false hopes; Amanda's sentimental reminiscences about her past and her unconfirmed claims about her children's extraordinary abilities; Tom's stories about where he goes at night; Amanda's refusal to say Laura is crippled; Jim's facile trust in night school courses as the road to success.
2. The scene could be played to bring out Tom's exasperation and discontent, Amanda's dominance and loquacity, and Laura's deference and gentle compliance.
3. Tom does not find fulfillment or satisfaction in his job. He yearns for adventure that ordinary life simply can't provide (as Amanda points out to him, people find adventure in their careers or "they do without it!"). Thus, he seems to fit Miller's

concept by being torn away from his instinctual desires and forced to seek his adventure in alcohol and mindless escapism. Statements that imply displacement or indignity might include these:

- Laura: And everybody was seated before I came in. I had to walk in front of all those people. My seat was in the back row. I had to go clumping all the way up the aisle with everyone watching! (Sc. VII)
- Jim: You think of yourself as having the only problems, as being the only one who is disappointed. But just look around you and you will see lots of people as disappointed as you are. For instance, I hoped when I was going to high school that I would be further along at this time, six years later, than I am now. (Sc. VII)
- Tom: I'm starting to boil inside. I know I seem dreamy, but inside—well, I'm boiling!— Whenever I pick up a shoe, I shudder a little thinking how short life is and what I am doing! (Sc. VI)
- Amanda: That innocent look of your father's had everyone fooled! He *smiled*—the world was *enchanted*! No girl can do worse than put herself at the mercy of a handsome appearance! (Sc. V)

4. Antigone's heroism is different because she is sure of her destiny—her role in society. She pursues her obligation regardless of the consequences. She battles a hostile society on her own terms.

5. Tom probably feels guilty that he left Laura to live with their overbearing mother, especially since Laura always treated Tom with understanding and affection. Throughout the play, Tom seems to dismiss Laura and her problems, taking a "what can we do?" approach and focusing more on his own needs and desires. It may be that with the separation he has come to realize that he loves his sister and should have paid more attention to her.

6. Choices will vary, but it seems easiest to pick Tom because he finally does something to alter his life, to fight his feelings of displacement and indignity. He is also the narrator, so we have a more complete sense of his motives and development. We really don't know what happens to Laura, Amanda, and Jim—not in the same way we do with Tom.

## Ideas for Writing [pp. 809–10]

Use the first idea for responsive writing to get students to review the play and as prewriting for a critical analysis. Use the questions in the ideas for critical writing as the basis for small-group discussions.

## Exercise on Providing Quotations [p. 812]

Quotations to support generalizations:

1. Amanda is not deeply and completely self-deceived:
   - "My devotion has made me a witch and so I make myself hateful to my children!" (Sc. IV)
   - "I wasn't prepared for what the future brought me." (Sc. VI)

- "Things have a way of turning out so badly. . . . Don't think about us, a mother deserted, an unmarried sister who's crippled and has no job!" (Sc. VII)
2. Human sexuality disturbs Amanda:
   - "I took that horrible novel back to the library—yes! That hideous book by that insane Mr. Lawrence. I cannot control the output of diseased minds or people who cater to them—BUT I WON'T ALLOW SUCH FILTH BROUGHT INTO MY HOUSE!" (Sc. III)
   - "Instinct is something that people have got away from! It belongs to animals! Christian adults don't want it!" (Sc. IV)
3. Characters in the play take both realistic and unrealistic action toward their goals:
   - Amanda takes some very real steps to prepare for the Gentleman Caller: "We can't have a gentleman caller in a pig-sty. All my wedding silver has to be polished, the monogrammed table linen ought to be laundered! The windows have to be washed and fresh curtains put up. . . ." (Sc. V). But she also pins a lot of her hopes on wishes and dreams: "Laura, come here and make a wish on the moon! . . . A little silver slipper of a moon. Look over your left shoulder, Laura, and make a wish!" (Sc. V)
   - Jim has some good ideas about the value of self-confidence, but he also believes that a night school course in public speaking "fits you for executive positions!"
4. Both times glass is broken in the play the forces of masculinity and sexuality are involved:
   - Tom has just presented himself as a gambling, boozing rake. Then he tries unsuccessfully to fling his coat on and storm out: "With an outraged groan [Tom] tears the coat off again, splitting the shoulder of it, and hurls it across the room. It strikes against the shelf of Laura's glass collection, there is a tinkle of shattering glass. Laura cries out as if wounded." (stage direction, Sc. III)
   - Jim takes Laura in his arms, telling her to relax as they dance. When she does begin to relax and enjoy it:
   "[Jim] moves her about the room in a clumsy waltz. . . . They suddenly bump into the table. Jim stops." (stage direction, Sc. VII)
5. Tom Wingfield may live as much in his imagination as Amanda or Laura do in theirs:
   - "People go to the *movies* instead of moving! Hollywood characters are supposed to have all the adventures for everybody in America, while everybody in America sits in a dark room and watches them have them! Yes, until there's a war. That's when adventure becomes available to the masses! Everyone's dish, not only Gable's! Then the people in the dark room come out of the dark room to have some adventures themselves—Goody, goody!—It's our turn now, to go to the South Sea Island—to make a safari—to be exotic, far-off!" (Sc. VI)
   - " . . . my secret practice of retiring to a cabinet of the washroom to work on poems. (Sc.VI)
   - "I know I seem dreamy, but inside—well, I'm boiling!" (Sc. VI)

238

## Video

→*The Glass Menagerie*. 134 minutes, color, 1987. Directed by Paul Newman. With Joanne Woodward, Karen Allen, John Malkovich. Available from Filmic Archives and Insight Media.

→*The Glass Menagerie*. TV production: 120 minutes., color, 1973. With Katherine Hepburn as Amanda, Sam Waterston as Tom, Joanna Mills as Laura, and Michael Moriarity as Jim. Distributed by ABC.

→*The Glass Menagerie*. TV production: 120 minutes, color, 1966. With Shirley Booth as Amanda, Hal Holbrook as Tom, Barbara Laden as Laura, and Pat Hingle as Jim.

→*The Glass Menagerie*. 107 minutes, b&w, 1950. With Gertrude Lawrence as Amanda, Jane Wyman as Laura, Arthur Kennedy as Tom, and Kirk Douglas as Jim. Distributed by 20th Century Fox Film Corp.

## Audio

→*The Glass Menagerie*. 2 cassettes. Dramatization performed by Montgomery Clift, Jessica Tandy, and Julie Harris. Available from Caedmon/Harper Audio.

## Websites

→*Tennessee Williams: Mississippi Writers Page*. An extensive catalog of links to web resources on the playwright. Includes lists of publications, stage productions, Internet resources, news. **www.olemiss.edu/mwp/dir/williams_tennessee/index.html**

→*Tennessee Williams (1911–1983)* from *PAL: Perspectives in American Literature: A Research and Reference Guide* by Paul P. Reuben.
**www.csustan.edu/english/reuben/pal/chap8/williams.html**

# A Casebook on *The Glass Menagerie*: Interpreting Amanda
[pp. 813–18]

This collection of brief critical comments about Amanda presents several different perspectives on her character. As your students may notice, the critics' reactions depend to some degree on the actress playing the role and her interpretation of the part. To explore these differing views further, have several groups of students act out or present an oral reading of the play's first scene involving Amanda, Tom, and Laura (see "Analyzing the Characters," question 2, p. 808). Or choose a different scene involving Amanda and Laura or Amanda and Tom. Instruct each group to interpret Amanda in a specific way: loving and gentle, overbearing and selfish, strong but caring, etc. Discuss the readings afterward, and ask students to decide which interpretation seemed most valid. Also ask them how their reactions to Amanda affect their feelings about the other characters.

Several famous actresses have portrayed Amanda on film: Katherine Hepburn, Shirley Booth, Joanne Woodward, Gertrude Lawrence. If you can locate videos of several filmed productions of the play or videos on YouTube, view the same scene involving Amanda and discuss the merits of each actress's portrayal. You might also include Jessica Tandy's superb audio performance.

Students can also gather reviews from other productions to supplement the critical comments offered in the casebook. Philip Kolin has compiled a useful list of resources in *Tennessee Williams: A Guide to Research and Performance* (Greenwood Press, 1998).

In developing their evaluation of Amanda, students might also consider what Williams himself said, especially since the play is clearly autobiographical and Amanda is modeled on the playwright's own mother. The following comment from an interview with Williams, reprinted in *Conversations with Tennessee Williams* (ed. Albert J. Devlin), offers a surprising defense of Amanda: "The mother's valor is the *core* of *The Glass Menagerie*. . . . She's confused, pathetic, even stupid, but everything has *got* to be all right. She fights to make it that way in the only way she knows how."

# Chapter 19   Writing About Culture [pp. 819–80]

In this chapter we emphasize how cultural factors—gender, class, race, ethnicity, religion, history, traditions, values, personal experiences—influence the writing of a literary work, as well as the way readers understand the work. A cultural approach to literature assumes that a text exists most interestingly as part of a social context.

## *Looking at Cultural Issues* [p. 820]

*M. Butterfly* is essentially a play about culture—or, more accurately, about the clash of cultures. You might begin by reading the news source that was the basis for the play (p. 829). You can find a photograph of the real Shi Pei Pu as he appeared in the opera production *The Story of the Butterfly* by doing a Google image search. You might also want to have students read a plot synopsis of *Madame Butterfly* before having them read Hwang's play. A knowledge of Puccini's original will help them to follow Gallimard's description of the opera (Act I, Scene III) and to trace the reversals that come at the play's end.

## M. BUTTERFLY by David Henry Hwang [pp. 820–67]

In his play, David Hwang critiques the sexual and racial attitudes that inform Western relations with Asia, captured most powerfully and seductively in the image of Puccini's Madame Butterfly. As Hwang explains in the "Afterword" to his play, the character of Butterfly has become a cultural stereotype of East-West relations: "Speaking of an Asian woman, we would sometimes say, 'She's pulling a Butterfly,' which meant playing the submissive Oriental number" (95).

    *M. Butterfly* explores the connection between the "Orient" of Western imagination and the political consequences that such images promote. The play's main character, the French diplomat Rene Gallimard, conducts his relationship with China in terms of Puccini's opera. In *Madame Butterfly* (1904), the American naval officer Pinkerton marries the Japanese geisha girl Butterfly; he then leaves for the United States, promising to return. Butterfly waits for him, meanwhile bearing his child. When Pinkerton sends his American wife to collect the child, Butterfly realizes that he will never return—and she commits suicide.

    When Hwang read of the French diplomat who had an affair with a Chinese actress, who turned out to be a spy—and a *man*—, the playwright concluded that the diplomat had fallen in love with a fantasy stereotype. By combining the diplomat's story with Puccini's plot, Hwang constructed the basic "arc" of his play: "the Frenchman fantasizes that he is Pinkerton and his lover is Butterfly. By the end of the piece, he realizes that it is he who has been Butterfly, in that the Frenchman has been duped by love; the Chinese spy, who exploited that love, is therefore the real Pinkerton" ("Afterword," 95–96).

    *M. Butterfly* is also a highly political play. Hwang doesn't just contend that the sexist and racist stereotype of a "submissive Oriental number" fuels the fantasies of Western men about Asian women (as demonstrated by the profitable business of supplying Americans and Europeans with mail-order brides from Asia); he also argues that this attitude has conditioned political relations between Asia and the West as well. In making this point, Hwang suggests that the debacle of the Vietnam War was related, in part, to cultural assumptions about the submissive nature of Asians in general. By fusing the erotic and political desire for domination in the character of Gallimard, the play presents a complex reading of the politics of race, gender, and sexuality in a brilliant theatrical production.

To help students understand the various levels of this play, you may want to give them the basic outline of Puccini's opera and discuss the romantic notions about Oriental women that it reinforced and fostered. Students will also benefit from knowledge about the true story the play is based on. It's important to note, though, that Hwang says he took his idea from a brief account in the *New York Times* ("France Jails 2 in Odd Case of Espionage": 11 May 1986) but did not do any further research into the incident. Students, like most people who read or see the play, will wonder how the French diplomat could not know that the "woman" he had fallen in love was really a man. It may help to remind them that Hwang did not invent this part of the story—nor the part about the child. The real-life diplomat, Bernard Bouriscot, continues to maintain that he did not know the true sex of the person he had the affair with.

### *Questions for Discussion and Writing*

1. What does the stage look like in *M. Butterfly*, and what does it represent? (Notice that the initial description of the setting says that the play takes place "in recall" and that in Act 2, Scene 11, Gallimard says, "You have to do what I say! I'm conjuring you up in *my* mind!")
2. Gallimard says that he has "known, and been loved by . . . the Perfect Woman!" (1.3). What does he mean by this? In what way may he be right?
3. How does Puccini's opera *Madame Butterfly* function in this play?
4. Gallimard and some other characters address the audience directly and even interact with them (as when Marc flirts with the women in the audience). What do these breaks in theatrical convention suggest about this play? How do they contribute to the play's ideas about illusions and role-playing?
5. Gallimard says he was "not handsome, nor brave, nor powerful" (1.5), and he conjures up the image of a pinup girl from a sex magazine. What does this scene have to do with the play's main themes?
6. When Gallimard and Song first meet (1.6), they discuss the plot of *Madame Butterfly* and Song tells Gallimard, "It's one of your favorite fantasies, isn't it? The submissive Oriental and the cruel white man." Is Song right?
7. How does Song conduct her seduction of Gallimard without revealing "her" secret?
8. Does Gallimard believe what he sees, or does he see what he believes?
9. In 2.3, Gallimard gives Toulon some political advice about Vietnam. Later Toulon tells Gallimard that he is almost comically wrong in everything he says. How have gender issues affected Gallimard's political thinking?

10. What's the significance of the spelling of Renee's name? Compare Song and Renee. Why does Gallimard go to Butterfly in 2.6, instead of to Renee? Gallimard says that Renee "questions the role of the penis in modern society." Does Butterfly also question the role of the penis in modern society?

11. Song says that women's roles are played by men in the Peking Opera because "only a man knows how a woman is supposed to act" (2.7). What does Song mean? In what ways does the play confirm this point?

12. In the final scene between them (3.2), Song tries to get Gallimard to admit that he is still attracted to his "Butterfly," even though "she" is a man. What is the point of this scene?

13. Just before he kills himself, Gallimard dresses, makes up as Butterfly, and says, "My name is Rene Gallimard—also known as Madame Butterfly." What is the point of this final switch of identities?

14. Does the fact that the play is based on an actual event make it more believable than it otherwise might be? Or is the plot just too improbable (even though it actually happened)? How does the playwright try to overcome the improbability of the story? Does he succeed?

15. Compare Song with Antigone. Analyze how the "women" in each play resist being defined by men.

## Making Connections

→ Compare Hwang's exploration and use of Asian culture with the depictions in the stories "The Bridegroom" and "Seventeen Syllables." Do Jin and Yamamoto refute or confirm the views that Hwang presents?

→ Compare Gallimard's illusions with those of the characters in *The Glass Menagerie*.

→ Is Gallimard a tragic character? How does he compare to Othello, especially in the discoveries each makes about himself?

## Video

→ *M. Butterfly*. 110 minutes, 1973. An uninspired film version, with screenplay by Hwang, starring Jeremy Irons and John Lone. Available from Warner Home Video.

## Audio

→ *M. Butterfly*. 118 minutes. John Lithgow and B. D. Wong re-create the roles they originated in the Broadway production. Available from L.A. Theatre Works: www.latheatreworks.com

## Prewriting [pp. 868–70]

Students sometimes get themselves in trouble by going directly to the library or to online databases when outside sources will be necessary for their literary essays. Thus, we encourage an activity like Linda Samuel's reading notes (p. 869) to make a start on what key words and topics are interesting enough to pursue further. An extension of this exercise might be to create a list of key terms to define the limits of a database search.

This prewriting step will help students stay with topics that they have themselves originated and that they can contribute their own thoughts to, instead of summarizing or parroting the sources they find.

### Exploring Cultural Themes [pp. 868–70]
We offer five sets of questions that guide the student in thinking about the piece of literature from a cultural point of view. Though we encourage the students to "work through this list systematically," in today's hypertext world such an activity is extremely time consuming and unlikely to be completed without duress. If time permits, divide the class into five groups and assign each group one of these sets of questions. Ask each group to come up with one meaningful cultural approach to *M. Butterfly* from their discussion of their questions. Alternatively, you could choose a different piece of literature that you've previously studied in class and ask each group to apply the questions to that. This would show that all literature lends itself to cultural inquiry.

### Posing Yourself a Problem [p. 870]
From the cultural approaches developed in the exercise earlier, ask students to revise their approach into one or more questions. Discuss how these questions can guide a search for sources.

Reading the abstracts, titles, and first paragraphs of articles with the question in mind will help a student cull the material and refrain from reading things that are beside the point. If you have wireless database access in your classroom, have students demonstrate some of this sorting system. Remember that getting mired in too many sources can result in incomprehensible literary papers or in the desperate decision to plagiarize.

### Writing [pp. 870–71]
The distinction we make here between the thesis question and the thesis statement is that the secondary sources students have now read should have guided them to an answer (or two) to the question they began with. Taking the time to write out the thesis statement along with the question will help students remember what it was they wanted to investigate. Thinking of the source material as evidence for the truth of the thesis sentence—like crime scene evidence pointing to the true culprit—may help keep the writer on point.

### Ideas for Writing [pp. 871–73]
Your choice about which writing ideas to encourage in your students will depend on the timeline of your course, the level of your students' writing, and the purpose of the course in your school's overall curriculum.

### Ideas for Responsive Writing
These ideas tend to rely mostly on personal experience and then relate it to what happens in the literary work. In this case, the common experience of basing a romance on illusion,

and the age-old strategy of becoming more desirable by making oneself unavailable, are narratives your students probably find familiar.

### Ideas for Critical Writing
These ideas assist students by providing a cultural focus to investigate within the play—in particular, a focus that is still relevant in their own culture, such as the nature of male friendships, the function of stereotypes, and the relation between fact and fiction.

### Ideas for Researched Writing
The researched ideas are just as they sound: though they may borrow themes from other types of writing ideas (earlier), they depend much more on doing research in outside sources. In these topics, we attempt to branch out into the culture of the theater for students whose interests lie in that direction—for example, researching the costuming and staging of *M. Butterfly*. In creating topics for students, we consider it important to reach outside what may be our own literary fascinations and brainstorm about what people in other walks of life might find interesting about the piece.

## Coordinating Your Introduction and Conclusion [p. 873]
In this section, we offer an experiment in deleting the original introduction from an old essay or a draft and then shifting a sentence from the conclusion to be used in writing a new introduction. With computerized writing and display options, this experiment is simple and could even be done and shared in class. Students could critique examples of the shift and suggest how elements of the conclusion can be used to improve the introduction.

## Sample Student Paper [pp. 874–80]
You can use this essay to illustrate how to use secondary sources thoughtfully and accurately. Although this paper was written in 2008, we've updated the form of the entries in the list of Works Cited to follow the most recent MLA style.

# ANTHOLOGY OF DRAMA

**OTHELLO, THE MOOR OF VENICE** by William Shakespeare [pp. 881–967]
*Othello* differs in several important ways from the other three major Shakespearean tragedies that it is usually ranked with. The protagonist is not a prince or king (as in *Hamlet*, *Macbeth*, and *King Lear*); he is a recently married general. The play has no supernatural visits, no fully developed subplot, little comic relief, and few minor characters serving as foils. The cast of *Othello* is small and the plot is concentrated. The action takes place in a few days in only two locations, unlike the years and far-reaching locales that are spanned in the other major tragedies. While all four plays share a thematic fascination with evil, *Othello* is the most focused on one particular form of evil—sexual jealousy. Othello's tragic fall does not threaten the social order: the catastrophe centers on the destruction of a specific, personal love through jealousy. The play is confined to an unusual degree to the fate of three main characters: Othello, Desdemona, and Iago.

Most students will be impressed with the rapid action and the tension of the tightly constructed plot. But they may have problems with the characters and their motives, especially those of Iago and Othello. Iago's envy for Cassio is clear, but the reasons for his jealousy of Othello are less certain. Critics have argued repeatedly about the plausibility of Iago's motivation. Some have said that it is insufficient and that his character is inconsistent. Coleridge used the phrase "motiveless malignity" to account for Iago's behavior. Others have found adequate cause in Iago's suspicions of his wife's fidelity (presuming she was having an affair with Othello), his sexual attraction to Desdemona, and his envy for Othello's position and success. While students may have reservations about the credibility of these motives, they should have little trouble seeing how cunning and crafty the villain is in his manipulation of people and circumstances. Iago belongs to a select group of villains who seem to delight in evil for its own sake. He takes pleasure in deceiving almost everyone in the play and amazes us with his virtuosity. Also, Iago may be so adept at working self-hatred in others because he suffers from it himself.

As for Othello, students may wonder why someone who appears to be intelligent, strong-willed, even-tempered, and honorable can fall so easily for Iago's schemes and deceptions. They may question how such a good character can be driven to such evil deeds. That Othello is black is a key force behind Iago's success. He is also a military man, simple and inexperienced in the ways of love and civilized society. As an outsider, both by race and temperament, Othello is not able to believe in the admiration and esteem that the sophisticated Venetians proclaim for him. When Iago persuades Othello to see himself as alien, the resulting loss of self-regard is devastating. His jealousy arises from a deep suspicion that others cannot love him, since he does not consider himself lovable. Because Othello has loved Desdemona as an extension of himself, his destruction of her is a destruction of himself. The murder of Desdemona is actually a prelude to his suicide. The horror and pity of *Othello* comes from the spectacle of a noble love made filthy by self-hatred, but the play's special terror arises from the fact that the savagery of the two central characters cannot be satisfactorily explained.

246

## Possible Responses to *Questions for Discussion and Writing*

1. Through Act 3, Scene 2, Othello is a grandly positive character. He is a leading figure in the Venetian establishment, a respected military man, and a loving husband. He acts with restraint and dignity when confronted by Brabantio, Roderigo, and the officers that Brabantio has gathered (1.2). Othello's response to Brabantio's insults and charges is both eloquent and persuasive: even the Duke says, "I think this tale would win my daughter too" (1.3.171). Desdemona confirms the mutuality of their love, revealing it to be both spiritually satisfying and sexually vigorous.

   With his suicide Othello acknowledges his fault and in doing so may recover something of his former nobility. He honestly admits that he "lov'd not wisely, but too well" and was "Perplex'd in the extreme" (5.2.345, 347). He shows a vestige of his pride when he refers to his former service to the state; and when he identifies with the "malignant . . . Turk" (5.2.354) he once slew, his death retains a moment of honor and atonement.

2. The attraction between Othello and Desdemona seems to be based, to a large degree, on their differences. Othello is very different from the Venetians (like Roderigo) who have courted Desdemona: he is an older black man who has had adventures and experiences that she has never been exposed to. Likewise, Desdemona is apparently unlike any woman Othello has known: refined, virtuous, tenderhearted—as well as young and beautiful and white. They are exotic and mysterious to each other. These differences and mysteries are also largely responsible for the tragedy that comes into their lives, since they account for the insecurities that Iago exploits to fuel Othello's jealousy. The differences are a source of wonderment for Desdemona (she is sure that the noble Othello must still love her) and a source of doubt for Othello (how can he be sure that someone like Desdemona can truly love him?). As Brabantio says to him, "Look to her, Moor, if thou has eyes to see; / She has deceiv'd her father, and may thee" (1.3.291–92).

3. As the embodiment of evil and villainy, Iago must destroy the one person in the play who stands for everything he does not: innocence, purity, loyalty, and virtue. He is a complete cynic who cannot stand to see someone who is truly virtuous. Some readers also think Iago is jealous of Desdemona because, like Cassio, she has displaced Iago from Othello's regard and affections.

4. Desdemona is simply too innocent and trusting for her own good. She has been bewitched, in a way, by Othello and has also become dependent on him. (She ran away from her home to marry Othello and then left with him, away from Venice to the military outpost in Cyprus.) The same cultural dissonance that makes Othello susceptible to Iago's lies also affects Desdemona. Having firmly and courageously defied the prejudices of the only society she had ever known, Desdemona is incapable of betraying her love and devotion to Othello. She recognizes that his jealousy is ignoble, but she continues to give him her love to its fullest extent, saying, "My love doth so approve him, / That even his stubbornness, his checks and frowns, / . . . have grace and favour in them" (4.3.19–21).

247

5. The protagonist's race was not very important in the play's main source, but it is frequently mentioned by Shakespeare, especially in Act I, where the nature of Venetian society is stressed. The obvious racist caricature offered, even before Othello appears, would be the same stereotypes that many in Shakespeare's audience held at that time. Othello's race helps establish him as an outsider in Venice, and this status makes him susceptible to Iago's wiles. The Moor is fatally naïve about Desdemona's world; and when Iago assures him, "I know our country disposition well" (3.3.202), Othello is ready to accept, at face value, the outrageous claim that adultery is commonplace among Venetian women. Also, once his mind has been poisoned by Iago's charges, Othello is not capable of understanding Desdemona's worth: he has seen and heard Venice's prejudice, but does not fully appreciate her courage in opposing it.

6. Suggest that students begin by defining "reason" and "instinct." One way to frame (and limit) this issue would be: Does Iago rely mainly on reason or on instinct to manipulate Othello and the other characters in the play? Students could also focus on the conflict between reason and instinct in Othello. Or they might identify Othello as a man of instinct and Iago as a man of (perverted) reason and develop an interpretation around that conflict.

7. Two "marriages" parallel that of Othello and Desdemona. Cassio is linked with Bianca, and although they are not formally married, the comparison is promoted by the fact that Iago substitutes Bianca for Desdemona when he uses the handkerchief to deceive Othello. Moreover, Bianca's jealousy of Cassio (which seems justified) contrasts with Othello's jealousy (which seems incredible). The marriage of Iago and Emilia plainly lacks affection, let alone love, but is marked by sexual jealousy, at least in Iago's overheated imagination: he remarks several times that he suspects his wife of adultery with either Othello (1.3.369–71 and 2.1.276–77) or Cassio (2.1.287–88)—although both suspicions seem as preposterous as the claims about Desdemona's infidelity.

8. The answers to questions 2 and 5 earlier provide a number of points that could be used in developing an essay on this topic. Add the observation about Othello as a military man: he has succeeded as a soldier (an all-male environment) but has trouble understanding the civilian world, especially since the duplicitous Iago is his chief intermediary between these two worlds.

### Additional Questions for Discussion and Writing
1. What incident first incites Iago to vengeance against Othello?
2. Where in Act I is Othello's race mentioned in a derogatory manner? What are the implications of these slurs?
3. What is Roderigo's relation to Iago?
4. What is Brabantio's initial reaction to the news that Othello and Desdemona are together?
5. Describe how Iago begins to succeed in his evil plans in the third scene of Act II.
6. How does Iago plant the seed of suspicion in Othello's mind (Act III)?

7. How does Cassio's personality make him susceptible to Iago's manipulation?
8. Contrast the Iago-Emilia relationship with that of Othello and Desdemona (see Act III, Scene III).
9. Explain the role of chance or fate in the tragedy.
10. How do you interpret Iago's statement, "I am your own forever" (end of Act III, Scene III)?
11. What is Bianca's function in the play?
12. When Othello, enraged by Iago's insinuations, grovels at the villain's feet, is he a tragic figure or merely pathetic?
13. What new trick does Iago devise to incite Othello's jealousy in the first scene of Act IV? Why does Othello fall for such an obvious deception?
14. Compare and contrast Desdemona with Emilia. Why is Desdemona so passive in the last part of Act IV?
15. What mistakes does Iago make in the first scene of Act V? How do these mistakes ensure his own fate?
16. Analyze Othello's speech at the start of Scene II, Act V. Why must he kill Desdemona quickly, rather than listen to her pleas?

## Making Connections
→ Write an essay in which you compare the tragedy of Othello with the tragedy of Antigone.
→ Compare Desdemona with Antigone.

## Videos
→ *Othello*. 93 minutes, b&w, 1952. With Orson Welles and Suzanne Cloutier; directed by Orson Welles. Available from Corinth Films and Filmic Archives.
→ *Othello*. 166 minutes, color, 1965; 16 mm film. With Laurence Olivier, Maggie Smith, Frank Findlay, and Derek Jacobi. Available from Swank Motion Pictures.
→ *Othello*. 208 minutes, color, 1982. With Anthony Hopkins, Bob Hoskins, and Penelope Wilton. BBC Shakespeare. Available from Filmic Archives, Time-Life, Inc., and Insight Media.
→ *Othello*. 198 minutes, color, 1989. With John Kani, Joanna Weinberg; directed by Janet Suzman. Available from Films for the Humanities & Sciences.

## TRIFLES by Susan Glaspell [pp. 967–78]
Susan Glaspell wrote this play at a time (1916) when women did not often write for the stage. The play's feminist point of view is also remarkable for its time. While the action centers on a murder investigation, the playwright skillfully introduces a second investigation, conducted by the two women who accompany the men inquiring into John Wright's death. At the beginning of the play Mr. Hale remarks that "women are used to worrying over trifles," but it is just such trifles that are the substance of the women's investigation.

The men hunt in vain for clues to the murder; the women quickly find what the men have missed. Their discovery is the result of their feminine sensibilities, which enable them to recognize the importance of what they find—a bird with a broken neck. They realize that Wright must have killed it and that the bird's death was probably Mrs. Wright's motive for murdering her husband. Glaspell also introduces the idea that the truly "awful thing" was not the murder of John Wright but the lonely and isolated life his wife had been forced to endure. Because they neglected Minnie Wright, the women feel implicated and decide to hide the incriminating evidence.

The play emphasizes the essential differences between men and women in rural life. The men are insensitive to the nature of women's lives. More important, their adherence to the letter of the law precludes a merciful administration of justice. The two women, with their sense of a higher purpose, band together to protect another woman from the injustice of man's law when applied to women. (At the time this play was written, women were not allowed to vote or serve on juries.)

A year after Glaspell wrote this play, she rewrote it as a short story titled "A Jury of Her Peers." Although the story is close to the play (after the first page, much of the dialogue is identical with that in the play), the women take more central roles earlier in the story than in the play. The story also takes us inside Mrs. Hale's mind to learn of her guilt for not having visited Mrs. Wright. The story seems to focus more on justice than on the "trifles" overlooked by the men. Perhaps this shift in thematic emphasis is why the author changed the title.

## Possible Responses to *Questions for Discussion and Writing*
1. The setting is stark, gloomy, and cold. It conveys the hard life that Mr. Wright imposed on his wife and sums up the relationship between the Wrights.
2. The men are conventional, efficient, officious, and condescending toward the women. They are so smugly certain of their own authority that they overlook the kind of evidence (the "trifles" of the title) that could be used to convict Mrs. Wright.
3. The women recognize the identical knots that Mrs. Wright used on her sewing and on her husband. In the last line of the play, Mrs. Hale reveals that key piece of evidence to Mr. Henderson, but as far as he's concerned, that's "not it."
4. Minnie Foster used to wear a white dress with blue ribbons and sing in the choir. All of the joy in her life was strangled out by the confining marriage and isolated existence that she had to endure with Mr. Wright.
5. Encourage students to define what they mean by "the right thing." Do the women choose to hide the evidence because they empathize with Minnie Wright or because they feel guilty that they didn't help her out? In other words, do they do the right thing for Minnie? for themselves? for women in general? for the cause of justice?

## Additional Questions for Discussion and Writing
1. Make a list of the events that occurred (or that you speculate might have occurred) before the play begins. Why did Glaspell choose to begin the play where she did?
2. How does the first entrance of the characters establish a distinction between the men

and the women? What do the different reactions to the frozen preserves tell you?

3. Why does Glaspell include Mrs. Peters's speech about the boy who killed her cat?

4. Susan Glaspell wrote a short story version of *Trifles* and changed the title to "A Jury of Her Peers." What is the significance of each title? Why do you think she changed the title? Which one do you prefer?

5. Could it be argued that this play is immoral? Write an essay in which you explain your answer to this question.

## Making Connections

→ Compare Mrs. Peters and Mrs. Hale with the women in *A Raisin in the Sun*. Which women seem to have the most control over their lives?

## Video

→ *A Jury of Her Peers*. 30 min., color, 1980. Filmed version of *Trifles*, directed by Sally Heckel. Available from Women Make Movies.


## A RAISIN IN THE SUN by Lorraine Hansberry [pp. 978–1033]

This play tells the story of a family's attempt to move from an all-black neighborhood to the white suburbs, a struggle that Hansberry's own parents fought all the way to the Supreme Court. Before the Hansberrys were granted the right to live in the house they had purchased, they were harassed and threatened daily. The play was first produced in 1959; its action takes place before the civil rights movement of the 1960s. Abortion was also against the law in this country at that time, meaning that Ruth's decision about her pregnancy could lead to a physically dangerous and illegal operation.

The play portrays the American Dream of working hard, saving your money, buying your own home, and having the kind of space and privacy that will permit you to live with dignity and pride. Although this theme seems to emphasize middle-class values and consumerism, Hansberry wrote her play to explore these issues and to demonstrate that the needs of black families parallel those of white families but also involve conflicts that most white families do not experience.

Hansberry's play is painfully honest. It shows that Walter Younger is affected by the same lust for possessions (and the power they can confer) that affects many Americans. He is also caught up in the old pattern of male dominance over women, although the women in his life do not tolerate his chauvinistic behavior. Mama opposes her son's plan to buy a liquor store—because it will further corrupt her own community and because she wants the security and identity that she feels her family deserves. In the end, Walter finds the strength to think of his family rather than his own selfish concerns. He refuses the offer of the Clybourne Park Improvement Association, not to express a desire to own a better house but to demonstrate that the Youngers are not socially inferior and that they have the right to live wherever they choose.

**Possible Responses to *Questions for Discussion and Writing***

1.  Hughes's poem captures both the simplicity and complexity of the effects of racism on the ability of black Americans to define and achieve their dreams. The main characters, Mama, Walter, Ruth, and Beneatha, contrast in their varied responses to their collective experience of this oppression. Students might be inclined to too easily match characters to lines—for example, Mama to the line "just sags like a heavy load"—but class discussion can complicate any simplistic or stereotypical connections.

2.  Each character takes his or her select piece of the deferred American Dream, from Walter's desire to be a respected business man; to Mama's desire to see her family united, somehow making progress from the generations before them; to Ruth's desire to rekindle a love that might help her to confront her difficult life; to Beneatha's desire as a woman to find both meaningful work and love in her life. One of the major contrasts to be discussed is the extent to which each character understands the differences between their personal dreams and the welfare of the family as a whole. Mama and Ruth serve the traditionally more selfless female role of nurturing and acting with empathy, while Beneatha and Walter strike out for themselves, as individuals, without sufficient awareness of the effects on others. Students might benefit from making lists of the positive and negative effects of each character's behavior as a way to support their answer to "Which one of these characters to you find most admirable?"

3.  While a better house in a better neighborhood is clearly a part of Mama and Ruth's definition of the good life, and Walter's entrepreneurial spirits seems centered in the money itself, the real impulse in both cases is finding meaning in a harsh world, in a society where self-respect, comfort, and the time to love seem to depend, at least to some extent, on material gain and consumer power, both of which are just out of reach for the Youngers. The place of George in Beneatha's life makes her harder to analyze. Though she wants to be a doctor, not to make money and buy things but to "sew up the problem," she has, up to this point, continued to date George. Two key turning points in the play undermine a view that consumerism and material values drive the plot of the play, when Mama realizes the effects of her buying the house on Walter's self-image and later when Walter realizes his own need to act on behalf of his own son. Mama says, "There ain't nothing worth holding on to, money, dreams, nothing else—if it means—if it means it's going to destroy my boy." This same insight turns Walter around at the end of the play.

4.  Several characters and events undercut the idea that mainstream white culture is the ideal to which blacks should aspire. While Lindner articulates key values of the American Dream, his hypocrisy suggests the extent to which white Americans have fallen short of their expressed values. In addition, George's superficial character reveals the potential problem with simplistic assimilation. Hansberry's contrast between George and Asagai, with whom she is clearly more sympathetic, further contradicts any reading of the play as being about a black family simply finding

success by assimilating into the white culture. However, Beneatha's naïve nationalism tells us that Hansberry is also suspect of blacks turning uncritically to Africa, a place they've never lived, for answers to their American problems. The values at the heart of the play connect the best of people in both America and Africa, including self-respect and love of and commitment to family and community. Additional research: two other key terms in black political history are *nationalism* and *accommodation*; both concepts are explored in the play, for example in Walter's reference to the accommodationist figure Uncle Tom.

5. Obama's election will certainly be raised as positive evidence of progress in American race relations. This discussion can be an opportunity for analyzing the kinds of family-level change his success might represent and enable. However, asking students to do some quick research into the demographics of black employment (especially black men) and housing discrimination will balance the discussion of the extent to which necessary change has been fully achieved.

6. Discussion of questions 1–5 will generate analysis of the intersection of race and gender in the play, especially in understanding the contrasting characters of Ruth and Walter and Beneatha and Walter. The "Thematic Table of Contents" sections on "Male and Female" and "Prejudice and Acceptance" can help students identify stories and plays to compare.

## *Additional Questions for Discussion and Writing*

1. Who is the play's protagonist? Who (or what) is the antagonist? Is the central conflict within the Younger family?
2. Why are Joseph Asagai and George Murchison in the play? What perspectives of the black experience in the United States do they represent?
3. The entire play occurs in the Youngers' apartment. Write an essay analyzing the effect of this setting on the characters and the action.
4. Choose the scene in the play in which you believe each major character most clearly reveals his or her true nature. Analyze the dialogue in that scene, and explain how the scene is most characteristic.
5. Write a scene or story that shows the Younger family ten years later. What has happened to their dreams? Where are they living, and what are they doing?

## *Making Connections*

→ Compare the use of setting in *Raisin in the Sun* to the setting in *The Glass Menagerie* and *Trifles*. In which play is the setting most important?

## *Videos*

→ *A Raisin in the Sun.* 128 minutes, b&w, 1961. With Sidney Poitier, Claudia McNeil, and Ruby Dee. Available from RCA/Columbia Pictures Home Video.
→ *A Raisin in the Sun.* 171 minutes, color, 1988. American Playhouse production with Danny Glover, Starletta DuPois, Esther Rolle, and Kim Yancey. See local retailer.
→ *A Raisin in the Sun.* 131 minutes, color, DVD, 2008. With Phylicia Rashad, Sean 'P.

Diddy' Combs, Audra McDonald, and Sanaa Lathan. Available from Sony Pictures and Amazon.com.

→ *Lorraine Hansberry: The Black Experience in the Creation of Drama.* 35 minutes, color, 1975. Includes clips of her plays. Available from Films for the Humanities & Sciences.

### Website

→ *Voices from the Gaps: Lorraine Hansberry.* Includes biography, criticism, bibliography, and related links.
**http://voices.cla.umn/artistspages/hansberryLorraine.php**

# A PORTFOLIO OF HUMOROUS AND SATIRICAL PLAYS

Much of the humor in these plays derives from their satiric purpose—making fun of and ridiculing certain people or institutions. You might want to begin the study of these selections with a discussion of humor: What makes you laugh? Do you know why? Examples from movies and television should be helpful—and probably illustrate the wide divergence of opinions about what's humorous and what isn't.

**BEAUTY** by Jane Martin [pp. 1035–39]
As a prereading activity, ask students to do a short write about these sayings, which the play seems to be exploring and questioning: "The grass is always greener on the other side of the fence"; "Beauty is only skin deep"; "Beauty is in the eye of the beholder." What do these proverbs mean? Is there any truth to them? After reading the play, then ask students to comment on what the play seems to be saying about these proverbs.

The play seems to be straight-on satire about the cultural obsession with physical beauty and sexual attractiveness. But the point of the satire is not that simple. The two trade more than bodies; they trade brains and personalities. As Carla/Bethany says, "I wanted to be beautiful, but I didn't want to be you." And Bethany/Carla says, "You have my brain. You poor bastard." Also, could the combined names (with the slash marks) suggest that the characters represent two sides of the same person? The theme would then involve a claim about self-knowledge or self-acceptance.

## Possible Responses to *Questions for Discussion and Writing*
1. It attacks the obsession with physical beauty, sexual attractiveness, and the preoccupations of outward appearances. It also delivers a strong comment about envy—the human tendency to be unsatisfied with what one has and to want what others have. A lot of advertising is based on creating and exploiting this tendency.
2. Carla fits the dumb-blonde stereotype; Bethany is the "plain Jane" type. Whether both are equal objects of the satire is an issue that might spark some disagreement, as will the question of who gets the better deal. Carla seems more self-aware and realistic about herself; she seems less obsessive and thus not the primary target of ridicule. But as Bethany points out, Carla's self-criticisms must be taken cautiously: "You're just trying to make us feel better because we aren't in your league."
3. She thinks that it's just a trick, that it doesn't really cost Carla anything to denigrate her own advantages.
4. Corresponding male stereotypes might be the technogeek and the dumb jock; or a bumptious egghead (Barney Frank) vs. a handsome smooth-operator (Mitt Romney, John Edwards). The two adult brothers in the TV sitcom *Two and a Half Men* (played by Jon Cryer and Charlie Sheen) present another example of contrasting male stereotypes. Students may prefer to rewrite the script themselves, rather than just explain how to adapt it.

**LOS VENDIDOS** by Luis Valdez [pp. 1040–48]

In 1964 Valdez founded El Teatro Campesino ("The Farmworkers' Theater") to assist the grape boycott and farmworker strike in Delano, California. The company devised a form of drama which they called *actos*, short satirical plays that portrayed the oppression of the field workers. According to Valdez the actos were used to "inspire the audience to social action. Illuminate specific points about social problems. Satirize the opposition. Show or hint at a solution. Express what people are feeling."

Los Vendidos is one of Teatro Campesino's most acclaimed and enduring actos. It presents a range of stereotypes that Anglo culture applies to Chicano experience: farmworkers, urban tough guys, revolutionaries, and the "new" Mexican American yuppie. In the surprise ending, however, the yuppie turns on the secretary, and the "Used Mexicans" turn out to be in charge of the shop—Honest Sancho is their front. Although *Los Vendidos* is no less political than the earlier actos, the focus is no longer on striking farmworkers. It is on the Chicano's relationship to Anglo culture. Furthermore, this play seems less concerned with offering a solution than with showing contrasting kinds of Chicanos, although it is clear where Valdez's sympathies lie.

The play's title sums up the conflicts inherent in the Mexican Americans' dual experience. "Los Vendidos" can be translated two ways: "those who are sold" (like the Mexicans in Sancho's lot, who are "used" and exploited by Anglos) and "the sellouts" (like Sancho and Miss Jiménez, who have sold out their cultural identity). This duality is reinforced by the play's mixture of Spanish and English—the two languages that Chicanos use to define themselves and to relate to the Anglo world. In other words, the play operates on the border between the two cultures, demonstrating through exaggerated comedy the complex social and political negotiations that Mexican Americans engage in today.

## Possible Responses to *Questions for Discussion and Writing*

1.  See the last paragraph in the play discussion.
2.  The types are Honest Sancho, the smarmy salesman; the docile, compliant farm worker; Pachuco Johnny, who wields a knife, deals drugs, and makes a good scapegoat; the Revolucionario or Early California Bandit, dangerous, virile, and romantic (like Pancho Villa or Zorro); and a modern Mexican American, the perfectly assimilated immigrant. Sancho's descriptions of these types are intentionally offensive, designed to expose Miss Jiménez's prejudices—and, by extension, those of the audience.
3.  The models come to life and menace the secretary and the audience; Honest Sancho is revealed to be a model that the others use to fool Anglos and get money from them. The stereotypes insist that they are more than machines, burros, and puppets to be exploited by the Anglos. The exploited have learned to be exploiters.
4.  There are several social and political messages. One is how Americans, especially politicians and companies, exploit Mexicans (and other immigrants) at the same time

256

fearing them and wanting desperately to Americanize them. Another message might be how oppression and racism contribute to revolution and rebellion.

5. Opinions will be divided about the alternate ending. It may seem more right-minded and politically correct, but it waters down the revolutionary message of the play.

### Additional Questions for Discussion and Writing

1. Do you think the play is a satire? Why or why not?
2. Did you find the play dated? Entertaining? Offensive? Explain your reactions.
3. How would different audiences respond to this play? Would Mexican Americans be offended or delighted? Would Anglos enjoy this play? Do you think Valdez wants to make his audience uncomfortable?

### Making Connections

→ Compare this play's treatment of racial issues and cultural stereotypes with that of *Othello* and/or *M. Butterfly*. Which approach do you prefer?

### Video

→ *Luis Valdez and El Teatro Campesino*. 26 min., color, 1991. Interview. Available from Films for the Humanities & Sciences.

### SURE THING by David Ives [pp. 1048–57]

This play experiments with the intriguing idea of applying instant replay to real-life encounters. What would happen if we could immediately revise what we say until we get the response we want? This is the fantasy that David Ives plays with in *Sure Thing*. In following this notion to its dramatic limits, the playwright manages to portray a variety of characters and explore a range of emotions in a brief one-act, two-character play. Ives takes the formulaic "boy meets girl" scene and complicates it in unexpected ways. The result is witty and insightful, as well as very funny. As students read they should look for the elements of traditional dramatic structure that Ives uses: point of attack, exposition, rising action, climax, falling action, denouement.

This is a play that students will enjoy acting out. Ask for volunteers, stop the play at several points, and call for a different duo to continue. You might divide the class into groups and have each group work on a section of the play. Then the groups could choose a couple to present their approach to the scene. It might also be fun to mix up the gender assignments: have a female play Bill and a male play Betty, or have the parts portrayed by two males or two females.

### Possible Responses to Questions for Discussion and Writing

1. A café, as opposed to a bus stop, conveys intent. This setting says the characters are sociable and are looking to hook up with someone (both say they come to the café a lot).

2. The dramatic premise—applying instant replay to a social encounter—makes it easy to arrive at the "right moment." Time is repeatedly readjusted to give the characters multiple chances to "get it right."

3. It signals that a speaker has made a faux pas, and the scene will be replayed to give the person another chance to get it right. In some productions, the listener rings the bell (or simply says "ding") to tell the speaker to try again. This approach underscores the influence of the listener on the speaker's attempts to be the perfect catch.

4. The plot follows the traditional scheme of boy meets girl, boy almost loses girl (many times), boy finally gets girl. Or you could put it the other way around: girl chases boy, girl almost loses boy, girl gets boy. The conflict involves the struggle to find an acceptable mate. It is resolved when both characters refashion themselves enough to meet the other's requirements. (Authenticity and honesty have nothing to do with this match.) The climax occurs when the two start to speak simultaneously (p. 1126), and the bell stops interrupting their conversation. At the end Betty says, "Sure thing" (the play's title), and they then speak together once more: détente has been achieved.

5. This approach will allow more students to participate in the performance.

## Additional Questions for Discussion and Writing

1. Is the title ironic? The same phrase—"sure thing"—is also used several times in the play. Does it always mean the same thing?

2. Do you think Bill and Betty are genuinely well matched or are they simply the product of self-revision?

3. Which character is the protagonist? What does the protagonist want? Is the other character the antagonist? Or is the antagonist some social force or convention?

4. How would you describe the comedy in this play? Is it romantic or farcical? Write an essay in which you explain why the play is funny.

5. Write another scene between Betty and Bill that takes place after they come out of the movies.

## Making Connections

Compare Ives's comic treatment of love and romance to the treatment of these same subjects in Raymond Carver's story "What We Talk About When We Talk About Love" and/or Margaret Atwood's "Happy Endings."

Compare the encounter between Bill and Betty with that of Jake and Mariana in the story "Love in L.A." by Dagoberto Gilb, focusing on the elements of performance and revision.

# CRITICAL APPROACHES FOR INTERPRETING LITERATURE

[pp. 1084–90]

Since our emphasis in this text is on writing, using literature as a rich source of content, we discourage lengthy forays into the world of literary criticism. However, students may find good ideas about how to approach a work of literature from reading this appendix, especially when they are stuck for a topic. If they have not had a literature class yet, they may be unaware that these schools of thought exist. Another time the appendix may be useful is when you see a student paper or comment that has the seeds of one of these critical approaches already within it, and reading about the approach can focus the discussion.

In the 10th edition of *Literature and the Writing Process*, we have labeled those writing prompts that pertain to specific critical approaches. In these prompts students are directed to review the relevant material in this appendix as a way to help them explore and develop the topic.

## Useful Reference Works

Brunel, Pierre, ed. *Companion to Literary Myths, Heroes, and Archetypes*. Trans. Wendy Allatson and Judith Hayward. London; New York: Routledge, 1996.

Cirlot, J. E. *A Dictionary of Symbols*. 2nd ed. Trans. Jack Sage. New York: Barnes & Noble, 1995.

Cooper, J. C. *An Illustrated Encyclopaedia of Traditional Symbols*. New York: Thames and Hudson, 1990.

Eagleton, Terry. *Literary Theory: An Introduction*. Anniversary ed. Minneapolis: U of Minnesota P, 2008.

Frazer, Sir James, and George W. Stacking. *The Golden Bough: A Study in Magic and Religion*. 1922. Rpt. New York: Penguin, 1998.

Guerin, Wilfred L. *A Handbook of Critical Approaches to Literature*. 5th ed. New York: Oxford UP, 2005.

Harmon, William. *A Handbook to Literature*. 12th ed. Boston: Longman, 2011.

Lentricchia, Frank, and Thomas McLaughlin. *Critical Terms for Literary Study*. 2nd ed. Chicago: Chicago UP, 1995.

Preminger, Alex, and T. V. F. Brogan, eds. *The New Princeton Encyclopedia of Poetry and Poetics*. 3rd ed. Princeton: Princeton UP, 1993.

Tresidder, Jack, ed. *The Complete Dictionary of Symbols*. San Francisco: Chronicle, 2005.

Urdang, Laurence, and Frederick G. Ruffner, Jr., eds. *Allusions: Cultural, Literary, Biblical, and Historical: A Thematic Dictionary*. 2nd ed. Detroit: Gale, 1986.

Walker, Barbara G. *The Woman's Encyclopedia of Myths and Secrets*. Edison: Castle, 1996.

# Directory of Audio and Video Distributors

For further information, consult the *Educational Film & Video Locator of the Consortium of College and University Media Centers,* published by R. R. Bowker; or the *Film & Video Finder*, published by the National Information Center for Educational Media.

Annenberg Media
P. O. Box 2345
South Burlington, VT 05407
www.learner.org

Audio Book Contractors
P. O. Box 40115
Washington, DC 20016
202-363-3429
www.audiobookcontractors.com

Audio Editions
P. O. Box 6930
Auburn, CA 95604-6930
800-231-4261
www.audioeditions.com

Caedmon/Harper Audio
P. O. Box 588
Dunmore, PA 18512
800-242-7737
www.harpercollins.com

Caedmon Records
    See Caedmon/Harper Audio

Corinth Films
3117 Bursonville Rd.
Riegelsville, PA 18077
610-346-7446
www.cornithfilms.com

Coronet/MTI Film & Video
    See Phoenix Learning Group

Filmic Archives
448 Pepper St.
Monroe, CT 06468
800-366-1920

Films for the Humanities & Sciences
P. O. Box 2053
Princeton, NJ 08543-2053
800-257-5126
www.films.com

Indiana University Instructional Support Services
Franklin Hall, Room 0004
Bloomington, IN 47405
812-885-2853
www.indiana.edu/-iss/instr_media.shtml

Insight Media
2162 Broadway
New York, NY 10024
212-721-6316; 800-233-9910
www.insight-media.com

Learning Corporation of America
    See Phoenix Learning Group

Listening Library
    See Random House Audio

MGM/United Artists Home Video
1350 Avenue of the Americas
New York, NY 10019
212-707-0300
www.mgm.com

Monterey Home Video
566 St. Charles Drive
Thousand Oaks, CA 91360
800-424-2593
www.montereymedia.com/video

National Public Radio
Listener Services
635 Massachusetts Ave NW
Washington, DC 20001
www.npr.org

New Dimensions Radio
P. O. Box 569
Ukiah, CA 95482
800-935-8273
www.newdimensions.org

New Letters on Air
University of Missouri at Kansas City
5100 Rockhill Rd.
Kansas City, MO 64110
816-235-1168
www.newlettere.org/onTheAir.asp
PBS Home Video
1320 Braddock Place
Alexandria, VA 22314
703-739-5380; 800-645-4727

Phoenix Learning Group
2349 Chaffee Drive
St. Louis, MO 63146
800-221-1274
www.phoenixlearninggroup.com

Pyramid Media
P. O. Box 1048
Santa Monica, CA 90406
800-421-2304
www.pyramidmedia.com

RCA/Columbia Home Video
    See Sony Pictures Home Entertainment

Random House Audio
400 Hahn Road
Westminster, MD 21157
800-726-0600
www.randomhouse.com/audio

Recorded Books
270 Skipjack Rd.
Prince Frederick, MD 20678
800-638-1304
www.recordedbooks.com

www.folkways.si.edu
800-365-5929

Smithsonian Folkways Recordings
600 Maryland Ave. SW, Suite 2001
Washington, DC 20024

Sony Pictures Home Entertainment
10202 W. Washington Blvd.
Culver City, CA 90232
www.sonypictures.com/homevideo

Spoken Arts
195 South White Rock Road
Holmes, NY 12531
800-326-4090
www.spokenartsmedia.com

Time-Life Video
Customer Service
1450 East Parham Rd.
Richmond, VA 23280
800-950-7887
www.TimeLife.com

Video Learning Library
15838 North 62nd Street, Suite 101
Scottsdale, AZ 85254
800-383-8811
www.videolearning.com

Warner Home Video
4000 Warner Blvd.
Burbank, CA 91522
818-954-6000
www.warnerbrothrs.com

Women Make Movies
462 Broadway, Suite 500
New York, NY 10013
www.wmm.com